CW01348200

Marian Protestantism

St Andrews Studies in Reformation History

Editorial Board:
Andrew Pettegree, Bruce Gordon and John Guy

Titles in this series include:

The Shaping of a Community: The Rise and Reformation of the English Parish c. 1400–1560
Beat Kümin

Seminary or University? The Genevan Academy and Reformed Higher Education, 1560–1620
Karin Maag

Marian Protestantism: Six Studies
Andrew Pettegree

Forthcoming:

Protestant History and Identity in Sixteenth-Century Europe
edited by Bruce Gordon

Antifraternalism and Anticlericalism in the German Reformation: Johann Eberlin von Günzberg and the Campaign against the Friars
Geoffrey Dipple

Piety and the People: Religious Printing in French, 1511–51
Francis Higman

Marian Protestantism

Six Studies

ANDREW PETTEGREE

SCOLAR PRESS

© Andrew Pettegree, 1996

All rights reserved. No part of this publication may be reproduced, stored in a retrieval system, or transmitted in any form or by any means, electronic, mechanical, photocopying, recording, or otherwise without the prior permission of the publisher.

Published by
SCOLAR PRESS
Gower House
Croft Road
Aldershot
Hants GU11 3HR
England

Ashgate Publishing Company
Old Post Road
Brookfield
Vermont 05036–9704
USA

British Library Cataloguing in Publication Data

Pettegree, Andrew
  Marian Protestantism: Six Studies.
  (St Andrews Studies in Reformation History)
  I. Title II. Series
  280.40942

  ISBN 1–85928–176–1

Library of Congress Cataloging-in-Publication Data

Pettegree, Andrew.
    Marian Protestantism: six studies/Andrew Pettegree.
      p.   cm. (St Andrews Studies in Reformation History)
    Includes bibliographical references and index.
    ISBN 1–85928–176–1
    1. Protestant churches—England—History—16th century.
  2. England—Church history—16th century. 3. Great Britain—
  History—Mary I, 1553–1558. 4. Refugees, Religious—Europe—
  History—16th century. 5. Refugees, Religious—England—
  History—16th century. I. Title. II. Series.
  BR377.P48   1996
  280'.4'09209031—dc20   95–41847
ISBN 1 85928 176 1   CIP

Typeset in Sabon by Poole Typesetting (Wessex) Ltd
and printed in Great Britain by Hartnolls Ltd, Bodmin

Contents

Preface	vii
List of abbreviations	ix
Acknowledgements	x
Introduction	1
1 The English Church at Emden	10
2 The Stranger Community in Marian London	39
3 The London Exile Community and the Second Sacramentarian Controversy, 1553–1560	55
4 Nicodemism and the English Reformation	86
5 The Latin Polemic of the Marian Exiles	118
6 The Marian Exiles and the Elizabethan Settlement	129
Conclusion: Marian Protestantism	151

Appendices

Appendix 1: Books Published for the English Exile Community in Emden, 1554–1558	168
Appendix 2: English and Scottish Newcomers Enrolled as Citizens of Emden, 1554–1558	170
Appendix 3: John Dowley's Submission to the French and Dutch Churches	172
Appendix 4: Checklist of Latin Polemic Published by the Marian Exiles Abroad, 1553–1559	183
Appendix 5: Two Letters of the Delegate of the Emden Reformed Church, from London, April/May 1559	197
Bibliography	200
Index	206

Preface

The publication of this book represents for me a long-intended return to the study of English history. Although I have been interested in the problems of mid-Tudor Protestantism for almost as long as I have been engaged in research, the last ten years of my writing have been devoted mostly to continental subjects: a choice dictated largely, as is the way in these things, by accidents of career and geographic location. Yet even from the point of English history these years have been extremely instructive, for the time I have spent on the German and Dutch Reformations has, I hope, greatly enriched my understanding of what was always a very international movement. I have tried to bring these experiences to bear in the studies contained in this book. For it is my clear sense – and this is one of the leading arguments of the book – that the periods of the reigns of Edward VI and Mary represent the time when English Protestantism was most integrated into the mainstream of the continental Reformation. If recent writers are probably right to argue that England was relatively infertile territory for the new evangelical doctrines in the first decades after Luther's protest, then the balance was richly redressed in the period under study. Indeed, for a brief moment, England became the central stage for the continuing Reformation drama, as continental Protestants seized the opportunity presented by the accession of Edward VI. By the end of Mary's reign English Protestantism was a much more deeply-rooted (if somewhat weather-beaten) plant than had been the case 12 years previously.

This is a collection of six separate studies, and it does not aspire to be a complete history of Protestantism during the reign of Mary. There are some aspects of the subject – such as the underground congregations of Mary's reign – where anything I could say would not add greatly to the established scholarship, and I have therefore resisted the temptation to tread over familiar ground. I have, however, taken the opportunity to draw attention in Chapter 1 to remarkable new information on the London underground church which has been discovered by Mr Brett Usher, and which he will publish in due course. Similarly I have less to say about John Foxe than would be necessary in a full study of Protestantism under Mary. This is largely a deliberate choice. It will be clear from the general tenor of the essays collected here that I believe that an over-reliance on Foxe has impeded a proper evaluation of mid-Tudor Protestantism. By presenting here a collection of essays which on the whole makes little use of Foxe as a source, I hope to have done something to suggest the potentially very wide range of materials available to students of this period of English Protestantism. Further (and sometimes appropriately sceptical) reflections on the true value of the *Acts and Monuments* as a work of history and literature will be available with the publication next year (also in this series) of the first fruits of the British Academy John Foxe project, and I am happy to express my own obligation to the stimulating and careful work being done as part of that enterprise. In the meantime I have contented myself here with expressing in the conclusion my own developing sense of the place of Foxe's martyr narratives in the wider history of Marian Protestantism. I have also taken the opportunity to spell out what I feel to be the implications of the more generous evaluation of Marian Protestantism that I propose here, for the wider debate on the nature of English Protestantism in the sixteenth century.

The preface of a new book is always a welcome opportunity to express intellectual debts. In putting together these essays I have profited enormously from the opportunity to discuss these and other issues with my colleagues in the Reformation Studies Institute in St Andrews, not least my co-editors in this series, John Guy and Bruce Gordon. Bill Naphy, Karin Maag and Rona Johnston, and at a further geographical remove, Alastair Duke, Patrick Collinson and Peter Truesdale, have been good friends and interested critics. Diarmaid MacCulloch was kind enough to read the whole text, and shared with me many additional pieces of evidence from his own capacious knowledge of early English Protestantism. Heinold Fast checked a number of references for me in the church and town archives at Emden. But on this occasion I would like particularly to acknowledge a special debt to four graduate students in the Reformation Studies Institute, all of whom have greatly enriched my understanding of this subject: David Watson, who taught me the need to to look more critically at the sixteenth-century martyrologists; Christopher Bradshaw, who has brought home to me the biblicism of the English Protestant polemicists; Alec Ryrie, from whose work on Protestantism in the 1540s this work has profited very directly; and Stephen Alford, who has sketched out a view of a radical Protestant regime in the 1560s which I find very persuasive. This book is in a very direct sense a tribute to the co-operation and collegiality possible in a community of scholars with common interests, and I am grateful to them all.

ADMP
St Andrews Reformation Studies Institute
1995

Abbreviations

ARG	*Archiv für Reformationsgeschichte*
BHR	*Bibliothèque d'Humanisme et Renaissance*
BIHR	*Bulletin of the Institute of Historical Research* (now *Historical Research*)
BSHPF	*Bulletin de la Société d'Histoire du Protestantisme Français*
CO	*Calvini Opera*
CR	*Corpus Reformatorum*
DNB	*Dictionary of National Biography*
EHR	*English Historical Review*
HJ	*Historical Journal*
JEH	*Journal of Ecclesiastical History*
NAK	*Nederlands archief voor kerkgeschiedenis*
SCJ	*Sixteenth Century Journal*
STC	*Short Title Catalogue of Books Printed in England* ... 1475–1640
TRHS	*Transactions of the Royal Historical Society*
WA	Luther, *Werke* (Weimar Ausgabe)

Acknowledgements

Chapter two, 'The Stranger Community in Marian London', previously published in *Proceedings of the Huguenot Society of Great Britain and Ireland*, 24 (1987), pp. 390–402.

Chapter three, 'The London Exile Community and the Second Sacramentarian Controversy, 1553–1560', previously published in *Archiv für Reformationsgeschichte*, 78 (1987), pp. 223–51.

Chapter five, 'The Latin Polemic of the Marian Exiles', previously published in James Kirk (ed.), *Humanism and Reform: The Church in Europe, England and Scotland, 1400–1643* (*Studies in Church History*, subsidia 8, Blackwells, 1991), pp. 305–29. By permission of the Ecclesiastical History Society.

Reproduced here with kind permission.

The introduction, conclusion, and chapters one, four, and six are original to this volume.

Introduction

The death of Edward VI in 1553 brought to an end the most concerted attempt of the early sixteenth century to remake England as a Protestant country. In the space of six years, the Catholic Mass, largely unaltered through the depredations of Henry VIII's erratic reforms, had been emphatically repudiated in two successive Protestant Prayer Books. An English order of service had become the familiar, if not always welcome, focal point of Sunday worship. Priests had married and taken on family responsibilities; large quantities of church property had passed into lay hands. In a short space of time, English religious life had been comprehensively reordered.

Such swirling change, introduced in accordance with theological precepts which paid scant regard to many traditional parts of English church life, swept away much of the fabric of the old religious order. To many, it must have seemed brutal and gratuitous, an act of religious vandalism made no less terrible by the explanatory sermons of the new evangelical preachers.[1] To men of this sort the accession of Mary Tudor, and her restoration of the old religion, was an occasion for frank relief, and sometimes, inevitably, for the settling of scores.[2] Others, and perhaps the majority, would have greeted this – as all other political alterations of the sixteenth century – with a sublime indifference; uncomprehending obedience would have been a wide-ranging (if, for the historian, uninteresting) experience. But for those who had given their enthusiastic support to the changed order, the Catholic restoration posed harsh choices. The rapid collapse of the Duke of Northumberland's attempt to set up Lady Jane Grey as Queen made clear that political resistance to the legitimate succession was doomed: Protestants had either to accept the inevitable and accommodate themselves to the new regime, or reconcile themselves to the perils and hardships of an uncertain future at home or abroad.

---

[1] Eamon Duffy, *The Stripping of the Altars: Traditional Religion in England, c.1400–c.1580* (New Haven and London, 1992), pp. 448–77.
[2] A. G. Dickens, 'Robert Parkyn's Narrative of the Reformation', *EHR*, 62 (1947), pp. 58–83. Susan Brigden, *London and the Reformation* (Oxford, 1989), pp. 326 ff.

How significant a phenomenon was this Protestantism of the unreconciled? How important were these small but determined groups of English men and women whose commitment to the new evangelical faith outweighed all the pressures which would have urged conformity with the new regime – convenience, family, the duty of obedience? This is an important question, not least because the historiographical tide in recent years has moved so heavily against any positive evaluation of the achievements of early English Protestantism. In large part, this interpretative shift has revolved around a more sympathetic reappraisal of the traditional English church life challenged, and inevitably denigrated, by the evangelical assault. Fine work by a succession of scholars has demonstrated that as Luther's criticisms convulsed much of Europe, English church life, and the English church hierarchy, were by no means moribund or defenceless.[3] To many on the continent, England in the 1540s must have seemed a rare bastion of orthodoxy (hence, in part, the eagerness of continental theologians to share in the destruction of traditional religion during the reign of Edward VI). On her accession in 1553 Mary could draw not only on a deep well of sympathy for her own position but affection for the old ways and a large measure of revulsion against the sheer destructiveness of Protestant change. To be reminded of this, in books of imposing scholarship and moving eloquence,[4] has been very valuable and proper, but an inevitable consequence has been the comparative neglect of the positive achievements of English Protestantism, and in particular of the reign of Edward VI. Yet for a short time during this reign, England's new Protestant leadership had become the European centre of efforts to institutionalize Luther's theological revolution. In six years they had made astonishing

---

[3] J. J. Scarisbrick, *The Reformation and the English People* (Oxford, 1984). Richard Rex, *The Theology of John Fisher* (Cambridge, 1991). Duffy, *Stripping of the Altars*. A comprehensive and accessible synthesis of this view of the Reformation is now available in Christopher Haigh, *English Reformations, Religion, Politics and Society under the Tudors* (Oxford, 1993). The comparatively healthy state of the English church is perhaps most evident when placed in a European context. See here, for an introduction, Andrew Pettegree (ed.), *The Early Reformation in Europe* (Cambridge, 1992). Peter Dykema and Heiko Oberman, *Anticlericalism in Late Medieval and Early Modern Europe* (Leiden, 1993).

[4] Notably Duffy's *Stripping of the Altars*, an impressive if unashamedly partisan evocation of the glories of the later medieval English church. See the insightful reviews by Susan Brigden in *London Review of Books*, 27 May 1993, Patrick Collinson in *Times Literary Supplement*, 15 January 1993.

progress towards at least the outward appearance of a Protestant state. And they could not have done so without a significant measure of support among the nation's opinion-formers.[5]

Edward's death in 1553 destroyed the political legitimacy of this reforming movement, but it could not undo the impact of six years of constant change. And here the fundamental transformation was as much human as legal, in particular in the lives of many hundreds of men and women who now felt themselves too committed to the new way simply to accept a return to the traditional church. On the whole, the professional politicians would bend, but English Protestantism would be kept alive by a variety of people who to varying degrees discovered a conscientious sticking point: churchmen, theologians and ordinary citizens who found ways of keeping the faith at home or abroad in exceptionally difficult circumstances. And their defiance, for all its limitations in terms of numbers, became one of the central political phenomena of the new reign, a constant factor in the political calculations of policy-makers throughout the period of Mary's Catholic restoration, until her death in 1558 undid much of her work, as Edward's had his.

The six studies collected here explore different aspects of this residual English Protestantism, and its significance both for the future of the English church and the wider European Reformation movement. The underlying assumption which links all six is that Marian Protestantism remained much more important, and was a much more diverse movement, than the small numbers involved would initially suggest. To date, studies of this movement have inevitably focused on the two groups who signalled their defiance in one of two obvious ways: either by stubbornly declaring their opposition to the changes wrought in England, and suffering the consequences even to the point of death – the English martyrs so movingly memorialized by Foxe; or by withdrawing, not much less bravely, to face the uncertain future of separation from home and family in exile. The fact that the size of both these groups may be calculated with a plausible if rather spurious numerical precision has permitted posterity to assume a rough total of some 1000 irreconcilables: 300 martyrs, recorded in

---

[5] Brigden, *London and the Reformation*, pp. 488–519. W. K. Jordan, *Edward VI. The Young King* (London, 1968). Idem, *Edward VI. The Threshold of Power* (London, 1970). The full history of the Edwardian Reformation remains to be written. The forthcoming biography by Diarmaid MacCulloch, *Thomas Cranmer: A Life* (New Haven and London, 1996), will be an important contribution to a more generous evaluation of the Edwardian reforming experiment.

Foxe, and a rather larger number of exiles listed in Garrett's classic if now rather dated register.[6]

All of this now seems rather too simple. Both sets of figures, from Garrett and Foxe, deserve closer scrutiny; taken together they are very far from describing the total phenomenon of Marian Protestantism. The figures for the exile seem, on the face of it, the most secure. The movement as a whole is reasonably well documented, partly because of the high status of those who left England, and their future importance for the restored English church, and partly through the assiduous efforts of the exiles themselves, who gave much attention to collecting materials which would explain their trials abroad. Miss Garrett's work was based on a great deal of conscientious archive work in the principal exile centres of Switzerland and southern Germany. But there remain obvious lacunae. Apart from the somewhat speculative superstructure of support for those left behind in England, hypothesized in Garrett's introduction, her work has been criticized for a naive assumption that all those who left England during Mary's reign were religious exiles. More likely, at least a proportion were engaged on travel for entirely traditional reasons; this probably applies most to the group of young noblemen who attended universities in Italy during this period.[7] Further, Garrett's list of genuinely religious refugees can be significantly enhanced from archival sources which fell outside Garrett's purview. In particular, the archives of north Germany cast important light on the life and personnel of at least one church largely ignored in the wider literature of the exile, the English church at Emden.

Emden was geographically somewhat separated from the main centres of exile, and played only a subsidiary role in the key disputes of the period, but it was clearly far from being an insignificant community. The material presented here makes it possible to reconstruct its daily life and composition to an unexpected extent.[8]

Our picture of the Protestant martyrs of Mary's reign also requires a degree of rather more subtle shading. Foxe lists some 300 individuals who died for religious offences during Mary's reign, but it is probably more helpful to divide these people into three distinct categories. The smallest number, and generally the first and most prominent individuals among the martyrs, were those leading mem-

---

[6] Christina Garrett, *The Marian Exiles* (Cambridge, 1938).

[7] Kenneth Bartlett, 'The Role of the Marian Exiles', in P. W. Hasler (ed.), *The Commons, 1558–1603* (3 vols, London, 1981), vol. 1, pp. 102–10.

[8] Chapter 1.

bers of the Edwardian regime whom the new government moved swiftly to neutralize at the beginning of the reign, and later decided to make an example of in the hope of terrifying lesser figures into submission. These included Ridley, Hooper and Latimer of the bishops, and John Bradford, John Rogers and Rowland Taylor of the preachers.[9] Cranmer became a reluctant addition to their number, though his waverings at the point of death suggest that more subtle handling would have secured the government a highly public apostasy and a notable propaganda coup. In the second group one may place those whose courageous adherence to the new faith eventually brought them, through open defiance or betrayal, to denunciation and death. Among these were members of the small secret congregations which enjoyed a sporadic existence in London and other towns at various points in the reign.[10]

The problems are posed by the remaining third group, of uncertain size, made up of a variety of religious dissidents of various hues and degrees of unorthodoxy. In many cases it is hard to claim these men and women as martyrs for Protestantism, at least of the sort recognized and authorized under Edward VI. It is hard to know just how many were free-thinkers and anabaptists of the sort the Edwardian regime also pursued, occasionally to their death.[11] But men and women of this sort were precisely those most likely to be denounced to the authorities, since they were often outsiders or marginal figures whom the local magistrates would inevitably have less scruples about surrendering to justice than respected local citizens of known evangelical leanings. Quite what many of these pitiable and unfortunate victims believed remains obscure, partly because they were not always articulate witnesses in their own defence, and partly because their real views might be artfully obscured by Foxe, who, eager for obvious reasons to emphasize the brutality of the Marian regime by maximizing the number of its victims, was therefore happy to make of these uncomfortable dissidents orthodox martyrs of Protestantism. Foxe's subtle abuse of his sources has been carefully demonstrated for

---

[9] D. M. Loades, *The Oxford Martyrs* (Oxford, 1970). W. J. Brown, *Life of Rowland Taylor* (London, 1959).
[10] J. W. Martin, 'The Protestant Underground Congregations of Mary's Reign', *JEH*, 35 (1984), pp. 519–38.
[11] The two capital victims of Edward's reign, George van Parris and Joan Bocher, were both radical dissidents of strong if sometimes eccentric views. W. K. Jordan, *Edward VI. The Threshold of Power*, pp. 327–30. I. B. Horst, *The Radical Brethren* (Nieuwkoop, 1972), pp. 109–37.

at least one group of Kentish martyrs by Patrick Collinson.[12] A further critical investigation might reveal other examples for different parts of the country.

But the real point here is that overconcentration on these two groups, exiles and martyrs, risks presenting an oversimplified picture of residual English Protestantism during Mary's reign. What of those who remained behind, not necessarily committing themselves to the hazardous secret congregations, but nevertheless keeping the faith in their hearts? That this represents a genuine if flexible commitment may be demonstrated by the numbers who promptly re-adopted Protestantism when it became safe to do so under Elizabeth.[13]

Such behaviour has never really been regarded as an authentic expression of belief, partly, no doubt, because conduct of this sort was so emphatically deplored by the reformers themselves. The leading role in this regard was taken by John Calvin, who between 1537 and 1542 published a series of sharp and pointed tracts denouncing such simple sympathizers as Nicodemites, after the Pharisee who came to Jesus by night. Instead Calvin urged on them the stern alternative of open witness to the faith, with its inevitable dire consequences, or retreat into exile. Calvin's lead was followed by most of the leading continental reformers, whose writings set the tone for a remorseless devaluation of such equivocal behaviour, a valuation which has been at least implicitly accepted by modern historians who refuse to see such individuals as real Protestants. What is not always recognized is that Calvin's writings were controversial at the time, bitterly resented and in fact openly repudiated in some evangelical circles. Nicodemism, despite Calvin, continued to be widely practised in most Catholic countries with a sizeable submerged evangelical movement. That this was true also of Marian England is strongly indicated by the number of writings directed by the exiles abroad to those who lingered in England, urging them to keep faith. Yet such behaviour, routinely denounced by those who had taken the decision for exile, was far from indefensible, and not without real value for English Protestantism. Where would the Elizabethan church have been without that celebrated trio of 'Nicodemites', Parker, Cecil and Elizabeth herself? Chapter 4 of this book presents the case for a fundamental re-evaluation of this phenomenon.

---

[12] Patrick Collinson, 'Truth and Legend: the veracity of John Foxe's book of Martyrs', in A. C. Duke and C. A. Tamse, *Clio's Mirror. Historiography in Britain and the Netherlands* (Zutphen, 1985), pp. 31–54.

[13] In the London foreign churches this involved a humiliating confession of fault, a not inconsiderable disincentive to the half-hearted. See Chapter 2.

Thus three different groups, exiles, martyrs and conformers, helped to keep English Protestantism alive, but it was mostly the exiles who ensured that it remained securely bonded into the European evangelical movement. In many respects this was to continue and secure the achievement of the Edwardian period, because it was during the reign of Edward VI that England had become critical to further Protestant advance in Europe. After years of lagging behind the lands of central and northern Europe, the establishment in England in 1547 of a regime sympathetic to evangelical reform provided a splendid, and in some respects unexpected opportunity; and this occurred, furthermore, at a time when the Protestant movement in Europe had suffered significant reverses, both in its German heartland and elsewhere. Luther had died in 1546, leaving a German Protestant church pensive and apprehensive at the impending onslaught of Charles V, now finally determined on a military solution to the religious disunity of the Empire. In April 1547 his armies would inflict a crushing defeat on the German Protestant princes at the battle of Mühlberg, a victory which threatened fleetingly to undermine the whole basis of the evangelical movement in Germany. These were critical and difficult years too for the much less robust evangelical movements in France and the Netherlands, where the peace of Crépy in 1544 had been the signal for an intensification and reinforcement of edicts of persecution. In both countries, but particularly in the Netherlands, the identification of small evangelical cells had led to trials, executions, and a new wave of emigration.[14]

These events could not but have a depressing effect on the leaders of the reform movement in Germany and Switzerland, and go some way towards explaining the enthusiasm with which continental reformers took up the mission to bring evangelical reform to England during Edward's reign.[15] The European dimension did not die with Mary's accession. On the contrary, the presence of so many leading figures from the English church on the continent significantly increased contacts with European centres of the Reformation during a decade when the alignment of European Protestantism was itself undergoing significant change. The English exiles were eager to expound their own version of recent events, and to link these into a developing view of the English past which provided the evangelical movement with a historical justification. Their desire to present this view to a continental audience explains the surge of Latin works

---

[14] Andrew Pettegree, *Emden and the Dutch Revolt* (Oxford, 1992), pp. 18–21.
[15] W. K. Jordan, *Edward VI. The Young King* (London, 1968), pp. 189–205.

written and published by the English exiles. This was a body of work every bit as considerable as the better known vernacular tracts, destined mostly for an English audience. The Latin polemic deserves to be better known and more widely studied, since it represents an important continental dimension of English Protestantism.[16]

The exiles were inevitably an unquiet presence. Deprived of the normal comforts and security of home, and often desperately poor, they fell, notoriously, to quarrelling among themselves.[17] But they were also drawn inevitably into the wider theological controversies then diverting the leading reformers in Germany and beyond. This was especially true of the foreign congregations established in London during Edward's reign and now in search of a new home, whose troubled peregrinations became a cause célèbre among the Reformed and the source of a major upsurge of polemical activity against the northern Lutheran churches who had turned them away from their gates.[18]

By taking the leading role in these debates Calvin thrust himself to the forefront of the Reformed movement for the first time, a movement with which the exiles, both English and foreign, were from this point unambiguously aligned. For this was not a decade when continental Protestantism stood still. Changes in both Lutheran and Reformed churches, and in particular in relations between them, meant that the restoration of Protestantism on Elizabeth's accession in 1558 would take place in a very different context to the bold experimentation of Edward's reign. This is a circumstance not sufficiently recognized in some studies of the Elizabethan settlement, the subject of the last essay in this volume. How changes in the European scene affected the thinking of English policy-makers, and the part played by returning exiles and re-emerging evangelicals, needs to be realistically reassessed if we are to understand what (despite what is sometimes asserted in the literature) was always intended to be an unambigously Protestant settlement.

It is now generally accepted that England only became a Protestant country in a full sense in the second half of the sixteenth century, when the changes made by the Edwardian regime, and remade by

---

[16] Chapter 5.

[17] The best account of these disputes is the classic *Brief Discourse of the Troubles at Frankfurt*, attributed to William Whittingham. STC 25442, Modern edn, London, 1908. See also Patrick Collinson, *Archbishop Grindal* (London, 1979), pp. 73–9. Jasper Ridley, *John Knox* (Oxford, 1968), pp. 189–214. The quarrels in Emden are described here in Chapter 1.

[18] Chapter 4.

Elizabeth, finally took root.[19] But that is not to say that the seeds planted in the earlier decades were not in themselves of importance in shaping the character of what later emerged as a distinctive branch of European Protestantism. The studies collected here present a case for the positive evaluation of the Protestantism of the middle decades of the century. Although the achievement of a limited group, it paved the way for England's eventual emergence as a Protestant nation.

---

[19] See especially Patrick Collinson, *The Birthpangs of Protestant England. Religious and Cultural Change in the Sixteenth and Seventeenth Centuries* (Basingstoke, 1988), and the literature cited there.

CHAPTER ONE

The English Church at Emden

The interested visitor to modern Geneva is made immediately aware of the close connections between the church in Calvin's city and the great European movement he spawned. The Great Wall of the Reformation, erected towards the end of the nineteenth century and now one of Geneva's principal tourist sites, makes tangible the close connections between Geneva and daughter churches from Scotland to Hungary. Here the four central figures of Calvin, Beza, Knox and Farel are flanked by statues and monuments to representative figures of the international Calvinist movement: William of Orange, Admiral Coligny, Stefan Bocskai.[1] A visitor to Calvin's own church, the Cathedral of St Pierre, will also have his attention drawn to Calvin's Auditorium, a small building nestling in its shadows and the site of some of the first teaching in Geneva's Academy, the new institution of higher education founded by Calvin in 1559 to provide the quality of training appropriate for the new Calvinist ministeriat.[2] But the Auditorium also had a distinguished pre-history, for it was here, between 1556 and 1559, that the small English-speaking exile church had its meetings, figuratively and physically under Calvin's protective wing.[3]

The same is hardly true of Emden, where little trace remains of the sixteenth-century connections between England and one of the principal northern outposts of the the Reformed faith.[4] Yet in the sixteenth century Emden played a significant role in English affairs on several occasions. The most obvious example came in 1562, when the English government found itself casting about for a replacement for Antwerp as principal continental market town for its exports. Relations with the Spanish government of the Netherlands, under strain

---

[1] Francis Higman, *A Guided Tour of the International Reformation Monument* (Geneva, 1994); *The International Reformation Monument, Geneva* (Geneva, 1993).

[2] On the Academy see now Karin Maag, *Seminary or University? The Genevan Academy and Reformed Higher Education, 1560–1620* (St Andrews Studies in Reformation History, 2, 1995).

[3] Charles Martin, *Les protestants anglais réfugiés à Genève au temps de Calvin, 1555–1560* (Geneva, 1915). The *Auditoire* is also sometimes known in the literature by its former name, the church of St Marie le Nève.

[4] This owes something to Bomber Command, which in 1943 and 1944 obliterated 75 per cent of the old city.

since the beginning of the reign, had now totally broken down, and English goods were forbidden the Antwerp mart.[5] The pretext was an outbreak of infectious disease in London, but the intention was clearly to bring the English government to heel. Rather than submit to such obvious pressure, the English authoritites cast around for an alternative mart town. Attention quickly fixed on Emden, a small port in north Germany where the local regime had been notably friendly since the beginning of Elizabeth's reign. An optimistic manifesto from one of the merchant promoters of Emden's claims had already circulated among influential councillors, and this in turn encouraged the Merchant Adventurers' Company to take further soundings.[6] The scheme certainly had its opponents. Writing from Antwerp, Richard Clough offered an altogether less sanguine view of Emden's facilities. According to Clough, Emden was wholly unsuited to the merchants' needs, the harbour small and inconvenient, its approaches difficult. The quay was small and the local citizenry 'rude both in word and deed, not meet to entertain merchants'.[7] When the mart went ahead, Emden, despite an enthusiastic welcome, rather confirmed these dire predictions. The merchants found the conditions primitive, the town malodorous, and the packhouses for their precious cloths were just cowhouses and stables, hurriedly cleared for the purpose. The Emden experiment was not a conspicuous success.

Perhaps Clough, in his zeal to promote an alternative solution, traduced Emden unfairly. The Merchant Adventurers were after all comparing their new temporary home with Antwerp, the greatest international entrepôt of the period, where they had lived in pampered ease. But the essential point was that the mart *did* go ahead: a decision which, in the circumstances probably owed as much to religious and personal connections as it did to austerely economic considerations. These connections had first been established during the reign of Mary Tudor, when a considerable English community had settled in Emden, and now in time of need they could be resurrected. The long after-effects of the Marian exile were by no means confined to the purely religious sphere.

The personal and religious connections activated so effectively in 1562 have not been sufficiently acknowledged because so little has been known or written about the English community in Emden.

---

[5] This story is well told in G. D. Ramsay, *The City of London in international Politics at the accession of Elizabeth Tudor* (Manchester, 1975).

[6] The 'book' of George Nedham is edited by G. D. Ramsay as *The Politics of a Tudor merchant adventurer. A letter to the Earls of East Friesland* (Manchester, 1979).

[7] Ramsay, *City of London*, p. 239.

Certainly Emden remains the least well known of the major Marian exile churches. The reasons for this may be put down to a combination of different historical accidents. Unlike Strasbourg or Geneva, which both entertained considerable groups of English exiles, Emden was not at this point a significant centre of European Protestantism and there was no great figure of the evangelical movement to raise the town's international profile. Unlike Wesel and Frankfurt, the other sizeable churches, the Emden church was not riven by disputes which resonated – like the troubles at Frankfurt – through later church affairs.[8] Geography also worked against the Emden community. Removed as it is from the major sixteenth-century centres of population and communication in Switzerland and the Rhineland, Emden was more easily dismissed as provincial and outside of the main nexus. It is significant that Christina Garrett did not visit Emden as part of the otherwise admirably thorough exploration of continental archives for her census of Marian exiles; an omission with serious consequences both for her survey and for Emden's perceived prominence in the whole exile community.[9]

This is a neglect from which Emden deserves to be rescued. It was clearly a far from uninteresting community. Documents preserved locally suggest that this may indeed have been one of the larger English exile churches, in which several of the most important figures of the exile would spend all or part of Mary's reign. The congregation, although not riven by fundamental disputes over church order as in Frankfurt, was prone to the usual division and quarrelling, as one fascinating document preserved in the local church archive makes clear.[10] Most of all, the Emden church was a much more influential force in the wider exile community than it has been given credit for. As a model of both church order and organization, Emden played a significant part in developing the ecclesiological understanding of English Protestants who had left England after 1553 and returned after Elizabeth's accession to participate in the regeneration of English Protestantism. As a printing centre, too, Emden was a significant thorn in the side of Mary's regime.

Emden's neglect owes something to the fact that the usual and most

---

[8] Partly through William Whittingham's influential and partisan account, *A brieff discourse of the Troubles at Frankfort* (1574). STC 25442.

[9] Notably in the very small number of exiles whom Miss Garrett acknowledges to have been in Emden. C. Garrett, *The Marian Exiles* (Cambridge, 1938).

[10] Emden, Archiv der Evangelische-Reformierte Kirche, Rep 320 A, no 6. Reproduced here in English translation as Appendix 3 (p. 172).

convenient sources for the exile have little to say about the most northerly of the congregations. It is not altogether clear when the English refugees who found their way to East Friesland first began to meet as a formal congregation. In a letter of 1555 to Nicholas Ridley, in prison in England, Edmund Grindal included an offhand and rather dismissive reference to the Emden church which, repeated through the various histories, has become the definitive judgement on the northern congregation. 'Master Scory and certain others that be with him in Friesland and have an English church at Emden, but not very frequent', by which Grindal is generally thought to mean, not very numerously frequented.[11] In either interpretation, Grindal was wrongly informed. The English church in Emden had been in operation for about a year at this point, and was both well organized and sufficiently numerous.

The first services in Emden probably took place in the spring or early summer of 1554, making it one of the earliest of the Marian exile congregations. According to an early German chronicle, 32 Englishmen with their families arrived in Emden in March 1554,[12] and a number certainly travelled with John a Lasco on his ill-fated journey through Denmark and northern Germany in the winter of 1553–54, presumably arriving in Emden at about the same time.[13] Services were most likely already underway by the time of the arrival of John Scory, former bishop of Rochester, who quickly took charge of the congregation as its minister.

The congregation was from an early date both reasonably attended and well organized. Hagedorn's reference to the arrival of 32 families would imply a congregation of over one hundred, and new arrivals through the reign augmented its numbers further. The Emden registers of new citizens yield the names of some 35 English and Scottish incomers who enrolled as citizens between 1555 and 1558.[14] This

---

[11] *Remains of Edmund Grindal*, ed. W. Nicolson (Cambridge, 1843), p. 239.

[12] B. Hagedorn, *Ostfrieslands Handel und Schiffahrt im 16. Jahrhundert* (Berlin, 1910), p. 123, quoting a manuscript chronicle of the Emden burgomaster Jan Tileman Hesslingk (1758).

[13] Lasco arrived in Emden first in December 1553, having left his companions in the care of Marten Micron and proceeded straight to Emden; the bulk of his fellow travellers arrived with Micron in the spring of 1554. Several English names are included among the partial list of those who sailed with Lasco which is printed as a footnote to the modern edition of Jan Utenhove, *Simplex et Fidelis Narratio* (Basle, 1560), an account of the London congregation's ill-fated voyage. See *Bibliotheca Reformatoria Neerlandica*, ed. S. Cramer and F. Pijper (10 vols, The Hague, 1903–14), vol. 9, pp. 89–90.

[14] Stadtarchiv Emden, Bürgerbücher. See Appendix 2, p.170.

information, however, offers no clear indication of the total size of the English congregation, since not all the newcomers would have wished to pay the fees and take the necessary oath to obtain citizens' rights, particularly if they only intended their stay to be of short duration. By no means all the Emden exiles were single men travelling without their wives and families, since the congregation subsequently appointed two schoolmasters to care for its children. The adult congregation was served by a worship regime which included two midweek prayer services as well as the regular Sunday service.[15]

Some of the most important figures of the exile either passed through Emden or settled there on a more permanent basis. Foremost among them was John Scory, bishop of Chichester, one of only two serving bishops to join the exile.[16] Scory's escape abroad was not without hazard and potential scandal, since at one point Scory had appeared ready to recant his Protestant beliefs and make his peace with the new regime.[17] But if Scory briefly weakened he swiftly thought better of it and by June 1554 he was on the continent, settled in Emden and promoted to a leadership role.[18] Almost from the point of his arrival Scory appears in local records as the undisputed spokesman of the English community in Emden. Most of the Englishmen who took out citizenship are entered in the Emden Bürgerbücher as having been presented by Scory.[19] Some local sources even refer to him as the English church's 'bishop'.[20] Probably what is intended here is something analogous to the office of superintendent which Lasco had performed in the London stranger congregations.[21]

It is clear that other leading figures of the exile, both in and beyond

---

[15] These details come from documents relating to the dispute of 1558: see Appendix 3, p. 173. The identity of the two schoolmasters is not revealed.

[16] The other was Ponet, bishop of Winchester. On Scory, Garrett, *Marian Exiles*, p. 285–6. *DNB*, vol. 17, pp. 846–7.

[17] Along with Barlow, bishop of Bath and Wells. John Strype, *Ecclesiastical Memorials* (3 vols in 6, Oxford, 1822), vol. 3, i. p. 241.

[18] Stadtarchiv Emden, Bürgerbücher, vol. 1, fol. 99^v, 20 June 1554. This entry corrects the previous assumption that Scory was still in England at the time that Bishop Bonner registered his recantation on 14 July. In fact he must have left England at least a month before.

[19] Thus Stadtarchiv Emden, Bürgerbücher, vol. 2, fol. 12^v: 'Stephanus Gren uth Engeland ... ex. com[mendatione] J. Schorij.' In this respect Scory played a parallel role to John a Lasco with members of his former London church. Cf. idem, fol. 4^r, 6^r, etc.

[20] Staatsarchiv Aurich, OAP 10, VIII, 216: 31 December 1558, Johannes Schorrii, 'der Engelschen gemene allhyr tho Embden bisshop', gives power of attorney to a local Emden citizen to deal with any remaining debts.

[21] John Strype, *Memorials of Archbishop Cranmer* (3 vols in 4, Oxford, 1848–54), vol. 3, p. 167, in fact refers to him as such.

Emden, thought none the worse of Scory for his brief moment of apostasy. In August of 1554 Scory was Grindal's candidate to lead the new congregation at Frankfurt, and indeed had indicated his willingness to move there before it became known that the congregation had offered the post elsewhere.[22] Despite this rebuff Scory continued to play a leadership role in the wider exile community, at one point leaving Emden to assist the more southerly churches for a while, before returning to Emden in 1557, possibly to supervise the publication of Cranmer's *Defensio verae et Catholicae doctrinae de Sacramento*, one of the principal Protestant manifestos of the exile years.[23] Scory would continue to act as a spokesman for the exiles even after their return to England in Elizabeth's reign, as the document presented in Appendix 5 of this collection makes clear.[24]

Scory's principal assistant in the new church was Thomas Young, not a prominent figure at the time though he would go on to be the first Elizabethan archbishop of York.[25] At the beginning of Mary's reign, Young had achieved a certain notoriety as one of the six members of the first Marian convocation who had publicly avowed their Protestant principles.[26] Consequently it has always been assumed that Young must have sought safety abroad, though no documentary trace of him had been established before his identification in these Emden documents. Young took out citizenship in Emden in 1554, and probably remained in East Friesland throughout Mary's reign.[27] His keen legal brain and disputatious temper are both remarked upon in the documents relating to the controversies within the community.

Other well-known figures of the exile spent at least some part of the reign in Emden before moving on elsewhere. The Protestant author John Olde followed his friend Thomas Becon to the continent and probably settled for a time in Emden before moving finally to Frankfurt.[28] So too did William Turner, dean of Wells, the man

---

[22] *Brieff discourse*, p. 31.
[23] (Emden, Ctematius, 1557.) STC 6005. Full bibliographical description (with list of surviving copies) in my *Emden and the Dutch Revolt* (Oxford, 1992), appendix nos 70, 71. Reprinted in *Writings and Theological Disputations of Thomas Cranmer*, ed. John Cox (Parker Society, 1844), pp. *1–99.
[24] See Appendix 5, p. 196.
[25] Garrett, *Marian Exiles*, p. 348. *DNB*, vol. 21, pp. 1305–7.
[26] October 1553. See Philpot's *True Report of the Disputation* in *The Examinations and Writings of John Philpot* (Parker Society, Cambridge, 1842), pp. 165–214.
[27] Stadtarchiv Emden, Bürgerbücher, vol. 2, fol. 12^r.
[28] Garrett, *Marian Exiles*, p. 241. *DNB*, vol. 14, pp. 979–80. For his writings published at Emden, see Appendix 1, p. 168.

credited with having introduced John a Lasco to the Duke of Somerset.[29] This connection stood him in good stead on his arrival in East Friesland, where Turner, a noted medical author in addition to his religious writing, served a brief period as physician to the Count of East Friesland before embarking on a perambulation that took him to most of the major exile centres in Germany. Other more transitory visitors included Thomas Cottisford, rector of St Martin's, Ludgate, who would occupy himself during the exile with writing and translation, and David Whitehead. Both these men apparently accompanied the Dutch exiles on their journey through Denmark and northern Germany, and it is possible that they left Emden in Lasco's company when he moved on to Frankfurt in 1555.[30] Cottisford was a far from insignificant individual; he had been a regular official preacher under Edward VI, and he also played a major part in compiling the last and most radical official catechism of the reign. Others who made fleeting visits to Emden included Cranmer's former steward, Robert Watson, whose account of his initial apostasy and later return to Protestantism was published in Emden as part of the literature of the exile, Sir John Cheke, and William Barlow, the later bishop of Bath and Wells, briefly in Emden before taking up his appointment as first minister of the English church in Wesel.[31] A more tragic instance was that of John Rough, who in 1557 returned from East Friesland to minister to the secret congregation in London. Within a matter of months he had been betrayed to the authorities and executed.[32]

The surviving records of the Emden municipality add a number of notable figures to those already known from other sources. Among the first group of exiles enrolled as citizens with John Scory were two Scots, David Simpson and John Willock. Simpson was a veteran of Lasco's voyage; Willock, an active preacher in England during the reign of Edward VI, would later achieve fame as one of the six Johns

---

[29] Garrett, *Marian Exiles*, pp. 314–5. *DNB*, vol. 19, pp. 1290–3. Whitney R. D. Jones, *William Turner. Tudor Naturalist, Physician and Divine* (London, 1988).

[30] See Cottisford's Epistle from Copenhagen, appended to his translation of *The Confession of Faith of Huldrike Zwingli* ([Emden], 1555), STC 26140. On Cottisford, *DNB*, vol. 4, pp. 1216–17 and the article by Leaver cited below. On Whitehead, *DNB*, vol. 21, pp. 96–8.

[31] On Watson, *DNB*, vol. 20, p. 940. His *Aetiologia* is Pettegree, *Emden*, appendix no. 58. On Barlow, *DNB*, vol. 1, pp. 1149–51.

[32] *DNB*, vol. 17, p. 313. *The Acts and Monuments of John Foxe*, ed. George Townsend and Stephen Cattley (8 vols, London, 1837–41), vol. 8, pp. 443–49.

commissioned to produce a draft of the First Scottish Book of Discipline.[33] Willock is also the only member of the Emden exile congregation known to have taken an active role in the military preparations for the Wyatt rebellion, and he seems to have fled England immediately after the collapse of this venture.[34] A local tradition has it that Willock at some point became one of the ministers of the English congregation;[35] if this was the case it can only have been fleetingly, since by 1555 Willock was back in Scotland conducting the diplomatic negotiations which resulted in the conclusion of a treaty of friendship between Scotland and East Friesland. But Willock also took the opportunity to maintain contacts with the small evangelical movement in the Scottish burghs, and by October 1558 he had returned permanently to take on a pivotal role organizing the new church. In the crisis of the Scottish Reformation the following year Willock was once again called upon to exercise his diplomatic skills, this time as part of Maitland of Lethington's delegation to the English Court pleading for military intervention on the side of the insurgent Protestant lords.[36] His established connections with the English church elite were no doubt of considerable value in repairing the damage done by John Knox's clumsy interventions earlier in the year.[37]

The English newcomers enrolled as citizens in Emden tended to be received in small groups, presented by their 'bishop' John Scory. The group enrolled shortly after Scory included two veterans of the first generation of English Protestantism: Christopher Coleman, a member of the so-called White Horse Group in Cambridge in the 1520s, and George Constantine, a survivor of several early heresy proceedings from the time of Henry VIII.[38] Neither Coleman nor Constantine had previously been identified as part of the exile during Mary's reign, and

---

[33] *The First Book of Discipline*, ed. J. K. Cameron (Edinburgh, 1972), p. 4. Duncan Shaw, 'John Willock', in his *Reformation and Revolution. Essays presented to Hugh Watt* (Edinburgh, 1957), pp. 42–69.

[34] Willock was indicted for treason on 10 February 1554. *Calendar of Patent Rolls, Philip and Mary* (4 vols, London, 1937–39), vol. 1, pp. 381, 499.

[35] P. F. Reershemius, *Ostfriesisches Predigerdenkmal* (Aurich, 1796), p. 527.

[36] J. A. B. Teulet, *Relations politiques de la France et de l'Espagne avec l'Ecosse au XVIe siècle* (5 vols, Paris, 1862), vol. 1, p. 384.

[37] See Chapter 6.

[38] John Fines, *A Biographical register of Early English Protestants and others opposed to the Roman Catholic Church* (2 vols, 1980, 1985, vol. 2 unpub.), vol. 1 (Coleman, Constantine). Susan Brigden, *London and the Reformation* (London, 1989), pp. 116–8.

the same is true of Stephen Green, a former canon of St David's deprived under Mary.[39] All in all, of 35 English and Scottish names registered in the Emden Bürgerbücher for the years 1554–58, more than two-thirds are not recorded in Garrett's register of Marian exiles.[40] All the evidence points to a lively and relatively numerous community, which included for some or all of the period some of the most influential figures of the exile.

The Emden church enjoyed an active and well-organized congregational life. The documents deposited in the Dutch church archive as a result of the dispute of 1558 described below reveal that the English congregation met three times a week in a house specially set aside for this purpose.[41] In addition to the main Sunday service the congregation met for prayers on Wednesday and Friday. Although, regrettably, no order of service has survived, it is possible to patch together a fair quantity of information regarding the church's congregational practice. It is clear, first of all, that the congregational life of the English church owed a great deal to the pattern and inspiration provided by the church order of John a Lasco's London foreign church. The arrival of the leading members of Lasco's London community in Emden had a considerable influence on church life in the town, and the local church order underwent a substantial revision to its practice to accommodate the newcomers.[42] The English church also adopted a congregational regime largely patterned upon Lasco's church order, which would shortly be published in Emden in several languages.[43] First and foremost the English congregation followed Lasco in establishing a complete hierarchy of church government and discipline according to the emerging Genevan Reformed practice. In the English

---

[39] Fines, *Biographical register*, vol. 2, G18.
[40] Appendix 2, p. 170.
[41] The location of the meeting place is not known. Possibly it was in part of the considerable monastic property in the city, which now in the post-Reformation period was being progressively taken over by the city for its own uses. See here Timothy Fehler, 'Social Welfare in Early Modern Emden: the Evolution of Poor Relief in the Age of Reformation and Confessionalization' (University of Madison, WI, PhD thesis, 1995).
[42] See my *Emden and the Dutch Revolt*, Chapter 2.
[43] Latin, French, and a shorter Dutch version by Marten Micron. Pettegree, *Emden and the Dutch Revolt*, appendix nos 5, 36, 57. The standard edition of the Latin text is in *Joannis a Lasco Opera*, ed. A. Kuyper (2 vols, Amsterdam, 1866), vol. 2, pp. 1–283. I know of no published English version, though it is likely that an English translation circulated in manuscript among the Emden exiles. According to the *DNB*, Thomas Cottisford had in hand a translation of Lasco's liturgy, but if so it was never published. The Bodleian library, Oxford, has a surviving manuscript translation of the *Forma ac Ratio* in a contemporary hand. Bodleian Ms Barlow 19.

church the two ministers, Scory and Young, were assisted by six elders and nine deacons.[44] The centrality of discipline was an essential element of the model of congregational life which Lasco had developed in London, to which he added an emphasis on congregational participation which went far beyond the more hierarchical instincts of Calvin.[45] This quasi-democratic element of Lasco's concept of church order was certainly influential in the English exile congregations, and played its part in many of the subsequent problems they faced.

Perhaps it is not surprising that Lasco's views on church government should have been influential in Emden. Many of the English exiles in Emden were personally known to him, and some would have had the opportunity to hear expositions of his ecclesiology in the regular series of public lectures he delivered in London during Edward's reign.[46] A recent discovery by Robin Leaver, one of the leading authorities on the congregational church music of the period, demonstrates that the English church also followed Lasco's recommendation in including in their form of worship a form of confession based on Daniel 9.[47] In the case of Emden this took the form of a metrical version devised by Thomas Cottisford, the survival of which is the only evidence of congregational singing in the Emden church.[48]

What can also be demonstrated through this discovery is the extent to which Lasco's views of church organization influenced the wider English exile community. A similar usage was adopted in at least two other of the exile congregations, Wesel and Geneva.[49] The recent discovery of an outline sketch of the church order adopted by the

---

[44] For the number of elders see Appendix 3, p. 175. The figure for deacons comes from a manuscript note of the Emden antiquary included with the document in the Emden archive. According to Harkenroth the community also had two schoolmasters.

[45] In the London procedure the election of ministers was consigned to the whole congregation, a model generally speaking not followed by other Calvinist systems. Calvin had very little faith in the unguided preferences of the congregation, who in Geneva were required only to signify their consent to the choice made by the Company of Pastors and the magistrates *by their silence*. For the London procedure, Lasco, *Forma ac Ratio*, Lasco Opera, vol. 2, pp. 52 ff.

[46] Pettegree, *Foreign Protestant Communities*, pp. 63–4.

[47] Robin Leaver, 'A penitential hymn from the English Exile Congregation in Emden, 1555', *The Hymn*, 41, 1 (1990), pp. 15–18. Lasco, *Forma ac Ratio*, p. 557.

[48] It is included at the end of a translation by Cottisford of a work by Ulrich Zwingli, *The accompt rekentnge and confession of the faith* ([Emden, Ctematius], 1555), STC 26140, pp. 106–9.

[49] Leaver, art. cit., 17. And cf. n. 104, below.

English church in Wesel reveals how far this too was patterned on Lasco's London church order, the *Forma ac Ratio*.[50]

Following Lasco's recommendations, the English churches in both Emden and Wesel put considerable emphasis on the practice of communal discipline. But this did not insulate either community from dissension among its members, indeed probably rather the reverse, since a system of participatory discipline encouraged expectations of a high standard of personal conduct – not least on the part of the ministers and elders – which they often found it difficult to live up to. Perhaps it was inevitable too that these unusual congregations, made up disproportionately of educated and committed men, often separated from their families and normal means of making a living, should be prone to fractiousness and division. Emden was no exception, and in 1558 the church was riven by a serious dispute. Although it did not have the wider ecclesiological ramifications of the more famous dispute at Frankfurt it was serious enough to require the intervention of the Emden Dutch church, in whose records the relevant documentation is still preserved.[51]

The dispute revolved around a complaint by a member of the congregation, John Dowley, that the ministers and elders had decided to abandon the normal place of worship as a result of a local outbreak of plague. Dowley has not previously been a well-known figure in the annals of the exile,[52] though the document of complaint he compiled demonstrates him to have been an articulate and determined individual. He was enrolled as a citizen of Emden with other Englishmen earlier in 1558, so perhaps he was a relatively recent arrival in the town.[53] Dowley claimed to speak for a number of members of the congregation who were offended at an action they clearly saw as both precipitate and inappropriate. Having failed to persuade the minister to reinstate the normal midweek services, Dowley and his dissident group met separately to pray for the sick. It was this unofficial gathering which seems to have outraged the church's leaders and led to a confrontation in open church, where Dowley was first denounced and then made his defences before the

---

[50] Lambeth Palace Library, Ms. 2523, fol. 1ʳ⁻ᵛ, 4ʳ⁻ᵛ. Discussed in Robin Leaver, 'Goostly Psalmes and Sprituall Songes'. *English and Dutch Metrical Psalms from Coverdale to Utenhove, 1535–1566* (Oxford, 1991), pp. 196–8.

[51] Appendix 3. And see *Die Kirchenratsprotokolle der Reformierten Gemeinde Emden, 1557–1620*, ed. Heinz Schilling (2 vols, Cologne/Vienna, 1989–92), vol. 1, pp. 63–4.

[52] He is not included in Garrett's register of exiles.

[53] Emden StA, Bürgerbücher, vol. 2, fol. 30ʳ.

whole congregation. The dispute escalated rapidly, as Dowley (according to his own account) first defended the validity of his criticisms and then offered to put the matter to independent mediators. When this too was rebuffed, Dowley finally appealed to the mediation of the Dutch church.

By this time (as was almost inevitable in disputes of this nature between the consistory and one or more members of the congregation) the original point of issue had been largely superseded by differences over fundamental questions of authority. Was it for the ministers and elders to take such decisions on behalf of the community? And how legitimate was their sudden and unexpected denunciation of Dowley in open church, without there having been time to progress through the various stages of brotherly admonition laid down in Matthew 18, the pattern for all Reformed systems of discipline?[54] That said, the original issue on which Dowley took his stand was far from trivial. By the time he wrote his letter of admonition to the ministers and elders Dowley had made explicit his criticism of their conduct in refusing to visit the sick during a time of plague, an issue which, given the terror of the disease, inevitably raised controversy among the Godly.[55] Some argued strongly, with Dowley, that the duty of care demanded that ministers fulfil this obligation, even unto death. Certainly a large part of Calvin's contempt for some of his less capable colleagues in Geneva arose from their refusal to carry out visitations of the sick during time of plague.[56] But often more practical considerations would prevail. In the case of Geneva it should be said that Calvin himself had been explicitly forbidden by the magistracy from visiting plague victims, since his own life was too precious to put at risk. And when the Dutch church in London lost both their ministers within months of the outbreak of a severe plague epidemic in 1563 they sensibly moved to

---

[54] As for instance Lasco's London church order and the Genevan Ecclesiastical Ordinances. See P. E. Hughes (ed.), *The Register of the Company of Pastors* (Grand Rapids, 1966), pp. 48–9. Lasco, *Forma ac Ratio, Lasco Opera*, vol. 2, pp. 170–222. Matthew 18 15:20: 'If thy brother trespass against thee, go and tell him his fault between thee and him alone. If he hear thee, thou hast won thy brother: but if he hear thee not, then take with thee one or two, that in the mouth of two or three witnesses, all things may be established. If he hear not then, tell it unto the congregation. If he hear not the congregation, take him as a heathen man, and as a publican.'

[55] The best treatment of early modern attitudes to plague is Leo Noordegraaf and Gerrit Valk, *De Gave Gods. De pest in Holland vanaf de late middeleeuwen* (Bergen, 1988).

[56] On this see now William Naphy, *Calvin and the Consolidation of the Genevan Reformation* (Manchester, 1994), pp. 68–9, 90.

the appointment of salaried plague visitors, a solution subsequently adopted in several similar communities.[57] In all the circumstances Scory and Young could perhaps be forgiven a degree of circumspection.

That said, neither minister showed himself in a very good light during the course of the dispute. Scory was prepared to denounce Dowley unheard as a liar before the whole congregation, and Young took the lead in hectoring both Dowley and his supporters. Once committed to the dispute the ministers and elders would not consent to mediation, although this was a well-established procedure in the churches they sought to emulate.[58] Neither would they accept the mediation of the local Dutch and French churches. When Dowley's appeal came before the Dutch consistory, the English ministers and elders refused to appear, arguing by letter that this was a purely internal matter. The Dutch consistory took a different view, entering into their minutes a judgement which essentially endorsed Dowley's position.[59]

And there the matter rested. Unlike some of these controversies, the dispute with Dowley did not rumble on; there is no further reference to the question in the Dutch church minutes. Within a few months most members of the English church would have left Emden: Scory, departing in December 1558, was one of the first to go. The English church did not long survive his departure, and there is little further trace of an English congregation in Emden in the reign of Elizabeth.[60] Presumably the whole community swiftly made its way back to England.

What, then, is the Emden church's significance to the exile, both as a whole and to the wider development of English Protestantism during this period? While the church certainly functioned as a model and exemplar to other, later-established English exile churches, its most immediate impact on the English political scene came through

---

[57] Naphy, op. cit., p. 90. Pettegree, *Foreign Protestant Communities in Sixteenth-Century London* (Oxford, 1986), pp. 206–9. The town church in Emden also subsequently moved to the appointment of salaried plague visitors, though this was not enough to prevent the plague deaths of all three ministers in August 1575. *Kirchenratsprotokolle*, ed. Schilling, vol. 2, pp. 566–7.

[58] As for instance the London stranger churches and the Emden church. Pettegree, *Foreign Protestant Communities*, pp. 195–8.

[59] *Kirchenratsprotokolle*, ed. Schilling, vol. 1, pp. 63–4.

[60] A single entry in the consistory minutes of the Emden church for 6 January 1584 refers to a baptism in the English community and to an English preacher. *Kirchenratsprotokolle*, ed. Schilling, vol. 2, p. 798. Possibly this was a congregation re-established on an *ad hoc* basis to cater for the English merchants now frequenting Emden.

Emden's growing importance as a printing centre. The Dutch exiles who migrated to Emden with John a Lasco included two men who had been prominent printers in Edwardian London, and who now, in Emden, collaborated in the establishment of a new printing house.[61] Gilles van der Erve (Ctematius) and Nicholas van den Berghe (known in England under his anglicized name, Nicholas Hill) quickly became in effect the official printers of the Emden Dutch church, turning out a variety of catechisms, psalters and exegetical literature for its use. They also put their considerable skills at the disposal of the English exile community. Van den Berghe, in particular, was a long-term London resident who had built a busy publishing house in England during Edward's and the latter part of Henry VIII's reign, and he was entirely comfortable with the publication of works in English or Latin.[62] His command of English printing made possible the development of a fruitful collaboration that saw Emden quickly emerge as the undisputed centre of production of vernacular exile literature.

Over the course of the next four years the Hill/Ctematius press turned out some 28 editions in English or Latin, originated by members of the exile churches and mostly intended for clandestine distribution back in England.[63] Members of Emden's English church featured strongly among the authors of these works. Among those who employed their leisure in this profitable fashion were the superintendent, John Scory, William Turner, John Olde and Thomas Cottisford. Most of the local authors divided their time between the composition of original works and translations, with the result that these Emden books include a significant group of works by continental reformers, translated into English for the first time. These include an edition of Ulrich Zwingli's *Confession of Faith*, translated by Cottisford, and John Olde's translation of Rudolph Gualter's fiercely anti-papal homilies on Antichrist.[64] Scory, meanwhile, concentrated his energies on translations of the church fathers: two books of St Augustine and an apposite series of sermons by the early

---

[61] See my *Emden and the Dutch Revolt*, Chapter 4.

[62] The STC Index volume lists 120 editions under Hill's name for the period 1542–53. E. Gordon Duff, *A Century of the English Book Trade* (London, 1948), pp. 72–3. Pettegree, *Foreign Protestant Communities*, pp. 86–92.

[63] See Appendix 1, p. 168.

[64] STC 26140, 25009. There were also two translations by Thomas Cottisford of works by Marten Micron, former minister of the London Dutch church and now a fellow exile in East Friesland: his short examination for intending new members of the church (STC 17864) and the Antitheses taken from his account of the death of the early Dutch Calvinist martyr, Joris van der Katelyne.

Christian writer (and martyr) Cyprian concerning endurance in the face of persecution.[65]

Scory's other purpose in rendering these works into English, as he explained in the preface to the Augustine translation, was to demonstrate that the church of Henry VIII and Edward VI was a true catholic church, its doctrines and practice wholly consistent with that of the apostolic church and early Christian centuries.[66] The same purpose informed much of the original writing of Emden's English authors, for example the two important writings of John Olde, his *Acquittal and Purgation of the Most Catholic Prince Edward VI* and the *Confession of the Most Ancient and true Catholic Old Belief*.[67] 'Forasmuch,' wrote Olde in his pungent and inimitable style, 'as the preachers now set up in England spew out the abominable poison of Antichrist's traditions, infaming thereby the order and use exercised by common authority under Edward VI, for banishing Antichrist', Olde valiantly took up the cudgels to defend the former regime.[68] The style and form of these works was fairly uniform: an exposition of the church practice of Edward's reign, demonstrating its consistency with the apostolic church, intermingled with predictable invective against the false supremacy of the Church of Rome.

A defence of the previous Protestant regime in England was inevitably one major preoccupation of the exile writers, which they pursued in their Latin as well as their English works. Their other principal concern was to offer comfort and counsel to those they had left behind in England. The fate of the Christian brethren who had seemed to support the Gospel in Edward's reign, but who were now content to reconcile themselves to Catholicism, was a constant, almost obsessive, preoccupation of the English exile writers.[69] Many urged resolution in the face of the present catastrophe, which they explained as a beneficial judgement of God, not as his repudiation of the evangelical cause. God had sent Mary as a scourge on a sinful nation, which by greed and negligence had shown itself unworthy of so good and Christian a king as Edward VI; but punishment was purgative and the time of trial would surely pass, as it had for the children of Israel despite their many offences against God's law.

Meanwhile the Protestant authors bent all their eloquence to persuade those still in England to witness to the truth. The English

---

[65] STC 921, 6152.
[66] *Two Books of the Noble Doctor St Augustine*, sig. 4^r.
[67] STC 18797, 18798.
[68] *Acquittal and Purgation*, sig. A2^r.
[69] This theme is addressed at greater length in Chapter 4.

exiles in Emden were deeply troubled by evidence of backsliding among the thousands who had committed themselves to the Gospel in the previous reign, and yet now made their peace with Mary. Thus Thomas Cottisford:

> With what a lamentable heart I consider the miserable state of England ... and what an infinite number (which within these two years past bare a fair face towards the true religion) are now suddenly turned back to worship the beast.
>
> Alas for pity, what a great number of God's people is this day within England, that in their hearts do detest and abhore that false worshipping and great dishonouring of God now violently (I will not say tyrannously) thrust into every church and chapel, and would with all their hearts (if they knew which way to bring it to pass) fly out of that Babylon now the great city of sin and confusion. And contrarywise it would pity any true Christian man's heart to remember how many there are within that realm (which are fully persuaded in their consciences concerning true religion), that might well enough escape and come away, and yet will not.[70]

The exiles' remedy was simple: those who were not strong enough to stand for their faith in England should join the exile abroad.

The exile writers do show some differences in emphasis in their treatment of these central questions. Whereas William Turner and a number of the anonymous tracts direct their attention towards the principal opinion-formers in England (and some of the most prominent apostates), the nobility,[71] John Olde had clearly abandoned hope of progress on this score. According to Olde, the nobility in England had been found conspicuously wanting.

> I could make a docket of remembrance how you, the nobility, might had answered and used these lecherous lying locusts ... Yet seeing you have already run too far against your own consciences, so that it seems almost too late for any admonition or remembrance to sink into your hearts, being afraid of every barking blast of Antichrist's barking beagles ... I will spare my pen.[72]

Yet on some occasions the Protestant authors did also show some recognition of the fact that standing fast for the faith was not always

---

[70] Cottisford in the preface to his translation of Zwingli's *Confession of Faith*, sig. A2ʳ.

[71] Turner, *Hunting of the Romish Fox* [Emden, Hill/Ctematius, c.1554], STC 24356. *New Book of Spiritual Physic* [Emden, Hill/Ctematius, 1555], STC 24361. Rainer Pineas, 'William Turner and Reformation Politics', *BHR*, 37 (1975), pp. 193–200.

[72] *Acquittal and Purgation*, sig. A4ʳ⁻ᵛ. This was actually one of Olde's less colourful descriptions of the Romish clergy. Compare this: 'Albeit no few in England have most faithfully resisted the babbling blasphemies and false forged fables of the mitred maskers and shaven swarms of shameless sodomites.' Ibid., sig. A3ʳ.

a straightforward choice. Some, of course, had not shown themselves entirely blameless, and their writings occasionally reflect a certain modest self-consciousness on this score. The most frank and generous in this respect is again John Olde.

> Nevetheless how faint and how weak a soldier I myself have been in this behalf, mine own experience (at my first entry into the Gospel) taught me ten or eleven years ago. By reason whereof, being afraid of mine own weakness, and partly being enforced from my vicarage by malicious force and rage of some unthankful people ... I departed from my vicarage somewhat before extreme trouble came.[73]

Robert Watson's *Aetiologia* was in effect a work of self-exculpatory autobiography, explaining how he had been forced into recantation before escaping abroad; though since Watson published it in Latin presumably his principal intended audience was among his fellow exiles.[74] Only John Scory shows no trace of self-consciousness in his *Epistle unto the Faithful in England*, exhorting them to patience in the face of the present tyrannous persecutions of Antichrist. There is no hint of his own fall from grace in his exhortation to resolution; instead Scory calls to mind the blessed martyrs who had gone before and offers them as models.[75]

In these respects the pamphlets published in English in Emden strongly reflect the exiles' continuing preoccupation with events in England. They seem to have had no doubt that the reverses suffered by the Gospel in their native land were temporary in nature; a conclusion to which they would be drawn as much by their reading of the Old Testament, with its strongly cyclical narrative of triumph and reverses, as by their analysis of current English history. The almost monotonous cycle of defeat and recovery recorded in the book of Judges, the tribulations of captive Israel in the book of Daniel, and the resolution of Abraham in the face of God's severest test, all offered comfort and hope to the grieving exile.

Given all this, and their anxieties that their brethren left behind should not in the interval of trial pollute themselves by truckling to Antichrist, it is striking that the Emden exiles seemed at no time inclined to flirt with radical political solutions to their current difficulties. Of the works of Knox, Goodman and Ponet on political resistance, only Knox's early and cautious *Faithful Admonition* is

---

[73] *Confession of the Catholic Old Belief*, sig. E7^{r-v}.
[74] STC 25111.
[75] *Epistle unto the Faithful*, sig. A6^{v}ff.

among the English works published in Emden.[76] For the most part the modest political statements encompassed in the books published in Emden are ostentatiously loyal and affirming of the political order.[77] The only indication that the exiles have used the exile years to reconsider their relationship with the established powers in church or state comes in certain cautious criticisms of the Edwardian church order. This is mostly in that area where the Edwardian church was deemed to have been most incomplete – congregational discipline – and clearly reflects once again the influence of John a Lasco and the Emden host church.

'We neglect not discreet and brotherly admonition,' writes John Olde in his *Acquittal of Edward VI*, recognizing that all was not fully established under Edward VI. 'For though all be not yet fully well herein as godly men could wish it, yet there is some Christian discipline practiced in the Gospellers' church.'[78] 'And what thing,' asks John Scory rhetorically in his defence of the Edwardian church, 'has God commanded by his written word to be done, that was then omitted (except only use of Christ's true discipline).'[79] Clearly this was a preoccupation that the exiles would carry back to England as a result of their first-hand experience of continental Europe's best Reformed churches.[80]

The scale and importance of Emden's English printing operation raises several interesting questions concerning the relationship of the exile congregation in Emden with other, until now better-known, English churches on the continent, and indeed the Emden community's contacts with Protestant groups still in England. Why was the apparently geographically remote town of Emden, far away from the real intellectual centres of English Protestantism, allowed to develop as the leading centre of vernacular English printing? The success of Emden in this respect demonstrates that its contacts, both with England and with other continental exile centres, were more extensive than have previously been recognized. Individual exiles moved quite freely between the various towns in Germany which harboured an English community, and there was clearly no difficulty maintaining contact by letter or in disseminating the exiles' published writings.

---

[76] Hill / Ctematius, 1554. STC 15069.
[77] Thus John Olde in the *Acquittal of Edward VI*, sig. E6ʳ: 'We heartily honour Princes and magistrates ... '
[78] *Acquittal of Edward VI*, sig. D8ᵛ.
[79] *Two Books of the Noble Doctor St Augustine*, sig. 7ʳ⁻ᵛ.
[80] And see below, p. 34 f.

When in 1556 the French martyrologist and Genevan exile Jean Crespin included in his latest selection of martyr stories some of the recent English martyrs, he had to hand in Geneva a number of their printed works, including some recently published exclusively in Emden.[81] The numbers in which these works have survived, making them despite their clandestine origins some of the least rare of early English Protestant literature, is another pointer to their wide dissemination at the time.[82]

Undoubtedly one reason for Emden's prominence was the availability of the Hill/Ctematius press, with its extensive prior experience of the publication of English Protestant works. Although the printers had not managed to bring with them from London any of their printing materials, their contacts in Antwerp and the support of monied Dutch exiles allowed them to re-equip extremely rapidly, and their books are undoubtedly among the neatest and best printed of the exile literature.[83] But the success of Emden as a printing centre also demonstrates the close nature of the exile community's continuing contacts with evangelical sympathizers who had remained in England. Tying down how such contacts functioned is extremely difficult, given the clandestine nature of the trade and the dangers involved, but it is clear that the Emden exiles both continued to receive communications from England and succeeded in bringing their books to the market.

The first part of this exchange had its fruits in the rapid appearance on Emden's presses of a sequence of works by the leaders of English Protestantism incarcerated at the beginning of Mary's reign and ultimately condemned to die a martyr's death. Emden's exile congregation honoured their memory by publishing *in extensio* accounts of their doctrines and trials: the output of the Emden presses included the first edition of Ridley and Latimer's prison conversations, Ridley's seminal *Brief Declaration of the Lord's Supper*, and a full account of the prison interrogations of John Philpot.[84] Also included in this Emden group was a separate publication of Cranmer's letter to Queen Mary, protesting his summons to Rome to answer charges of heresy;

---

[81] See J. F. Gilmont, *Jean Crespin: un éditeur réformé du XVIe siècle* (Geneva, 1981), pp. 137–40.

[82] Lists of surviving copies are in Pettegree, *Emden and the Dutch Revolt*, appendix.

[83] Contrast, for instance, the far scrappier books produced at Wesel. Listed in Leaver, 'Goostly Psalmes and Spirituall Songes', p. 200.

[84] STC 21046, 21047.3, 19892.

a summons to which as the indignant editor (probably John Olde) points out, the imprisoned archbishop was hardly in a position to answer.[85]

It is interesting to speculate how these texts could so quickly have reached the exiles abroad. Nicholas Ridley was executed with Hugh Latimer on 16 October 1555, but by the end of the year his *Brief Declaration of the Lord's Supper*, 'written by the singular learned man, and most constant martyr of Jesus Christ, Nicholas Ridley, ... a little before he suffered death', had already been published in Emden. The following year the Hill/Ctematius press also published Ridley's prison dialogues, this latter with a typically pungent preface and conclusion furnished by John Olde. In this case too the text must have been passed from friends in England to the exiles abroad very soon after it had first been taken down.

The efficiency of such contacts indicates the existence of some sort of network of contact between the exiles and their evangelical brethren in England. When Christina Garrett first proposed the existence of a formal group of 'sustainers', operating to supply money to the exiles from the remains of their English properties, this notion was widely criticized, perhaps because her theories ran ahead of the then available evidence and because she sought to name the individuals who she believed co-ordinated this effort.[86] But undoubtedly such contacts were in operation. Exiles abroad found means to enjoy their property, often administered on their behalf by friends and family left behind in England.[87] The government's attempts to inhibit the passage of money and goods to the exiles abroad provoked one of the few serious parliamentary revolts of the reign: a rare public act of defiance to the new regime from the otherwise discreet and cautious William Cecil.[88] Both government and the exiled evangelicals recognized the importance of this issue, and not just to property rights in the abstract.

Having secured rights to their residual property the exiles also clearly found ways to bring their publications to their intended English readership. A proclamation of 1555, stimulated by the discovery of one of the earliest exile manifestos, took stern and

---

[85] STC 5999.

[86] Garrett, *Marian Exiles*, pp. 6–16.

[87] The services provided by William Cecil for his father-in-law Sir Anthony Cooke in this regard are discussed in Chapter 4.

[88] Jennifer Loach, *Parliament and the Crown in the Reign of Mary Tudor* (Oxford, 1986), pp. 147–58. See chapter 4, below.

determined measures to inhibit the trade in Protestant books.[89] After the proclamation had enumerated a comprehensive list of banned authors (but not, alas, titles), the Stationers' Company was supplied with a list of questions to pose to all booksellers – whether, for instance, they had in stock books from a number of named continental centres, Emden included.[90] But the continuing vitality of Emden's English printing after this date testifies to the ineffectiveness of these measures. How these books made their way to England remains mysterious, but it is likely that they made use of the normal channels of trade. In the case of Emden this would have meant either via the entrepôt of Antwerp, or exploiting a growing direct trade between London and East Friesland. Goods, men and materials passed back and forth much more freely than is often realized. When John Rough returned to London from East Friesland to minister to the secret congregation there, he had initially intended a short visit to buy yarn for his stocking-making trade, the implication being that this sort of casual journey back and forth was entirely routine.[91]

The community may well also have made use of colporteurs, travelling pedlars who carried a small stock of forbidden texts to known sympathizers, sometimes gathering mail to carry back to the exile centres in return. The distribution of clandestine books from Geneva, by this time an established centre of the heretical book trade, relied heavily on humble folk of this sort, their journeys financed and co-ordinated by the publishing entrepreneur, Laurent de Normandie.[92] The Dutch church in Emden established a similar network to bring books to their potential readers in the Netherlands. But the practice, though efficient, was also dangerous. Several French and Dutch colporteurs met their deaths after they were apprehended in possession of forbidden texts, and at least one member of the Emden exile church, Elizabeth Young, came hazardously close to a similar fate when she was apprehended in England carrying books from Emden.[93]

Although the exile authors clearly found sufficient readers to encourage them to continue with their work, the exile presses were by

---

[89] *Tudor Royal Proclamations*, ed. P. L. Hughes and J. F. Larkin (3 vols, New Haven, 1964–69), vol. 2, pp. 57–60.

[90] Foxe, *Acts and Martyrs*, vol. 7, p. 128.

[91] Ibid., vol. 8, p. 444.

[92] Heidi-Lucie Schlaepfer, 'Laurent de Normandie', in Gabrielle Berthoud et al. (eds), *Aspects de la propagande religieuse* (Geneva, 1957), pp. 176–230. C.f. Jeannine Olson, *Calvin and Social Welfare. Deacons and the Bourse française* (Mississauga, Ont., 1989), pp. 50–69.

[93] Foxe, *Acts and Monuments*, vol. 8, pp. 536–48.

no means entirely market driven. On the contrary, the evidence suggests that the exile propaganda effort was the result of a quite carefully targeted and organized campaign. There clearly was some thought given among the leading figures of the exile to what type of work could most appropriately be published, and by whom.[94] The quality of the work being turned out by Hill and Ctematius, combined with a sympathetic local regime and good communications back into England made Emden a sensible strategic choice for the vernacular publishing; this helps explain why a town which had until 1554 no printing press at all so quickly became such an important centre of Protestant printing. The exiles' Latin works also formed an important part of this propaganda effort. The climax of the Emden propaganda campaign was the publication in 1557 of a new edition of Thomas Cranmer's *Defensio de verae doctrinae de sacramentis*, a translation of his *Defence of the True and Catholic Doctrine of the Lord's Supper*.[95] This, one of the most important of Cranmer's doctrinal works, was first published in 1550 as an explanation of the central Eucharistic doctrine of the first Edwardian Prayer Book. Cranmer's work had quickly provoked two replies, one from Richard Smith, formerly Regius Professor of Divinity at Oxford, and the other from Stephen Gardiner, writing under the pseudonym Marcus Antonius Constantius. This in turn produced a further response from Cranmer, and a new Latin translation of the *Defensio* in which he introduced some new material. Cranmer's annotations were further bolstered in the Emden edition of 1557 by a copious range of additional citations from the church fathers supportive of Cranmer's positions, many relating to the arguments at his disputation with his Catholic opponents in Oxford in April 1554.[96] The Emden editors, in addition, silently introduced a number of corrections into Cranmer's own citations.

The production of this new edition was very likely a committee work, involving Scory, Olde, and other of the Emden authors whose familiarity with the church fathers is clear from their own publications. The Emden congregation included a considerable residual

---

[94] See here the most interesting letter of John Ponet to John Bale, suggesting that while Bale should continue his scholarly work, other exiles should be encouraged to work on 'Ballets, rymes, and short toyes' that 'do muche good at home amonge the rude peple.' E. J. Baskerville, 'John Ponet in Exile; a Ponet letter to John Bale', *JEH*, 37 (1986), pp. 442–47.

[95] Emden, Ctematius, 1557. STC 6005, 6005 (var).

[96] See Cranmer, *True Defence*, ed. Henry Wace (London, 1907), pp. 61, 74, 75, 108–11, 114, 121–3, 126, 133–5, 138–9, 144–5, 147, 152, 201.

group of what might be called Cranmer's affinity: Scory, Olde, Cottisford and Watson spring to mind, and these would have been expected to take an interest in this important project. Scory, in particular, was a Cranmer protégé, from the time of his appointment as one of the six preachers in Canterbury through to his elevation, in succession to Ridley, to the bishopric of Rochester. Early in 1554, and shortly before his departure from England, he witnessed the will of William Morice, brother of Cranmer's secretary Ralph.[97] Scory had exhibited considerable devotion to the writings of his patron, though not always to Cranmer's advantage, since it was Scory's eager circulation of Cranmer's Declaration on the Mass in the autumn of 1553 that had precipitated the archbishop's arrest.[98] Now, in exile, Scory's devotion was if anything redoubled, and he was very likely the moving spirit behind the publication of Cranmer's most magisterial theological work.

The Emden *Defensio* became, in effect, the official manifesto of the exile. The edition was published in two variants with a fairly large print run. Its careful and deliberate dissemination around the centres of European Protestantism is reflected in the number of copies which still survive in European libraries.[99] Included along with the dedication of 1553 was a list of the leading figures of the exile, who hereby adopted Cranmer's work almost as a confession of faith.[100]

The success of the Emden *Defensio* is rivalled only by another compact but formidable Latin work, John a Lasco's *Forma ac Ratio*. This major publishing achievement, an expository version of the church order of the London stranger church, with an extensive commentary by Lasco, was only partly published at Ctematius's Emden press. The work was about two-thirds finished when Lasco removed to Frankfurt, taking with him the incomplete sheets. The book was subsequently completed and published, with a dedication to the King of Poland, at a local Frankfurt printing house. The contemporary impact of this work, perhaps the most influential church order of the whole exile period, is again suggested by the number of surviving copies: to date I have tracked down more than 40.[101]

The true influence of Lasco's work is as yet only dimly reflected in

---

[97] I owe this information to Diarmaid MacCulloch.
[98] Ridley, *Cranmer*, pp. 351–3.
[99] A total of almost 50 copies so far identified. See Pettegree, *Emden*, p. 270.
[100] *Writings and Disputations of Thomas Cranmer*, ed. J. Cox (Parker Society, 1844), appendix, p. 8.
[101] Pettegree, *Emden*, pp. 261–2.

scholarly work on other contemporary church orders; it is no doubt a subject which will bear further examination.[102] Certainly the leaders of other English exile congregations were deeply aware of Lasco's work when they set about their own church-forming. The extent to which the church at Wesel patterned its worship on the church order devised and promoted by Lasco has already been discussed above, and the same seems to have been the case of the much more famous church order of the English church at Geneva. To cite just one example: the method adopted for the election of ministers in the Genevan English congregation (inevitably a sensitive matter given the Geneva congregation's troubled pre-history at Frankfurt) followed the pattern laid out in Lasco's *Forma* and not that of the main Genevan church. Given what is known of the English exiles' admiration for Calvin this might seem somewhat surprising, and certainly renders incomprehensible the remark of William Maxwell in the introduction to his edition of the church order of the English church in Geneva that there is no discernible link with Lasco's order.[103]

The influence of Lasco's church order was by no means purely confined to the English congregations abroad. A fascinating document recently unearthed by Brett Usher, and to be published by him in a forthcoming collection of essays, reveals that the main London underground congregation also adopted a form of church government which borrowed extensively from Lasco's model.[104] According to this document, in 1562 Bishop Grindal was invited to confirm retrospectively an ordination performed in the London church, and then affirmed by the church's 'superintendent and *presbyterium*'. This is the clearest possible reference to a superintendent and governing council of elders, the obvious local model for which was Lasco's former London church. One of the ministers of the London underground congregation was the Swiss scholar Augustine Bernher, and he would have been fully familiar with the London stranger church's former practice.[105] Mr Usher's discovery is all the more striking since

---

[102] The latest study of Lasco's *Forma* is in Dirk Rodgers, *John a Lasco in England* (New York, 1994). For remarks on its wider influence see especially pp. 79–80. Dr Rodgers is currently preparing for publication an edited translation of the *Forma*.

[103] Maxwell, *The Liturgical Portions of the Genevan Service Book* (London, 1931), p. 76. Clearly this is a relationship which would bear further examination.

[104] Brett Usher, 'In a time of persecution: new light on the secret Protestant congregation in Marian London', forthcoming in David Loades (ed.), *John Foxe and the English Reformation* (St Andrews Studies in Reformation History, 1996). I am extremely grateful to Mr Usher for sharing this exciting discovery with me in advance of publication.

[105] Foxe, *Acts and Monuments*, vol. 8, p. 559. On Bernher, *DNB*, vol. 2, pp. 392–3.

Foxe says so little about the form of worship followed in the London underground congregation, the inference being that it continued to follow the Edwardian Prayer Book.[106] But clearly, in the new circumstances of Mary's reign, the congregation in London, like the English exile churches, drew on the experience of other 'gathered' churches such as Lasco's. The appointment of elders was a case in point; so also was the appointment of deacons to gather alms for the poor, a further characteristic practice of Lasco's London church.[107]

Foxe's reticence is not surprising, given the conscious rejection of presbyterian models of church organization in the official Elizabethan church as it emerged in 1559. But it would have been surprising if Lasco's order – by now so familiar to many of those committed to the re-introduction of Protestantism in England – had not been among the Protestant church orders under discussion as English statesmen and churchmen pondered the proper form for a reborn English church in 1559. Two aspects of Lasco's model order seem particularly to have commended themselves to those who favoured a fundamental reordering of the English church at this point: his stress on congregational discipline, and his identification of a role for a superintendent above the level of the parochial ministry (and presumably superseding episcopal authority). The presence of a strongly ordered system of congregational discipline had been one of the leading features of Lasco's church order, and its absence, as we have seen, had been noted by English Protestants abroad as one of the principal deficiencies of the Edwardian church.[108]

During the period of reflection provided by Mary's reign English Protestants in their new gathered churches sought to make good this deficiency. The exercise of communal discipline was, as we have seen, an important if potentially incendiary aspect of community life in the English exile churches, and there is evidence that the practice was also introduced into the underground church in London. When one mem-

---

[106] As was directly alleged in the articles against the deacon Cuthbert Symson. Foxe, *Acts and Monuments*, vol. 8, p. 458. See also the report of Bonner's spy: 'Commonly the usage is, to have all the English service without any diminishing, wholly as it was in the time of King Edward the sixth.'

[107] Foxe, *Acts and Monuments*, vol. 8, p. 559, and in the account of the martyrdom of Cuthbert Symson, deacon of the church, ibid., pp. 454–8. Symson was charged with keeping the congregation's register of members, a practice which again was patterned on that of Lasco's London church, but which in the context of an underground community could prove hazardous if the register fell into the hands of the authorities. A mishap of this nature in 1557, for instance, led to the destruction of the important Dutch Calvinist congregation in Antwerp. Pettegree, *Emden and the Dutch Revolt*, p. 64.

[108] Above, p. 27.

ber of the congregation, troubled in conscience after having attended Mass, asked the minister John Rough for guidance, he advised her to confess her fault to the whole congregation, 'and so be received into their fellowship again'.[109] Rough, of course, had direct experience of the functioning of Lasco's church order in Emden, and his advice suggests that the London congregation had introduced the practice laid down in Lasco's *Forma*. On another occasion Rough went as far as to excommunicate an errant member; a perilous undertaking, for it was not unknown for a member spurned in this way to take revenge by denouncing the congregation to the authorities.[110]

Notwithstanding their extensive experience of the best Reformed churches during the exile, it was never likely that returning English Protestants would make much progress if they desired to see such a system generalized in the restored English church. In the political context of 1559 the introduction of a full presbyterian system was never a viable option, but there is evidence that a number of those involved in the settlement were attracted to the concept of superintendency. Both Armigail Waad and Robert Beale promoted the vision of a reformed episcopacy, stripped of a large part of their lordly properties, a scheme which resonated uncomfortably with the new government's wish to enrich the public purse with a new round of forced exchanges of church land.[111] This was a notion which even won some support in the new Protestant establishment, at least judging by John Aylmer's trenchant recommendation to the new bishops in his *Harborowe for Faithful and True Subjects*:

> Come off you Bishops, away with your superfluities, yield up your thousands, be content with hundreds as they be in other reformed churches, where be as great learned men as you are. Let your portion be priestlike and not princelike. ... That every parish church may have his preacher, every city his superintendent to live honestly and not pompously.[112]

William Cecil was heavily involved with the programme of exchanges, but he may also have been attracted to the notion of superintendency on more theological grounds. At the time of the English intervention in Scotland, Cecil certainly commended to the Lords of the Congregation a pattern of reformation in which bishops

---

[109] Foxe, *Acts and Monuments*, vol. 8, pp. 727–8. J. W. Martin, 'The Protestant Underground Congregations of Mary's Reign', in his *Religious Radicals in Tudor England* (London, 1989), p. 138.
[110] Ibid., pp. 450–1.
[111] Felicity Heal, *Of Prelates and Princes. A Study of the Economic and Social Position of the Tudor Episcopate* (Cambridge, 1980), p. 207.
[112] *Harborowe*, STC 1005, sig. O4^{r-v}.

were reduced to the status of superintendent, and given only modest incomes.[113] Even without this prompting, it is almost certainly the case that the leaders of the new Protestant establishment in Scotland had Lasco's work to hand when they set about the composition of the First Book of Discipline in 1559. Again, this influence is largely unacknowledged, but the model of Lasco's order was certainly more immediate, and more immediately available, than other church orders sometimes credited with influencing the Scottish settlement.[114]

Lasco's *Forma* may thus be seen to have had a wide and profound impact, long before its incorporation into the developing church order of the Dutch Reformed church, or, indeed, its adoption by English critics of the Elizabethan church as an ideal form of church government.[115] The fact that this is not widely recognized may also serve as a parable for the Emden English congregation itself, constructed during the few short years of Mary's reign to a high degree of organization and participation that later puritans might have envied, only to be swiftly abandoned on Elizabeth's accession.

Perhaps more than anything else, geographical separation has obscured our understanding of the importance of Emden's history as an exile church and publishing centre in the Marian period. For scholars attuned by the contemporary voices of Calvin, Knox and Whittingham to look for the intellectual core of the exile experience in Geneva and Strasbourg, Emden must have appeared insignificantly remote and parochial, and so it has remained to the twentieth century. But at the time this physical separation would have been more apparent than real. The lines of communication linking both Emden and England, and Emden and the major Rhineland communities, were already more than adequate and improved steadily as Emden grew into its new role as a major importing and exporting town during precisely these decades. Indeed as travel along the more traditional routes between England and the continent through France and the Netherlands became perilous for Protestants, Emden grew into its new role as a transit town, the apex of a triangle linking the two major Protestant territories of the region. In 1571 the leaders of the Dutch exiled Calvinist church would choose Emden for their first

---

[113] Heal, *Of Prelates and Princes*, p. 207.

[114] James K. Cameron, *The First Book of Discipline* (Edinburgh, 1972). C.f. Rodgers, *John a Lasco in England*, pp. 162–4.

[115] Patrick Collinson, 'Calvinism with an Anglican face: the stranger churches in early Elizabethan London and their superintendent', in Derek Baker (ed.), *Reform and Reformation: England and the Continent, c.1500–c.1750* (Oxford, 1979), pp. 71–102.

major synodical gathering for precisely this reason. Its geographical location made it equally convenient for delegates from both England and the Rhineland communities.[116]

Emden prospered in this new role. By 1568 the town elders were prepared to contemplate both a major extension to the physical size of the city, and an ambitious Renaissance town hall, the façade of which was modelled, somewhat cheekily, on that of the new town hall at Antwerp.[117] At about this time too, a local Emden bookseller felt sufficiently confident to issue a prospectus proposing Emden as a supply centre for the import of works of continental theology into England, anticipating that the northern town would again supersede Antwerp in this respect.[118] For those who believed that international Protestant solidarity should have beneficial economic consequences all of these developments would have been very agreeable. For if the English exiles settling in Emden during Mary's reign witnessed only the first flowering of this economic prosperity, their presence and the subsequent much closer economic ties between England and East Friesland certainly contributed to it. The fact that Emden was even considered as a potential alternative venue for the long-established Antwerp mart in 1563 may be entirely attributed to the religious connections established during the reign of Mary, and now revived for other purposes.

In the long term Emden was undoubtedly the major beneficiary from this connection. The city fathers and ministers who welcomed the exiles, in contrast to the behaviour of the Lutheran Hanseatic towns, were richly rewarded for their act of humanity. The whole episode, the founding of churches, the settling of a considerable number of new residents (English and Netherlandish), and the rapid development of a whole network of economic connections with the more established centres of trade, is a tribute to the flexibility of the sixteenth-century economic system in maritime Europe.

For English Protestants the consequences were hardly less beneficial. Secure in their northern refuge, the exiles found the leisure and relief to build a church which would be a significant model for churches elsewhere in the Reformed tradition, and to publish the writings which would form an enduring monument to the movement for which they had left their homelands. Travelling hopefully to a

---

[116] Pettegree, *Emden and the Dutch Revolt*, p. 183.

[117] The new town hall was completed in 1574 and destroyed by bombing in 1943–44. The rebuilt modern building preserves some of its features and character.

[118] Andrew Pettegree, 'Emden as a centre of the sixteenth-century book trade: a catalogue of the bookseller Gaspar Staphorst', *Quaerendo*, 24 (1994), pp. 114–35.

land of which they had previously known nothing, the exiles found in Emden a place in which to build the model church societies which had largely eluded them in England. These churches in turn would have a lasting influence on the future development of ecclesiastical structures, both directly in the subsequent church orders of the Dutch Reformed church, and more widely through the dissemination of Lasco's *Forma ac Ratio*, an unacknowledged masterpiece of Protestant church order. Of course, exile is only ever intended to be a temporary experience, and the English would abandon their temporary home in 1559 with such alacrity that little trace of their community would remain. But it is tempting to speculate how many, surrounded by the cares and compromises of office and responsibility in their native lands, would in due course look back to these years as an era when the community ideal of the new Reformed churches had been explored to a degree hardly possible at home. It is a significant, if little known, episode in the development of the Reformed tradition.

CHAPTER TWO

The Stranger Community in Marian London

The reign of Mary Tudor was a uniquely difficult period for London's foreign residents. For most of the sixteenth century foreign immigrants to England could be sure of a warm enough welcome. The very different regimes of Henry VIII, Edward VI, and Elizabeth all maintained a fairly consistent policy towards the newcomers; they welcomed them for their skills and industry and, in the second half of the century, because many of them were Protestant refugees from persecuting Catholic regimes.[1] But for the five years of Mary's reign a very different atmosphere prevailed. The protection on which the strangers had relied was withdrawn, and instead the government pursued a policy of frank hostility towards the thousands of foreigners settled in the capital. New immigration was barred, and many of those already living here were required to return to the continent. It was a sudden and no doubt bewildering turn of events.

The reasons why Mary's government chose to make a sharp break with the otherwise tolerant tradition of English society are soon apparent. Mary was strongly committed to restoring England to Catholicism; indeed, this was the first and overriding priority of her whole reign. The foreign immigrants settled in the capital were seen as a potential impediment to the implementation of this policy, and for this reason government hostility was assured. During the preceding reign of Edward VI Protestant refugees from the continent had been openly encouraged to come and settle in England, and large numbers had done so. These included a number of eminent continental theologians such as Martin Bucer and Peter Martyr Vermigli, both of whom had been appointed to prestigious posts in the universities and encouraged to play an active part in the establishment of a Protestant church in England.[2] But just as alarming from the point

---

[1] See my *Foreign Protestant Communities in Sixteenth-Century London* (Oxford, 1986). Also J. Lindeboom, *Austin Friars* (The Hague, 1950). F. de Schickler, *Les Églises du refuge en Angleterre* (3 vols, Paris, 1892).

[2] W. K. Jordan, *Edward VI: the Young King* (London, 1968), pp. 189–205. C. Hopf, *Martin Bucer and the English Reformation* (Oxford, 1946). M. W. Anderson, *Peter Martyr, a Reformer in Exile* (Nieuwkoop, 1975).

of view of the new government was the fact that large numbers of more humble Protestant refugees had also settled here, most of them in London, giving the capital's established foreign community an unacceptably radical tinge. For this reason they were seen as a serious threat to the new order, and Mary's government wasted no time in sending them on their way back to the continent. It was accomplished with the minimum of violence, but by the end of 1553 a large proportion of London's foreign residents had been persuaded to depart.

For the thousands of foreigners peacefully, and as they thought permanently, settled in London this must indeed have been a dark and dismal prospect; uprooted from their homes and propelled without ceremony back to an uncertain future on the continent, back towards lands where fear of persecution and death had forced many of them to leave in the first place. But this is not the only sense in which it is possible to speak of a dark chapter in the history of London's foreign community, a brief but turbulent interruption in our otherwise honourable tradition of hospitality to persecuted minorities. For in fact surprisingly little is known of the fate of those expelled by Mary's government. Apart from a handful of the more conspicuous refugees, we do not know where most of them went; nor indeed, is it known with any certainty how many of London's foreign residents actually obeyed the government's injunctions to depart the kingdom. Most historians of the period, in so far as they touch on these events at all, tend to assume that with the publication of the government's last proclamation against the foreigners in 1554 the problem was effectively solved, that most of the Protestant refugees had by then left the kingdom and made their way to new homes in the more hospitable German exile towns.

Yet when the evidence is more closely examined, there is remarkably little to justify either of these assumptions. A search of records in the principal German exile towns, Emden, Wesel and Frankfurt, reveals little sign of a major influx of foreign refugees from London in 1553 or 1554; indeed, hardly more than a handful of names familiar from any London source crop up in these German archives.[3] Even the more obvious expectation that the vast majority of the exiles abandoned London in the face of the government's hostility begins to look doubtful. On the contrary, it appears that a considerable number of

---

[3] Emden, Stadtarchiv, Bürgerbücher; Archiv der Reformierte-Evangelische Kirche, Kirchenratsprotokollen. Frankfurt, Stadtarchiv; Wesel, Kirchenarchiv.

foreigners defied the injunctions against them and simply remained in England throughout the reign.

So there are reasons enough for taking a rather closer look at the fate of London's stranger population during Mary's reign. The circumstances that enabled a substantial minority of London's foreign residents to hang on grimly throughout the reign are worth exploring, not least for the light this sheds on the effectiveness of government in enforcing its policies in this crucial area. But it also raises interesting questions about the foreign community itself: what sort of men were likely to want to remain in such a changed environment? And what does this tell us about their religious convictions and priorities?

It is best to begin by outlining the actions taken by the Marian government against the foreigners settled in London at the beginning of the reign, before considering the effectiveness of these measures and the foreigners' response. What sort of problem did the immigrant community pose to the new regime?

When Mary took possession of her capital in the summer of 1553, there were probably as many as 10 000 foreigners living in London, out of a total population of around 100 000. This may seem a high number and, indeed, a very high proportion of the total population of the capital, but if anything, this is probably a low estimate. Hard figures are difficult to come by, but it has been estimated that about 5000 foreign nationals were settled in the city in the early years of the century, and this number increased rapidly during the years immediately preceding Mary's reign, particularly during the reign of Edward VI; so the estimate of 10 000 in the capital by 1553 is unlikely to be an exaggeration.[4]

The great increase in the city's foreign population was the result of a conscious policy pursued by the Edwardian Privy Council, who were committed to the introduction of a fully Protestant church settlement in England. They therefore made a point of extending a friendly welcome to any persecuted for the faith in the Catholic lands of Europe, with the result that many were encouraged to cross the Channel and make a new home in the English capital. By 1550 so many had gathered in London that the English government acceded to requests that they should be allowed to worship in their own native languages and permitted the establishment of two foreign churches, one for the French-speaking refugees and one for the Dutch.[5]

---

[4] *Foreign Protestant Communities*, pp. 17, 78.
[5] *Ibid.*, pp. 23–45. Lindeboom, *Austin Friars*, pp. 1–28.

These two communities, the French and the Dutch, made up the vast bulk of the foreign population of the city. Most of London's immigrant population came from the lands directly across the Channel, from France or more often from the Low Countries (for in addition to the Dutch-speaking Flemings many of the 'French' immigrants were actually from the French-speaking or Walloon provinces of the Netherlands). There were also a number from other lands, such as German merchants and a small well-established Italian merchant community, but these tended to hold aloof from the stranger churches. The core of the foreign population was formed by the substantial French and Dutch communities, and by 1553 these were more cohesive and visible than ever before, largely as result of the foundation of the stranger churches.

This then was the situation which faced the new Queen when she rode into London on 3 August: a substantial foreign community, amounting perhaps to 10 per cent of the population, and which certainly included an appreciable number of committed Protestants. It did not take long for the new government to decide that the foreign Protestants in the capital posed a serious potential threat to the security of the regime, and a severe impediment to the successful re-establishment of Catholicism. Although the foreigners seem to have played no part in the ill-advised attempt to exclude Mary from the succession in favour of Lady Jane Grey, they were some of the first to feel the chill wind brought about by the change in government. Within weeks the French and Dutch churches had been shut, and it was made clear to their ministers, and to the leading foreign theologians in Oxford and Cambridge, that they should take steps to remove themselves from the kingdom.[6]

Most of the foreign theologians were happy to oblige; they could see that under the prevailing circumstances there was little future for them if they remained in England. Peter Martyr, the Regius Professor of Divinity at Oxford, retired to his former chair at Strasbourg, while his colleague Bernardino Ochino made for Geneva.[7] For the ministers of the London foreign churches it was not quite so simple, since they had their congregations to think of. Neither the ministers nor their superintendent, the distinguished Polish theologian John a Lasco, were prepared to abandon their responsibilities without making provision for the members of their church, and two anxious weeks

---

[6] W. F. Turnbull et al. (eds), *Calendar of state papers Spanish* (London, 1861–1950), vol. 11, p. 173.

[7] P. McNair, 'Ochino's Apology: three kings or three wives?', *History*, 60 (1975), p. 360.

went by while they cast around for the means to get the most vulnerable of them away to safety. At last two Danish ships were found about to return home and hurriedly chartered. On 17 September Lasco and 165 members of the two congregations embarked at Gravesend, all the passengers the little vessels could hold. Those for whom no room had been found returned to London to plan their own means of escape.[8]

Over the next three months it is clear that many more members of the foreign churches did manage to make their way back to the continent by their own initiative. The government did nothing to stand in their way: on the contrary, instructions were swiftly forwarded to the mayors of Dover and Rye to allow the departing foreigners an unobstructed passage.[9] Many of the foreign Protestants presumably slipped quietly away by this route, following the coast road down through Kent and then finding a passage across to France or the Low Countries. On the other side of the Channel the influx was sufficient to cause some concern to the local authorities.[10] But this rapid exodus did not account for all the members of the foreign churches for whom no room had been found on Lasco's ships. Instead some seem simply to have remained in London, resolved for the time being to lie low and see how things would develop.

This, however, was not a response that the government was prepared to tolerate. Mary's councillors were determined to be rid of the more committed foreign Protestants, and they went to some trouble to hasten them on their way. Both Gardiner, the Lord Chancellor, and Bonner, the new bishop of London, played an active role in this regard. Bonner had apparently furnished himself with a list of the leading foreign heretics, compiled with the help of informers, and he took considerable pains to track them down.[11] Gardiner, meanwhile, relied on more subtle tactics, as he later recalled for the benefit of Renard, the imperial ambassador. When he heard that a foreign minister was lingering in the capital he summoned him to appear before him, judging, shrewdly enough, that the minister would take

---

[8] F. A. Norwood, 'The London Dutch refugees in search of a home, 1553–1554', *American Historical Review*, 58 (1952–3), pp. 64–6.

[9] J. R. Dasent, *Acts of the Privy Council of London* (11 vols, London, 1890–93), vol. 4, p. 349.

[10] J. Decavele, *De dageraad van de reformatie in Vlaanderen, 1520–1565* (2 vols, Brussels, 1975), vol. 2, pp. 342, 392–3.

[11] See the account of Jean des Forges to the French consistory in 1560. E. Johnson, *Actes du consistoire de l'église Française de Threadneedle Street, vol. 1, 1560–1565* (Publications of the Huguenot Society of London, 38, 1937), p. 22.

the hint and depart.[12] Such a device was sufficient to account for the distinguished French theologian Pierre Alexandre, a former client of the disgraced Archbishop Cranmer, and we may imagine that during the autumn of 1553 many other more humble foreign Protestants followed his example.

For those who still chose to remain in London, life became progressively more difficult. In December, parliament repealed the Edwardian Prayer Book, making attendance at Mass compulsory and further inhibiting the foreigners' freedom of action. Up to this point the leaders of the foreign community seem to have hoped that it might prove possible to keep some sort of community going, perhaps meeting informally in a private house. There were still members of both foreign churches left in London, and both the French and the Dutch had initially left behind one of their ministers to cater to their needs. But by the beginning of 1554 any such hopes were fast receding. Both communities were sorely troubled by informers ready to betray any irregularity to the authorities, so that when the Dutch minister Delenus came to write to Lasco early in 1554 he was already beginning to doubt whether any useful purpose was served by his remaining in London.[13] His mind was made up by the political events of January, and especially Wyatt's rebellion, a last-ditch protest by opponents of Mary's regime which might, if better organized, have caused it serious problems.[14] As it was, the revolt left the regime badly shaken; the loyalty of London had been in doubt up until the last moment, and the foreign Protestants who lingered in London were a convenient scapegoat for the capital's alarming unreliability. Within a week of the revolt's collapse, therefore, the Privy Council determined on a general expulsion of those foreign refugees who still lingered in the capital, a determination carried into effect by the proclamation of 17 February.[15] All foreign residents without the benefit of denizen status were ordered to leave the country within 14 days. Foreign printers and preachers were singled out for special attention, and in fact the last of the foreign ministers, Peter Delenus and his father Gualter, left England within days of its publication. Their departure marked the end of any attempt to maintain an official foreign church community in London during Mary's reign.

---

[12] *Calendar of state papers Spanish*, vol. 11, p. 217.

[13] J. H. Hessels, *Ecclesiae Londino-Batavae Archivum* (3 vols in 4, Cambridge, 1889–97), vol. 2, pp. 40–44.

[14] David Loades, *Two Tudor conspiracies* (Cambridge, 1965), pp. 67–74.

[15] P. L. Hughes and J. F. Larkin, *Tudor royal proclamations* (3 vols, New Haven, 1964–9), vol. 2, pp. 31–2.

With the proclamation of February 1554 and the departure of the last of the ministers the official campaign against the immigrant community was brought to a close. It seems now to have been assumed that the foreign Protestants in England at the beginning of the reign had been effectively dealt with; Simon Renard reported to the emperor at the end of February that the capital was much quieter since the foreigners had been expelled, and this probably represented the official view.[16] Gardiner and his colleagues now turned their attention to the wider problems connected with the restoration of Catholicism and its enforcement. The foreign community never again attracted a significant amount of government attention.

To some extent the government's confidence was justified. The foreigners who remained in London for the rest of Mary's reign caused no further trouble; they never, for instance, played more than a negligible part in the small Protestant underground movement. But if the authorities believed that all the remaining foreign residents had left London in the wake of the proclamation of February 1554, then here they were mistaken. This, indeed, was not what the proclamation had ordered. The proclamation of February had only required those who had not applied for denizen status to leave; but this was to exclude from the order a substantial category of foreigners, which included many former members of the foreign churches. Denization was a sort of quasi-naturalization and conferred significant economic and legal advantages; consequently most foreigners who envisaged settling permanently and could afford the fees applied to be registered.[17] During Edward's reign there were over 800 new denizens enrolled, and this included many of those who also joined the foreign churches.[18] As a result, many of the better-off members of the foreign Protestant congregations were perfectly entitled to remain in London even after the hostile proclamation of February.

Just how many of London's foreign population actually did so is a question which in the absence of reliable statistics is difficult to answer with assurance. Sixteenth-century statistics of population are never very reliable, and Mary's reign was no exception. Here it is particularly frustrating that no records have survived from the parliamentary subsidy of 1555, the only one of the reign, since this would

---

[16] *Calendar of State Papers Spanish*, vol. 12, p. 126.
[17] Pettegree, *Foreign Protestant Communities*, pp. 15–16. I. Scouloudi, *Returns of strangers in the metropolis, 1593 etc.* (Publications of the Huguenot Society, 57, 1985), pp. 1–16.
[18] W. Page, *Letters of denization and acts of naturalization for aliens in England, 1509–1603* (Publications of the Huguenot Society, 8, 1893), pp. lii–liii.

theoretically have recorded the names of every adult male immigrant then resident in London. However, subsidy returns have survived for two years close enough to either side of the reign to give an idea of relative population movements: 1552, the last Edwardian tax assessment, and the first in Elizabeth's reign in 1559. Comparing these two we find a significant thinning out of the foreign population, amounting to perhaps 50 or 60 per cent of the total.[19] But on this basis it is also clear that a substantial proportion had remained in London throughout; not the swollen roster of the Edwardian period, but a number probably comparable to the number of foreigners settled in the city before the first great influx of religious refugees.

Obviously those who remained in London throughout Mary's reign were likely to be among the less religiously committed members of the foreign community. A substantial body of foreign citizens were well established in London long before the Protestant refugees arrived; indeed, London had had a thriving foreign community right back to the Middle Ages. Those who had come to London in the early decades of the sixteenth century had done so essentially for traditional economic reasons – to find work, or to profit by the buoyant market for new skills and luxury goods. Some of these longer-term residents joined the new foreign church in 1550, but most did not, preferring to get on with their work in peace. Indeed, there remained throughout the Reformation period pockets within the stranger community, whole districts or occupational groups, which had little or no contact with the new church. Having remained oblivious of the religious changes of Edward's reign such men could equally have been expected to ignore the new upheaval in 1553, and indeed most of these sorts of foreign artisan do appear to have worked on regardless. An examination of the records of the Coopers' Company reveals no departures which one could associate with the change in regime in 1553.[20]

These long-established foreign residents of little or no religious commitment would have accounted for many, if not most, of those who remained in London during Mary's reign. But what of the members of the foreign churches? Were they all so committed to Protestantism that they quickly followed their ministers into exile? The answer to this question seems to be no; indeed, there is conclusive evidence that, on the contrary, a substantial number chose instead to

---

[19] R. E. G. Kirk and E. F. Kirk, *Returns of aliens dwelling in the city and suburbs of London* (4 vols, Publications of the Huguenot Society, 10, 1900–08), vol. 1, pp. 234–46, 260–7.
[20] See below, n. 22.

remain in England in defiance of both their ministers' wishes and the government's intentions. This group will be considered later; but first it is worth asking how they were able to continue in the face of such evident and (initially at least) active government hostility.

In the first place it is clear that the foreigners could count on a fair amount of sympathy from beyond their own community. Interesting in this connection is the case of Francis Bertie, one of the leading foreign Protestant merchants, who later recalled his story for the benefit of the French consistory.[21] At the beginning of Mary's reign Bertie found himself denounced to Bishop Bonner and arrested; but then, after two of the leading Catholic foreign merchants had interceded on his behalf with Renard, the imperial ambassador, he was released. Bertie had obviously been able to count on a feeling of solidarity among the foreign merchants, which took no account of religious differences between them. The Catholic merchants from the Low Countries might not share Bertie's convictions, but they had no wish to see him suffer for them.

And this did not apply only to foreign merchants. Bertie might have been exceptional in having rich and influential friends, but many other more humble foreigners could also rely on a degree of protection as a result of local economic factors. For it had quickly become apparent that the government's policy of harrying foreign residents into leaving England could cause problems for many outside the immigrant community, especially those English employers who relied on skilled foreign workmen. The proclamation of February 1554, which ordered the immediate departure of all foreign residents who did not have denizen status, was a case in point. If fully implemented this would have had disastrous consequences for many London citizens and indeed for the whole economy of the city, since in several trades crucial to the London economy foreign artisans made up a large proportion of the skilled workforce. Brewing, for instance, had always relied heavily on foreign expertise, ever since beer brewing was introduced into England from Germany in the fourteenth century, and in the associated trade of cooperage something like 30 per cent of the journeymen workers were foreign born.[22] So it was with their own interests very much at heart that several city companies immediately began to lobby to have workers in their trades exempted from the expulsion order, apparently with considerable success. As long as the journeymen foreigners were registered with the city

---

[21] *Actes du consistoire*, p. 23.
[22] G. Elkington, *The Coopers, Company and Craft* (London, 1933), pp. 240–1. Guildhall Library London, Ms 5606 (Coopers Company Accounts), vol. 1.

companies the government seems to have allowed them to stay, even if they were not denizens. Far from the proclamation of February 1554 causing wholesale departures among the foreign journeymen coopers, the number registered with the company actually rose during Mary's reign.[23] Two years later the mayor published an order that no foreigner should be employed in the city but exempted from its provisions not only foreign brewers, but textile workers, felt-makers and cap-thickers as well.[24]

In these important city crafts the interests of Londoners reluctant to deprive themselves of the foreigners' skills triumphed over the government's concern at their potential for sedition. The city authorities in fact gave the Privy Council little help in enforcing its policy against foreigners. In July 1554 two foreign shoemakers were arrested by the constable for loitering during the nightwatch. They were in serious trouble, as they were discovered to be non-denizens who had remained in England in defiance of the Queen's proclamation. They were committed to prison, but nine days later the mayor was authorized to release them and it seems no further action was taken.[25] This is an interesting case and a highly significant result, which tells us a great deal about the effectiveness of the Marian government's religious legislation. For however little actual opposition there had been in parliament and elsewhere, the enforcement of these measures was another matter altogether. In particular, the crucial support of local authorities could not necessarily be relied on, especially when, as here, government policy cut across vested economic interests. Considerations of this sort gave the foreign population in London a measure of protection that they could not have expected when the government first published its proclamation expelling most of them from the country.

It appears that among the foreigners who took advantage of these loopholes to remain in England were quite a large number of former members of the French and Dutch churches. This may seem rather a surprising assertion, given the trouble that the authorities had taken to be rid of them. But the evidence comes from a most reliable source: the minutes of the consistory of the French church in London.

When the French church reopened in the first years of Elizabeth's reign, one of its first collective acts was to receive back those members who had remained in London during Mary's reign and who had

---

[23] Coopers Company Accounts, vol. 1, fols 181, 191, 202.
[24] Corporation of London Record Office, Letter Book S, fol. 93ᵛ.
[25] Corporation of London, Repertoires of the Court of Aldermen, vol. 13, part 1, fols 179, 183.

compromised their beliefs by attending Mass. Fifty such acts of repentance are noted in the French minutes, and in the case of 34 of them their names are also recorded.[26] We will return to this interesting group in a moment. In the Dutch church far fewer cases are recorded, less than ten, which may suggest that the Dutch church members were rather more inclined to follow their ministers abroad in 1553. But they were by no means completely blameless; certainly there were other members of both churches who had remained in England during Mary's reign, but who did not choose to rejoin the church in 1559. A search of company records and similar documents has turned up a number of cases of this sort.[27]

But let us look a little more closely at this most interesting group of Frenchmen, those who remained in England during Mary's reign, but then rejoined the French church in 1560. What can we discover about them, that might give us a clue about their motives? Here we are greatly assisted by the fact that the names of 34 of these apostate Frenchmen are recorded in the consistory minutes. I have tried to trace all that may be discovered about them: their age, professions, economic circumstances, how long they had been in England, where they came from and so on. Obviously not all this information is available in all circumstances, but a gratifying amount can be found about what was, after all, a group of very ordinary people. Here we are indebted to the Elizabethan government's careful regulation of the foreign community in the 1560s, for had they been English we would know very little about them; as it is, we know enough to make some interesting generalizations about the sort of church member likely to be tempted to remain in England under a Catholic regime.[28]

The first point to note is that a large proportion of this sample had been in England a considerable time. The joiner Jacques Bontemps had been in London since 1528, the buttonmaker Hugh Bertrand since 1536. At least ten of them, probably more, had been in England a decade or more, that is since the reign of Henry VIII and long before the foreign churches were first set up. Such long residence would have been a considerable disincentive to throw it all up because of a change of government, particularly as many of them had invested both time and capital in building a successful new life in England. Most, at least 20 out of the 34, had taken out patents of denization. This was not cheap, since the whole process of becoming a denizen cost about £5,

---

[26] *Actes du consistoire*, pp. 5, 13, 15, 37, 39, 52.
[27] Pettegree, *Foreign Protestant Communities*, p. 165.
[28] This information, derived mainly from the *Returns of aliens* and *Denizations* is set out in Table 3 of my *Foreign Protestant Communities*, pp. 131–2.

the equivalent of three months' wages for a journeyman workman at the time.[29] Not that most of this group would necessarily have fallen into this category – the majority seem to have prospered to the extent that they would have been employing their own journeymen. Where a tax assessment survives for members of this group most paid on assessed wealth of £5 or £10, whereas foreigners generally paid a poll tax of fourpence on a nominal assessment of 20 shillings. So these were men of some substance, with an established business and place in society, all good reasons for a reluctance to throw it all up in 1553. One other contributory factor may have been the fact that quite a surprising proportion of this group worked in trades where their equipment was not very easily transportable. They included five who were smiths of one sort or another, coppersmiths or goldsmiths. There was also a crossbow-maker, a typefounder and a printer. On the other hand there was only one weaver, a significant under-representation of this important trade, but one where skills were relatively easily transported. Those with equipment or an established clientele could be forgiven for seeing the whole question with different eyes.

Of course such practical considerations could be overcome if a man's commitment to his faith was sufficiently strong. Take the case of Simon Percy, a French coppersmith who had been working in Southwark since 1530. He had every reason to wish to remain in England. He had been there more than 20 years, he had built up a prosperous business and had every prospect of continuing to make a comfortable living. Since 1541 he had also been a member of the Founders' Company, signalling a degree of acceptance into the local trade fraternity.[30] Yet in 1553 he threw up all of this and followed the ministers of the church into exile, settling the following year at Emden. Percy's was a courageous decision: the local records in Emden record that he had to be excused the usual modest fee on registering as an inhabitant on grounds of his poverty, so obviously he had not contrived to take much of his wealth with him.[31]

Yet for the more prosperous members of the foreign churches Percy's conduct was probably less typical than that of the group of Frenchmen I have discussed above. That is not to say that their decision did not cost them considerable mental anguish. Revealing in

---

[29] *Calendar of State Papers Spanish*, vol. 10, p. 265.

[30] *Returns of aliens*, vol. 1, pp. 146, 351, 472. C. G. Parsloe, *Wardens' Accounts of the Worshipful Company of Founders of the City of London, 1497–1681* (London, 1964), p. 95.

[31] Emden Bürgerbücher, vol. 2, fol. 6.

this respect is the testimony of one Guillaume Maubert, who was elected deacon in 1560 and then required to stand down on account of his apostasy during Mary's reign. Maubert did not deny the fact, but protested that he had intended to go into exile after the ministers. Indeed, he had got as far as Dover before his resolve crumbled and he returned to his home in Southwark, where he had lived 20 years and now had a thriving business as a currier. Having decided to remain in England he did eventually conform; or as he put it in his testimony to the consistory, 'did as others did during the persecution'.[32] It is a very human and very comprehensible story: the good intentions, the second thoughts, the final reluctant submission. Living as we do in a century which has furnished so many examples of this kind, of an uneasy suppression of conscientious objections in the face of superior force, who are we to reproach his evident lack of heroism?

Many of those who remained in London probably hoped that they would be able to live out the reign in quiet obscurity, without the need to compromise their beliefs. As we have seen in the case of Maubert, such hopes usually proved over-optimistic, but they were understandable enough. The behaviour of those who remained behind and compromised with the new regime was of course heartily disapproved by the church's leaders. John a Lasco, the former superintendent of the church now established in the German exile town of Emden, went as far as to publish an old tract in which he discussed whether a true Christian might attend the popish Mass, and solemnly warned against such behaviour.[33] But the publication of Lasco's work, and of Pierre du Val's *Petit dialogue du consolateur*, which he dedicated to the French community in London,[34] suggests a recognition on the part of the foreign ministers that a large number of their congregations had not followed them into exile.

Be that as it may, those who remained generally made their peace with the regime in the end; few, if any, found their way into the small secret Protestant congregations. A careful reading of Foxe's *Acts and Monuments*, the principal source for the history of Marian Protestantism, supplies only a handful of foreign names. The German student Augustine Bernher, a former disciple of Hugh Latimer, lingered in England long enough to earn a reputation as 'a diligent

---

[32] *Actes du consistoire*, p. 5.

[33] *Het ghevoelen Joannis a Lasco ... of het den christenen, na dien zy het word Godes ende de godlooszheit des Pauwstdoms bekent hebben ... dat zy zick in den pauwstlichen godsdiensten ... vinden laten* (Emden, 1557).

[34] *Le petit dialogue d'un consolateur consolant l'Église en ses afflictions*. See Schickler, *Églises du refuge*, vol. 1, pp. 73–5.

attender on the Lord's prisoners'; and a foreign merchant, one Bartley, offered Edwin Sandys a temporary refuge when he was on the run from Gardiner.[35] Two Frenchmen were briefly imprisoned for religion in the Tower, where one of them, Lion, offered his fellow prisoners the dubious comfort of singing psalms in French. There was only one foreign victim of the persecution: Lyon Cawch, a young Flemish merchant living in London, who was arrested and executed with 13 English Protestants at Stratford-le-Bowe.[36] Perhaps the most interesting reference in Foxe is to a Dutch shoemaker by the name of Frog who attended the clandestine congregation led by John Rough. On occasions the meetings took place in Frog's house, conveniently situated in the liberty of St Katherine's outside the city wall.[37]

All in all it cannot be claimed that those foreigners who remained in England during Mary's reign made a very distinguished contribution to the Protestant underground. Generally speaking, those whose commitment to their faith overrode all other considerations followed their ministers abroad; those who remained behind did not, on the whole, aspire to martyrdom. But, and this is the point I believe to be of a wider relevance, this does not mean that those who fell into this category can be ignored when we come to write the history of Marian Protestantism. These men, for all they eventually compromised with the state religion, had cared enough about their faith to join the churches in 1550 and many of them cared enough to endure the public humiliation of an act of repentance in order to rejoin in 1560. Their Protestantism was, it is true, of a pragmatic and conditional nature; but it was probably no less sincere for all that.

We do well to dwell on this for a moment, for it may be that this point is of relevance not just when discussing the conduct of members of the stranger community, but also more generally in comprehending the growth of Protestantism in lands where it was forced to exist in defiance of state authority. This element of passive support is something all too easily left out of account. In the case of Mary's reign, historians of Protestantism have been content to concentrate almost exclusively on two groups, the exiles and martyrs, both small and each in their way untypical. What we now know of the history of the stranger community in London suggests that our attention should also be directed to a third group: men and women who remained in England and avoided martyrdom even if that meant compromising

---

[35] John Foxe, *Acts and Monuments* (8 vols, London, 1837–41), vol. 7, p. 262, vol. 8, p. 596.

[36] Ibid., vol. 7, p. 744, vol. 8, pp. 151–6, 523.

[37] Ibid., vol. 8, pp. 458, 459.

their faith for the time being, but who were nevertheless in their own way sincere Protestants. They tended to be, like these Frenchmen, of middling wealth and social status; reluctant therefore to throw up a comfortable standard of living for an uncertain future abroad, and not inclined to court a death sentence by open defiance. But when the time came they would rally to the cause once it had become safe to do so. Until that happy day they were content to keep alive their faith in their hearts.

This sort of behaviour was forcefully deprecated by the leading reformers. Calvin warned repeatedly against 'Nicodemism' as he called it, publishing no fewer than five tracts between 1536 and 1562 urging such secret supporters to commit themselves fully to the cause.[38] But the fact that Calvin and his colleagues confronted the issue so often in their writings indicates how widespread a problem this was in France, the Netherlands and, as we have seen, in England, indeed everywhere where Protestantism could only exist in defiance of state power.

Ultimately, if we are to understand Protestantism in these various countries, we have to take such secret supporters seriously. For when the opportunity came they might take an important hand in events. It is worth remembering here that when Protestantism was restored in England, much of the achievement of establishing the Elizabethan church belonged to men and women who had remained in England through Mary's reign: Cecil, Archbishop Parker, Elizabeth herself. Returning exiles would help to set the tone, but no more than these prominent 'Nicodemites'. So also in the French church. After Elizabeth's accession, leading members of the Edwardian church hurried back to England to petition for the church's restoration, but they found that a community had already gathered to meet informally, made up of those who had remained in London through the dark days of Mary's reign.

Even before these wider implications are explored, the history of the foreign population during Mary's reign offers considerable food for thought, not least as a case study of how ordinary people may react to dilemmas of faith and commitment in an age of rapid religious change. But equally important in the long run was the fact that during this most difficult period the foreign community had demonstrated a quality that was to become a hallmark of the refugee congregations over the next two centuries: their extraordinary resil-

---

[38] C. M. Eire, 'Prelude to sedition? Calvin's attack on Nicodemism and religious compromise', *ARG*, 76 (1985), pp. 120–21.

ience. The same stubborn durability which helped them overcome government hostility in Mary's reign, would sustain the foreign community through plague and economic agitation later in the century, and the challenge posed by Archbishop Laud in the next. The hard lessons of Mary's reign were not without their value.

CHAPTER THREE

The London Exile Community and the Second Sacramentarian Controversy, 1553–1560

The foreign Protestant communities first established in London during the early decades of the English Reformation have had a long and distinguished history. Celebrations to mark the 300th anniversary of the Revocation of the Edict of Nantes in 1685 have called attention to the rich variety of the exile contribution to English cultural, economic, and intellectual development; and students of the Reformation have also begun to recognize the significance of an earlier generation of Protestant refugees.[1] In the 30 years between 1550 and 1580 the Protestant exile community in London played a particularly important role in the formation and development of Reformed Protestantism. To their embattled co-religionists in France and the Netherlands the churches in exile provided a vital source of support and encouragement; it is conceivable that the Reformed community in the Netherlands would not have survived the effective persecution of the decades preceding the war of independence against Spain without the support of the exile communities, and certainly the liturgical models developed in the exile churches had a formative and enduring influence on the doctrine and practice of the emerging Dutch Reformed Church.[2] The foreign communities in London were also not without influence on the religious climate in England, as the wary controls exercised by the Elizabethan government over their contacts with English radicals bear witness.[2a] If, despite their unconquerable meddlesomeness, the exiles remained welcome, this was very largely because the economic benefits that these industrious and

---

[1] Irene Scouloudi (ed.), *The Huguenots in Britain* (London, 1987); Robin D. Gwynn, *Huguenot Heritage* (London, 1985); Andrew Pettegree, *Foreign Protestant Communities in Sixteenth-Century London* (Oxford, 1986).

[2] A. A. van Schelven, *De Nederduitsche vluchtelingenkerken der zestiende eeuw* (The Hague, 1909); L. Knappert, *Het ontstaan en de vestiging van het protestantisme in de Nederlanden* (Utrecht, 1924); E. M. Braekman, 'Les Sources de la Confessio Belgica', *Bulletin de la Commission de l'Histoire des Eglises Wallonnes*, 5:7 (1961), pp. 3–24.

[2a] Patrick Collinson, 'The Elizabethan Puritans and the Foreign Reformed Church in London', *Proceedings of the Huguenot Society*, 20 (1958–64), pp. 528–55.

often highly skilled newcomers brought to the communities in which they settled could not easily be overlooked.

The achievement of the French and Dutch churches in their early years was an impressive one, yet without irony it can be said that the London exile community had its most immediate impact on the international scene between 1553 and 1558, when the London exile churches had temporarily ceased to exist. For in 1553, only three years after the first establishment of the foreign churches in London, the accession of a Catholic Queen in England brought a peremptory end to the noble experiment inaugurated by the ministers of Edward VI. The leaders of the exile community were forced to contemplate the need for a new place of refuge, and in the changed religious climate of the 1550s it was to prove by no means easy to find. Driven from town to town by suspicious and hostile Lutheran ministers, the London exiles quickly became a cause célèbre, and sparked a controversy which engaged many of the leading figures of the Protestant world; poor wanderers to their friends, the refugees became 'the devil's martyrs' to their embittered critics.[3]

The peregrinations of the London refugees in search of a new home make an unedifying tale of mistrust and persecution; furthermore, as church members often eventually made their own way to safety or travelled in small groups it is by no means easy to trace their movements. Nevertheless it is worth attempting to follow the exiles on their ill-fated journey, and not simply because the London exiles had such a formative influence on the German exile communities. On a wider field, the consequences of the London exiles' brief but turbulent sojourn in Germany, particularly for the relationship between Lutheran and Reformed, would be felt long after the death of Mary had allowed the re-establishment of Protestantism in England, and reopened London to Protestant exiles from across the Channel.

The tribulations experienced by the London exiles in Denmark and Germany were all the more painful because in England they had been treated with quite exceptional generosity. In the years following the accession of Edward VI as many as 10 000 foreign Protestants had taken refuge in England, crossing the Channel in increasing numbers as the Catholic authorities in France and the Spanish Netherlands pursued a steadily more effective policy of persecution. Most settled in London, and in 1550 the English government, responding to the petitions of the leading refugee ministers supported by prominent

---

[3] See p. 78.

English sympathizers, made over to the exiles churches in which the French- and Dutch-speaking refugees could enjoy worship in their native languages.[4] The exiles were quick to contrast their reception in Germany after 1553 with the lavishness of the Edwardian government, but it must be said that the refugees' friends at Court often had their own motives for their activities on the strangers' behalf. English radicals saw the foreign churches as a chance to establish a model Reformed community which would act as a spur to further change in the as yet only partially reformed English church, while others of the young King's advisers had a more prosaic intention, hoping that the foreign churches would be an effective instrument to control the radical sects which flourished among the capital's foreigners.[5] However mixed the motives which accompanied the churches' foundation, the exiles were quick to grasp the opportunity offered them, and thrived. The Royal Charter establishing the community provided the refugees with two large and prominent city churches, in addition to a substantial income for their first superintendent, the distinguished Polish reformer John a Lasco.[6] Four ministers were also appointed: the biblical scholar and royal servant Gualter Delenus together with Marten Micron for the Dutch community, Francis Perussel and Richard Vauville for the French. Together Lasco and his colleagues supervised the enrolment of members, and by the time the churches had been renovated and services could begin both communities had elected deacons to care for the poor and elders to assist the ministers in the running of the community. Within a couple of years the ministers and elders were presiding over two smoothly running church communities, with their own liturgy, catechisms and confession of faith.

The death of Edward VI brought an abrupt change to this satisfactory state of affairs, for it was soon clear that the accession of a Catholic Queen spelled disaster for the foreign church communities. The new Queen's advisers saw the foreign Protestants in the capital as a major obstacle to the restoration of the old faith, and even before the Mass was officially restored the French and Dutch churches were shut up, and the ministers informed that they should take steps to

---

[4] J. Lindeboom, *Austin Friars. History of the Dutch Reformed Church in London, 1550–1950* (The Hague, 1950).
[5] Pettegree, *Foreign Protestant Communities*, pp. 23–45.
[6] H. Dalton, *Johannes a Lasco* (Gotha, 1881); B. Hall, *John a Lasco, A Pole in Reformation England* (Friends of Dr Williams Library, 25th Lecture, 1971); Oskar Bartel, *Jan Laski* (Berlin, 1981).

remove themselves from the Queen's dominions.[7] This was no easy matter. Both foreign communities had grown considerably since the foundation of the churches in 1550, and a mass exodus of all the church members and their families would have involved something in excess of 4000 people.[8] Casting around for a means to get at least the most prominent, and thus the most vulnerable, members of the church out of the country, the ministers discovered two Danish ships lying in the Thames and preparing to set sail. These were hurriedly chartered, and on 17 September Lasco, Micron, and 175 members of the two communities departed from Gravesend. Those for whom no room could be found on board were left to make their own way to the continent, while two ministers, Delenus and Perussel, remained behind to care for those who chose, for the time being, to remain in England.

The problems which were to plague the unhappy voyagers began almost immediately when a storm in the North Sea separated the two small ships and carried them towards the inhospitable coast of Norway.[9] It was not until the end of October that the bedraggled travellers were reunited at Elsinore, whence the main body of the exiles found their way to Copenhagen. Lasco, Micron and Utenhove meanwhile journeyed wearily on to Kolding, where the King was holding court, to present their petition for the restoration of the community on Danish soil.[10] Initially at least they were well received, but a sermon by one of the Lutheran court preachers which the exiles interpreted as a veiled attack on themselves soon soured the atmosphere, and when two days later Lasco and his colleagues requested a

---

[7] *Calendar of State Papers relating to the negotiations between England and Spain*, ed. R. Tyler et al. (London, 1892 ff.), vol. 11, pp. 118, 169, 173.

[8] This is a conservative estimate. The Dutch church register of 1550 lists 351 male members, and the community would have at least doubled in size by 1553. No register of members of the French church survives, but it was later always about the same size as the Dutch. If the two churches together numbered about 1500 male members by 1553, then 4000 is a low estimate of the total strength of the community. Contemporaries spoke of much higher numbers: Bullinger, for instance, suggested 15 000 would have to leave England. *CO*, 14. col. 598.

[9] The basis for all subsequent accounts of the refugees' perambulations is the narrative published by Jan Utenhove, a close friend of Lasco's and one of the first elders of the London Dutch community. *Simplex et fidelis narratio de instituta ac demum dissipate Belgarum, aliorumque peregrinorum in Anglia Ecclesia* (Basle, 1560). Modern edn in *Bibliotheca Reformatoria Neerlandica* (*BRN*), ed. S. Cramer and F. Pijper (10 vols, The Hague, 1903–14), vol. 9, pp. 29–186. See also F. A. Norwood, 'The London Dutch Refugees in search of a Home, 1553–4', *American Historical Review*, 58 (1952–3), pp. 64–72, and the articles by Mönckeberg and Kayser cited below.

[10] Norwood, 'London Dutch Refugees', pp. 66–7.

public disputation to compare their observances with the local Lutheran rite the King was easily convinced that the exiles could not be tolerated on their own terms. On 15 November the refugees received the answer to their petition: permission to remain in Denmark was granted, but only on condition that they conformed to the local rites. The exiles hastened to prepare a reply, but their implied criticisms of the Danish order only precipitated a final order to leave the kingdom. A generous gift towards their travelling expenses could hardly assuage the disappointment Lasco and his companions felt at this unexpected rebuff.[11]

Lasco and Utenhove took ship direct from Kolding and found their way via Holstein and Bremen to Emden. Here they found other former members of the London church who had come direct from England, and a friendly reception from both Lasco's former patron Countess Anna and the local Reformed community.[12] For the main body of the exiles left behind in Copenhagen, however, the worst part of their journey was still to come. The refugees had been well received by the inhabitants of the Danish capital, and the arrival of the King's order to depart was a cruel and unexpected reverse. An anguished protest, even the sympathetic mediation of the Danish senate proved unavailing; only Lasco's children, their tutor, and a few seriously ill brethren were allowed to remain, and for the rest there was no alternative but to continue their journey through the worst of a northern winter. No ship could be found to take the whole party, which was forced to split into three smaller groups for the perilous voyage across the Baltic.[13] The first group put in at Warnemünde, but neither there nor at nearby Rostock were the local authorities prepared to risk allowing the exiles to remain. At the end of December they moved on to Wismar, where a second group of the exiles had a much more encouraging reception. The Wismar authorities had hitherto shown a degree of toleration, even to the extent of allowing the anabaptist Menno Simons and his followers to settle in the town. The Mennonites now took the lead in welcoming the half-frozen travellers into their homes. So things might have remained, had not the exiles insisted on pursuing their apparently inexhaustible passion for dis-

---

[11] Ibid., 67–8; The conduct of the Lutheran ministers receives a spirited defence from Karl Mönckeberg, 'Johannes a Lasco und seiner Fremdengemeinde Aufnahme in Dänemark und Norddeutschland', *Zeitschrift für kirchliche Wissenschaft und kirchliches Leben*, 4 (1883), pp. 588–604. See also Richard Kruske, *Johannes a Lasco und der Sakramentsstreit* (Leipzig, 1901), pp. 84–93.
[12] Dalton, *Lasco*, pp. 439 ff.
[13] List in *BRN*, vol. 9, pp. 89–90; Norwood, 'London Dutch Refugees', p. 69.

putation. A first doctrinal discussion demonstrated that none of the exile group could rise to the challenge of an opponent of Menno's stature, so an emissary was quickly despatched in search of Micron, who by this time had joined Lasco in Emden. Micron hastened back to Wismar and for two days engaged Menno in a wide-ranging doctrinal debate.[14] The result was almost inevitable. On the second day the disputation ended in angry scenes. The town council, now thoroughly alarmed, repented of its earlier generosity and ordered the exiles out. In the last week of February they reached Lübeck, where the third group from Copenhagen was now located. The refugees had been allowed to remain only on the most grudging terms and against the vehement protests of the town's Lutheran ministers, and the arrival of Micron and his band proved the last straw. A new dispute with three of the town's ministers provided the occasion for a peremptory order to depart. On the first of March the exiles moved on once more, this time to Hamburg.

Hamburg was an orthodox Lutheran town, but the exiles still had hopes of a favourable reception. Several former members of the London churches had apparently been allowed to settle in the town, and Micron himself had passed through several times on his trips to and from Emden without incident.[15] It was in Hamburg, however, that the exiles found their most bitter and able opponent: Joachim Westphal, pastor of St Katharine's and subsequently superintendent of the Hamburg church.[16] Westphal was one of a number of orthodox Lutherans increasingly alarmed at developments within Protestantism since Luther's death in 1546, and in particular by the apparent success of the leading Swiss churches in promoting a doctrine of the Eucharist which deviated sharply from that of the Wittenberg reformer. Nowhere was this development more evident than in England, where a small group of reformers with close links to Zurich and Geneva – Lasco and the other leaders of the foreign community prominent among them – had lobbied with considerable vigour and skill for rapid progress towards a fully Reformed church order. It was

---

[14] Both men wrote an account of the confrontation. Micron's *Waerachtigh Verhaal* has recently been republished, *Documenta Anabaptistica Neerlandica, 3: Marten Micron*, ed. W. F. Dankbaar (Leiden, 1981). See also J. H. Gerretsen, *Micronius* (Nijmegen, 1895).

[15] Mönckeberg, 'Johannes a Lasco', p. 598; idem, *Joachim Westphal und Johannes Calvin* (Hamburg, 1865), p. 26.

[16] On Westphal see Herwarth von Schade, *Joachim Westphal und Peter Braubach* (Hamburg, 1981), pp. 21–53.

the publication by Lasco in 1552 of a series of sermons in which he sharply attacked Luther's Eucharistic doctrine that spurred Westphal into action.[17] Lasco's sermons were primarily intended to express his support for the consensus on the Eucharist agreed by Calvin and Bullinger in 1549 and now for the first time published in England, the *Consensus Tigurinus*. The consensus was ostensibly a declaration of doctrinal agreement between the churches of Geneva and Zurich, but Calvin clearly hoped that it could be the basis of wider agreement with the German Lutherans, and these implications were not lost on Westphal.[18] In 1552 he published his *Farrago*, a collection of Eucharistic formulae taken from the writings of non-Lutheran reformers, purporting to show their confusion and the contradictions between them; it was intended more as a warning to the German churches of the progress being made by Calvin and the Reformed than as a systematic refutation of their doctrine. Westphal followed this in 1553 with his *Recta Fides de Coena Domini*, an exegesis of orthodox Lutheran doctrine on the Eucharist.[19]

Neither of these tracts seems to have had much immediate impact. Lasco first heard of the *Farrago* when Hardenberg sent him a copy from Bremen at the end of 1553,[20] and it was early 1554 before either work was mentioned in the correspondence of the leading Swiss reformers. It was the sufferings of the London exiles at the hands of the northern Lutheran ministers which brought the works belatedly into the public eye and gave them a dramatic contemporary relevance. Events in Hamburg added one more chapter to the exiles' long catalogue of woes. A two-day disputation between Westphal and Micron ended in predictable bitterness and denunciation, and the town council ordered the refugees out of the city shortly afterwards. A group that arrived from England about this time, led by the minister Gualter Delenus, were not even allowed into the city and citizens were forbidden on pain of fines to offer them food or shelter.[21] The weary travellers at last made their way

---

[17] Lasco, *Brevis et dilucida de sacramentis ecclesiae Christi tractatio* (London, 1552). See *Joannis a Lasco Opera*, ed. A. Kuyper (2 vols, Amsterdam, 1866), vol. 1, pp. 99–232.

[18] O. E. Strasser: 'Der Consensus Tigurinus', *Zwingliana*, 9 (1949–53), pp. 1–16; Ulrich Gäbler, 'Das Zustandekommen des Consensus Tigurinus im Jahre 1549', *Theologische Literaturzeitung*, 104 (1979), pp. 321–32.

[19] Von Schade, *Westphal*, pp. 27–30; Mönckeberg, *Westphal und Calvin*, pp. 19–23.

[20] *Lasco Opera*, vol. 2, 696.

[21] Rudolf Kayser, 'Johannes a Lasco und die Londoner Flüchtlingsgemeinde in Hamburg', *Zeitschrift des Vereins für Hamburgische Geschichte*, 37 (1938), pp. 9–13.

to Emden, where at least they could be sure of a welcome. Reinforced by a steady stream of new exiles from the Netherlands, Emden would for 30 years play a leading role among the German exile communities. The London exiles had little difficulty integrating themselves into the community, and were soon performing important functions as elders, or as deacons of the special *Fremdendiakonie*, set up to dispense help to newly arrived refugees.[22]

The exile leaders were not slow to voice abroad their bitter sense of outrage at the way they had been treated in Denmark and the German towns. At the beginning of March, before the arrival of Micron and the main body of the refugees, Lasco had sent an account of the Danish misadventure to both Bullinger in Zurich and Calvin in Geneva.[23] He took the opportunity to inform the Swiss reformers of the publication of the *Farrago*, and enclosed for good measure a copy of Westphal's *Recta Fides*. Lasco urged that one or other of his mentors should answer Westphal's tract, but the Swiss reformers seem at first to have been unsure of the appropriate response. At the end of March Calvin informed Bullinger that he had got hold of Westphal's book, and asked him whether he thought a reply necessary; Bullinger's immediate reaction was that Westphal was on the whole better ignored.[24] This exchange of letters seems to have taken place before either had received Lasco's letters: what convinced Calvin that a reply was indeed necessary was the news of the exiles' treatment on their northern peregrination.[25] For as Calvin wrote to Bullinger on 29

---

[22] Van Schelven, *Vluchtelingenkerken*, pp. 114–30; D. Nauta: 'Emden, Toevluchtsoord van Ballingen,' in D. Nauta and J. P. van Dooren (eds), *De Synode van Emden October 1571* (Kampen, 1971), pp. 7–21. Of the former members of the London community at least five served as elders in Emden (Josias Dauwe, Joest Roese, Wilhelm de Vissher, Gerard Mortaigne and Gilles van der Erve) and a further four were among the first administrators of the *Fremdendiakonie*. Archiv der reformierten Kirche Emden, Kirchenratsprotokolle, Bd. 1; *Stukken betreffende de Diaconie der vreemdelingen te Emden, 1560–1576*, ed. J. J. van Toorenenbergen (Marnix Vereeniging, series 1, part 2, 1876).

[23] Lasco to Bullinger, 6 March 1554: CO, vol. 15, no. 1919; Lasco to Calvin, 13 March 1554: CO, vol. 15, no. 1930.

[24] Calvin to Bullinger, 28 March 1554: CO, vol. 15, no. 1935; Bullinger to Calvin, 22 April 1554: CO, vol. 15, no. 1944.

[25] See Ernst Bizer, *Studien zur Geschichte des Abendmahlstreits* (Gütersloh, 1940), pp. 276–7. As Bizer points out, it is extremely unlikely that Calvin could have received Lasco's letter of 13 March when he wrote on 28 March. Confusion has arisen because no. 1931 has been misdated; this letter must have been written after no. 1954, in which Bullinger records the arrival of Lasco's letter of 6 March. Calvin apparently first heard about Westphal's book from Beza. See Mönckeberg, *Westphal und Calvin*, p. 30.

April, however poor Westphal's work in itself, if it could have such an effect on the hearts of princes as was apparent in the case of the King of Denmark, it could not go unanswered.[26] A few weeks later Bullinger could reassure Lasco that a reply would be forthcoming and that Calvin had the job in hand.[27]

Calvin went enthusiastically, if not hastily, to work. In October a first draft was despatched to Zurich, and the detailed criticisms of Bullinger and his colleagues were swiftly incorporated into a revised version.[28] In December Bullinger declared himself satisfied with the revision, and in the early weeks of 1555 Calvin's *Defensio sanae et orthodoxae doctrinae de Sacramentis* was simultaneously published in Zurich and Geneva.[29] If the *Defensio* was intended to put an end to the controversy Westphal had unleashed, neither the style nor the tone were particularly well judged. Although Calvin had removed some of the personal invective at Bullinger's insistence, contempt for the person and arguments of his opponent were barely concealed. Whilst refusing to name Westphal (a mistake in Bullinger's opinion), Calvin referred to his opponent as 'a son of the devil' and asked rhetorically whether he really believed that Christ's flesh was eaten 'like the oxen of his native land'. Bullinger's misgivings proved fully justified; Westphal was not easily silenced and soon returned with enthusiasm to the fray. Meanwhile there were already worrying indications that the conflict would not remain confined to an exchange of bitter pamphlets. Once again the London exiles were at the heart of the controversy.

By no means all the former members of the French and Dutch churches in London had found their way to Emden in the months following Mary's accession. If the two church communities together numbered something over 4000 men, women and children at the time of their dissolution, then the 175 who took ship with Lasco were only a small if influential proportion of the community.[30] Others made

---

[26] Calvin to Bullinger, 29 April 1554, CO, vol. 15, no. 1947.
[27] Bullinger to Lasco, about 15 May 1554: CO, vol. 15, no. 1931. See n. 25.
[28] Calvin to Bullinger, October 1554: CO, vol. 15, no. 2022; Zurich ministers to Calvin, 24 October 1554: CO, vol. 15, no. 2034.
[29] Mönckeberg, *Westphal und Calvin*, pp. 34-44.
[30] See above, pp. 58 f.

their own way from England to Emden, but an examination of the early records of the Emden Reformed community and the lists of new citizens of the town reveals only a small number of names familiar from the first membership list of the London Dutch church.[31] No membership list survives for the Edwardian French community, so that a similar comparison with the names of French refugees in Emden is not possible, but the French church in Emden remained, in any case, very small indeed.[32]

For many of the Dutch exiles in London and most of the French-speaking Walloons a new exile in Emden was an unattractive prospect and some chose instead to return at least temporarily to their former homes in the Netherlands. Ghent, Bruges, Antwerp, and the industrial villages of the Flanders Westkwartier all showed signs of increased Reformed activity as a result of the return of refugees from across the Channel, but the lay and ecclesiastical authorities were alert for possible trouble and a wave of arrests underlined the risks the Reformed would run if they intended to remain.[33] For many, return to the Netherlands proved only a brief respite before a new exile and through 1554 and 1555 former members of the London community joined increasing numbers of new refugees heading westwards towards the cities of the lower Rhine across the borders of the German Empire. Settlements of Dutch and Walloon exiles in Aachen, Duisburg and many smaller towns in Jülich and Cleves date from about this time, but the most significant contingents of refugees were attracted to two towns which had already given some encouragement to immigrants from the Netherlands, Wesel and Frankfurt.

In Wesel a small community of Walloon linenweavers, established in 1545, already enjoyed the privilege of meeting separately for

---

[31] A search of the Kirchenratsprotokolle and Bürgerbücher in Emden revealed only 24 names familiar from either the London register or the list of those who sailed with Lasco (printed *BRN*, vol. 9, pp. 89–90). A further 23 Dutch householders included in this second list but not identified in the Emden records probably also settled there, but even with their families these 50-odd former members of the Dutch church represent only a small proportion of the probable strength of the community by 1553.

[32] Only 38 members took part in the election of a minister in December 1555. French church at Emden to Perussel, 12 Dec 1555: *CO*, vol. 15, no 2357 bis.

[33] Johan Decavele, *De Dageraad van de Reformatie in Vlaanderen, 1520–1565* (2 vols, Brussels, 1975), vol. 1, pp. 325 ff., 340–5, 392–6.

religious services in their own language.[34] A certain hardening of opinion within the town's Lutheran establishment had not as yet succeeded in disturbing the generally harmonious relations between the Walloons and the town authorities, but the new influx of the 1550s was on a scale for which the town was hardly prepared. The first of the new exiles arrived in Wesel in October 1553. This seems to have been an organized group as their leader Francis Morellus presented a Confession of Faith to the city council on their behalf; the council professed themselves satisfied with this doctrinal statement and were prepared, under certain conditions, to allow this new group to worship in a separate community.[35] The fact that this group arrived so soon after the expulsion of the foreign Protestants from England, however, makes it highly doubtful that we are dealing here with refugees from the London church. Indeed, an examination of the sources for the early years of the Wesel and Frankfurt exile communities suggests that the degree of continuity between the membership of these churches and the former London churches was, as at Emden, much less than has previously been assumed.[36] Despite these promising beginnings, however, the Wesel community was soon embroiled in the repercussions of events in England, not least because when they came to choose a minister to serve alongside Morellus in the new church, they elected one of the former ministers of the French church in London, François Perussel.

Perussel had been delegated to remain in London after the departure of the other church leaders to care for church members who lingered in the capital. By the end of the year, however, he too had been forced to leave the country, and after a short stay in Antwerp he proceeded to Wesel to take up his new ministry in the first weeks of 1554.[37] Shortly after his arrival the new church made a formal

---

[34] On the Wesel exile see W. Neuser, 'Die Aufnahme der Flüchtlinge aus England in Wesel (1553) und ihre Ausweisung trotz der Vermittlung Calvins und Melanchthons', in *Weseler Konvent, 1568–1968* (Düsseldorf, 1968); F. W. Cuno, *Geschichte der wallonisch- und französisch-reformierten Gemeinde zu Wesel* (Geschichtsblätter des Deutschen Hugenotten-Vereins, V 2–4, 1895). Walther Hoffweg, 'Calvins Beziehungen zu den Rheinlanden', in *Calvinstudien*, ed. J. Bohatec (Leipzig, 1909), makes use of the best first-hand account of the Wesel disputes, Perussel's *Historia de Wesaliensis Ecclesiae dissipatione*, printed in *Frankfurtische Religions-Handlungen* (2 vols, Frankfurt, 1735), vol. 1, pp. 277–89. On the Wesel Reformation in general see Albrecht Wolters, *Reformationsgeschichte der Stadt Wesel* (Bonn, 1868).
[35] The Confession is printed by Wolters, *Reformationsgeschichte*, pp. 440 ff., where it is incorrectly attributed to the old Walloon community.
[36] See below, pp. 67–9.
[37] Perussel to Pierre du Val, 29 September 1554, Van Schelven, *Vluchtelingenkerken*, p. 424.

request to the council to be allowed to celebrate their own communion service. This was not a privilege that had been extended to the old Walloon community, and the council was not prepared to go so far to oblige the newcomers; the council meeting of 19 February refused the request and reaffirmed its earlier decision that the refugees must attend communion in the city churches.[38] This was not a condition that the exiles could accept with equanimity. The difference in language between the French-speaking exiles and the local church presented an obvious barrier to full participation in the local sacramental rite, but their decisive objection was to the local ceremonies, which to the Reformed refugees smacked too much of the vestiges of popery. A meeting of the leading members of the exile community, hastily convened at the house of Augustin le Grand, decided that it would be better to look for a more congenial place of refuge than to remain in Wesel on such terms. Whilst Perussel was to remain to care for the community in the meantime, Morellus was despatched to begin the search.[39]

It was only at this point, when a decision to leave Wesel had already been taken, that a letter arrived which threw the exiles once more into confusion. Some little time before Perussel's arrival the community's leaders had sought Calvin's opinion as to how they should resolve their differences with the local ceremonies, and the Genevan reformer now made clear that he thought it better to accept the disputed Lutheran practices than to sacrifice the chance of establishing a Reformed community on their account.[40] This totally unexpected development presented Perussel with a cruel dilemma. Simply to ignore Calvin's advice was impossible, but to accept communion at the hands of the town's ministers would be an intolerable deviation from the strict Reformed practice which Perussel had upheld in London and elsewhere. In his perplexity Perussel turned to his former London colleagues, and despatched Calvin's letter to Lasco in Emden with a request for further guidance. Lasco replied on 6 July, and his carefully reasoned judgement was quite contrary to that of his Genevan colleague.[41] Calvin, he suggested, had misunderstood the situation in Wesel if he believed the doctrinal differences between the

---

[38] Neuser, 'Aufnahme der Flüchtlinge', p. 33.

[39] Hollweg, 'Calvin's Beziehungen', p. 154; Perussel, *Historia*, para. 2.

[40] Calvin to Wesel, 13 March 1554; *CO*, vol. 15, no. 1929; Hollweg, 'Calvins Beziehungen', pp. 154–5; Neuser, 'Aufnahme der Flüchtlinge', pp. 31–2; Perussel, *Historia*, para. 3.

[41] *Lasco Opera*, vol. 2, pp. 703–7; Hollweg, 'Calvins Beziehungen', p. 156; Neuser, 'Aufnahme der Flüchtlinge', p. 33.

exiles and the local church to be small; to Lasco, the town's refusal to permit a colloquium to discuss their differences was sufficient evidence of their intractability. In any case the Wesel exiles were not a new community, but an established church seeking the restoration of a settled form of worship. To Lasco the Wesel community was nothing less than a part of his London church in search of a new home, and to forgo one of the essential attributes of a true church, free exercise of the sacraments, was quite out of the question.

With this last and crucial proposition, however, Lasco seems to have been mistaken, as became clear when Perussel called together the leading members of the community once more to discuss the reformers' verdicts. Faced with such an embarrassing divergence of opinion between Lasco and Calvin the community's elders decided, rather surprisingly, that the differences were more apparent than real: specifically they argued that Lasco's criticisms of Calvin's judgement were based on misapprehensions about the true state of affairs in the town. The fact that the town had initially accepted the exiles' Confession of Faith was sufficient evidence of the basic unity of doctrine which Lasco doubted, and the local ministers had expressed no doctrinal objection to the exiles' own ceremonies. More fundamentally, the Wesel community could hardly be regarded as a continuation of the London community, as no more than three of its members were actually London exiles; when this was understood Lasco's most serious objection to Calvin's judgement could be set aside.[42] Having accomplished this rather uneasy reconciliation of their mentors' opinions to their own satisfaction, the leaders of the Wesel exiles called together the whole community to decide how they should proceed further. After three days of debate, the exiles resolved to remain in Wesel, but only if the council eventually conceded their right to a separate Communion service. In the meantime, as a gesture of good faith, Perussel and other leading members of the community were to attend the town Communion for what it was hoped would be a transitional period of six months.[43]

Even if the Wesel church was not, as Perussel's account seems conclusively to demonstrate, a remnant of the dispersed London church, its leaders seem to have been infected with something of the London ministers' unquenchable spirit. For although the exiles had

---

[42] Perussel to Du Val, 29 September 1554, Van Schelven, *Vluchtelingenkerken*, p. 425. See also CO, 15. 2357 bis (a suggestion that Perussel should serve where most of his former church had settled, i.e. in Emden; yet the French church in Emden was less than 40 strong).

[43] Van Schelven, *Vluchtelingenkerken*, pp. 425–6.

resolved to proceed with a degree of circumspection, and the tone of the proceedings was decidedly and uncharacteristically conciliatory, the privileges they hoped to win were in essence not different from those enjoyed by the exiles in London: free exercise of their own rites, while reserving their criticisms of the local observances. Such a generous measure of toleration was in fact hardly feasible in the changed circumstances of the 1550s. In May 1554 the Wesel town council had reaffirmed its support for the Confession of Augsburg, and even while Perussel was continuing negotiations with sympathetically disposed members of the local clergy more militant ministers were doing their best to incite the native population to hostile demonstrations against the newcomers. Incidents of this sort induced several leading members of the community to quit Wesel and move on to Frankfurt, and Perussel was tempted to follow suit.[44] A recuperative visit to Antwerp encouraged the minister to pledge his continued service to the church until Easter 1555, but as this deadline drew nearer without any sign of progress in the deadlocked negotiations with the town authorities, the prospects for the community looked increasingly gloomy. However, help was at hand, though from a most unexpected source. The ecumenically minded Catholic theologian George Cassander visited Wesel in the summer of 1555, and he finally persuaded the council to carry out their earlier pledge to allow the exiles to worship in separate communities. In October the Heiliggeistkapelle was finally made over to the French-speaking exiles and their services could begin.[45] The English-speaking exiles were meanwhile permitted to meet in the Augustinerkirche, the church already used by the old established Walloon group.[46]

The council's decision did not actually settle the crucial issue of the strangers' observances, as the exiles were not permitted to celebrate Communion in their own churches. At least, though, a final confrontation had been avoided at a time when the refugees' expulsion had seemed imminent, and Perussel was persuaded to remain and continue his ministry to the French community. As a result it would not be in Wesel where the tensions between the exiles and their hosts first came to a head, but in Frankfurt, where initially at least the refugees had received a comparatively cordial welcome.

The first group of exiles to arrive in Frankfurt in the spring of 1554

---

[44] Perussel, *Historia*, para. 8.
[45] Hollweg, 'Calvins Beziehungen', pp. 157–8.
[46] Ibid. For the English exiles in Wesel see Christina H. Garrett, *The Marian Exiles* (Cambridge, 1938).

certainly hailed from England.[47] They were not, however, former members of the London churches, but the remnant of the small community of weavers established in Glastonbury on the initiative of the Protector, the Duke of Somerset.[48] The Glastonbury project was the first planned settlement on English soil with an unashamedly economic motive. In addition to houses, land and other financial inducements, however, the skilled foreign workmen were also allowed to establish an independent church community on the pattern of the London churches, and in January 1552 Valérand Poullain, a former minister of the French exile church in Strasbourg, was appointed as the first superintendent of the community and minister of their church.[49] It was the strongly religious character of the settlement which ensured that it would not survive the change of religion in 1553. On 5 September the Privy Council gave orders that the foreign weavers be evicted from their property, and by the end of the year Poullain, after lingering through the autumn in London, had led his small but loyal band back to the continent.[50] The search for a new place of refuge led Poullain via Antwerp and Wesel to Cologne, where a chance meeting with a member of the Frankfurt ruling council suggested the possibility of a favourable reception in the free city on the Main.[51] On 15 March Poullain appeared before the Frankfurt council to present a petition on behalf of his community, and three days later a special session of the council gave permission for the Glastonbury weavers to settle in the town, and to meet together for worship.[52] Hurried negotiations with the former prioress secured for

---

[47] On the exile community in Frankfurt see Frederick Clemens Ebrard, *Die französisch-reformierte Gemeinde in Frankfurt am Main, 1554–1904* (Frankfurt, 1906); Karl Bauer, *Valérand Poullain* (Elberfeld, 1927); Gustav A. Besser, *Geschichte der Frankfurter Flüchtlingsgemeinden, 1554–1558* (Halle, 1906).

[48] The continuity of membership between Glastonbury and Frankfurt may be demonstrated by comparing names in the Patent Rolls with the Frankfurt Bürgerbücher. Of the foreigners made denizen with Poullain on 31 December 1551, 15 were enrolled as citizens of Frankfurt between May 1554 and April 1555. *Calendar of Patent Rolls, Edward VI* (6 vols, London, 1924–9), vol. 4, p. 138; Stadtarchiv Frankfurt, Bürgerbuch 6, ff. 96–104.

[49] Bauer, *Poullain*, pp. 148–58; Ebrard, *Französisch-reformierte Gemeinde*, pp. 30–48; W. K. Jordan, *Edward VI, The Threshold of Power* (London, 1970).

[50] *Acts of the Privy Council of England*, ed. J. R. Dasent (11 vols, London, 1890–93), vol. 4, p. 341; Bauer, *Poullain*, pp. 168–70.

[51] Bauer, *Poullain*, pp. 170–8; Ebrard, *Französisch-reformierte Gemeinde*, p. 51.

[52] Bauer, *Poullain*, pp. 181–2; Poullain's petition is printed in Ebrard, *Französisch-reformierte Gemeinde*, pp. 156–8. *Die Eingliederung der Niederländischen Glaubensflüchtlinge in die Frankfurter Bürgerschaft, 1554–1596*, ed. H. Meinert (Frankfurt, 1981), p. 3.

the community the use of the Weißfrauenkloster, and services began on 19 April, attended by a large sympathetic crowd of Frankfurt citizens.[53]

Despite these promising beginnings Poullain's community was not destined to enjoy its generous privileges in tranquillity for long. In the months following Poullain's arrival a steady stream of new refugees continued to flow into Frankfurt, and the scale of the immigration soon put the initially harmonious relations between the town and the foreign community under increasing strain. The original privilege of free worship had been limited to Poullain and his 24 families from Glastonbury, but by the end of 1555 there were close on 2000 refugees in the city; this amounted to something like 10 per cent of the total population, and with the mounting pressure on prices, rents and jobs inevitably attributed to the new arrivals, the orthodox Lutheran ministers seized the opportunity to incite anxious native craftsmen against the immigrants.[54] A first attack by the intractable Lutheran Hartman Beyer and his ally Matthaeus Ritter in the spring of 1554 had been headed off by Poullain's allies on the council, but it was clear that the ministers continued to harbour a grudge; in August 1555 the exiles were forced to complain to the council that the town's ministers had taken to denouncing them from the pulpit.[55] By this time too, the changing character of the exile was giving rise to considerable friction within the exile community itself. The new arrivals in Frankfurt included among them a substantial number of prosperous merchants and skilled craftsmen, and these self-confident and relatively well-educated newcomers were increasingly inclined to resent the monopoly of power within the community exercised by Poullain and the well-meaning but barely literate Glastonbury elders.[56] Poullain's autocratic response to criticism only exacerbated the difficulties, and although an attempt was made to restore peace by summoning the mild-mannered Richard Vauville to serve as a second minister in March 1555, Vauville's inclination to take Poullain's side meant that he too was soon the object of increasing criticism.[57]

The summer of 1555 was, indeed, a difficult time for Poullain. Not only was he faced with a challenge to his authority within the community and increasing hostility in the town, but now also events

---

[53] Bauer, *Poullain*, pp. 184–5; Ebrard, *Französisch-reformierte Gemeinde*, pp. 53–4.
[54] Heinz Schilling, *Niederländische Exulanten im 16. Jahrhundert* (Gütersloh, 1972), pp. 52–4, 126–31.
[55] Bauer, *Poullain*, p. 209.
[56] Bauer, *Poullain*, pp. 231ff.
[57] Ibid., pp. 236–8.

beyond his control seemed to be threatening to thrust Frankfurt to the forefront of the wider struggle between Lutherans and the Reformed. Once again it was the former ministers of the exiled London church who were largely responsible. The vast majority of the refugees who had settled in Frankfurt during 1554 and 1555 were French-speaking Netherlanders, but there were also a small number of Dutch-speaking 'Flemings', and these too hankered after a church of their own. In April 1555 John a Lasco journeyed from Emden to organize a community on their behalf.[58] Again, few of the members of the new church seem to have had any direct connection with the London Dutch church, but this did not deter Lasco from organizing the church in the image of his former London community.[59] In the summer of 1555 Lasco summoned Marten Micron from Norden to assist with the organization of the new church, although it was Peter Dathenus, appointed by Lasco as minister, who preached at the church's inaugural service in September.[60]

To the Hamburg minister Joachim Westphal, now the established champion of the orthodox Lutherans, the presence of his two old adversaries in Frankfurt seems to have been an intolerable provocation, the more so as Westphal had close links with the town and its ministers. The minister Hartmann Beyer was a trusted friend since their student days in Wittenberg, as was the printer Peter Braubach, who had published Westphal's work since 1551 and continued to act as a reliable agent for the Hamburg minister throughout the conflict with the refugees.[61] In July 1555, shortly after Lasco's arrival in Frankfurt, Braubach published Westphal's *Justa defensio*, his considered response to Calvin's *Defensio sanae* of earlier in the year.[62] Calvin described the *Justa defensio* in a letter to Farel as a 'ferocious book', but it probably did less to inflame the atmosphere than a new *Farrago* published by Braubach during the course of the summer.

---

[58] In June Lasco was enrolled as a 'beisass' of the town. Frankfurt Stadtarchiv, Bürgerbuch, fol. 106; Meinert, *Eingliederung*, p. 12.

[59] Of the names recorded on a membership list of April 1556, only Claes de Schildere (Nicolas Pictor) appears to have come from England, and he spent some time in the Netherlands in the interim. Decavele, *Dageraad*, I. p. 393; R. M. van den Abeele, 'Nederlands vluchtelingen te Frankfort in de XVIe eeuw', *Onze Stam* (Familiekundige Bijlage van 'Ons Heem'), 1 (1950), pp. 1–9.

[60] Ebrard, *Französisch-reformierte Gemeinde*, p. 75. The Dutch shared the Weißfrauenkloster with the French-speaking community.

[61] Von Schade, *Westphal and Braubach*, pp. 63–7, 88–96. Braubach ensured that Westphal's works came promptly off the press even after the council had banned the publication of works of religious controversy in the town. See below, p. 78.

[62] Ibid., p. 33; Mönckeberg, *Westphal und Calvin*, pp. 44–52.

Compiled by the Bremen minister Johann Timann and intended as a complement to Westphal's book of the same title, this *Farrago* was a compendium of Lutheran writings on sacramental doctrine demonstrating (in contrast to the Reformed) their unity and conformity to scripture. More provocatively Timann also appended letters of support from pillars of the Lutheran establishment which denounced the exiles and singled John a Lasco out for special criticism. Westphal himself had contributed a letter in which he described the exiles from England as vagrants and vagabonds; to Bugenhagen and the Danish court preacher Buscoducensis they were 'members of satan' and 'sacramentiperdae'.[63] Lasco was not the man to remain silent in the face of such criticism. In Frankfurt he finally published his account of the rites and doctrine of the dispersed London community, and this was now prefaced with a letter of dedication to the King of Poland in which he loudly denounced the ignorance of his detractors.[64] Peter Braubach indignantly refused to print the work but his rival Egenolff proved more pliable, and the *Forma ac Ratio* appeared soon after the letter of dedication was finished on 6 September.[65]

The Swiss reformers regarded these heated exchanges in Frankfurt with increasing concern. Calvin's dedication of his *Evangelienharmonie* to the Frankfurt council at this time must be seen in this context as an attempt to preserve the standing of the Reformed among the patrician group which had until now been the refugees' most influential patrons, but the favourable response to Calvin's gesture could not obscure the fact that the developing situation in Frankfurt and the Empire looked increasingly ominous for the refugee communities.[66] In September 1555 Frankfurt formally adopted the religious Peace of Augsburg, and when the divided and turbulent English exile community chose this unpropitious moment to appeal for the use of one of the town churches for their services, the Lutheran ministers seized the chance to present a comprehensive denunciation of the refugees and

---

[63] Kruske, *Sakramentsstreit*, pp. 106–7; Mönckeberg, *Westphal und Calvin*, pp. 65–7.

[64] *Forma ac Ratio tota ecclesiastici Ministerii, in peregrinorum potissimum instituta Londini*. STC 16571. *Lasco Opera*, vol. 2, pp. 1–283. Kruske, *Sakramentsstreit*, pp. 107–10.

[65] Most of the sheets of the *Forma ac Ratio* had been printed in Emden (by Ctematius). Lasco apparently brought these with him and had Egenolff print the introduction and the final section.

[66] Karl Bauer, *Die Beziehungen Calvins zu Frankfurt am Main* (Schriften des Vereins für Reformationsgeschichte, 133, 1920), pp. 19–21.

their doctrine.[67] In October the conflict took a further ominous turn when the ministers formally drew the council's attention to the economic strains which resulted from the foreigners' presence; for the first time too there were those who openly advocated following the example of Denmark and the northern German towns and expelling the refugees.[68] The council showed no inclination to abandon its enlightened policy of protection, but the threat posed by an alliance between the ministers and anxious craftsmen had to be taken seriously. In February 1556 the council finally bowed to the insistent pressure of the ministers and invited the exiles to explain whether or not their doctrine was consistent with that of the Frankfurt Concord of 1542.[69]

The now quite obvious deterioration in relations between the exiles and the town authorities prompted Calvin to attempt a direct intervention. In the first weeks of 1556, Calvin had published his second rebuttal of Westphal, the *Secunda defensio*,[70] and he now sought to exploit his high reputation in Frankfurt to combat the progress Westphal and the orthodox Lutherans were making in the town. On 29 February Calvin wrote to the Frankfurt council, ostensibly to thank them for the gift of 40 gulden with which they had honoured his dedication of the *Evangelienharmonie*, but really to protest that the council had permitted the publication of Westphal's latest tract and Timann's *Farrago* in the town. In both this and a further letter to the Frankfurt ministers Calvin expressed his willingness to come to Frankfurt if this could help iron out any apparent doctrinal differences between himself and the town's ministers.[71]

The Frankfurt ministers returned a measured and cautious reply to Calvin's letter, and made no mention at all of his offer to come to Frankfurt.[72] Within a few months, however, Calvin had been convinced that a journey to Germany was necessary, not as a result of any change of mind on the part of the town's ministers, but rather because the continuing bitter disputes within the Walloon community threatened to exhaust the town's dwindling fund of goodwill towards the

---

[67] Ebrard, *Französisch-reformierte Gemeinde*, p. 79. For the English church in Frankfurt see Garrett, *Marian Exiles*; Rudolf Jung, *Die englische Flüchtlings-Gemeinde in Frankfurt am Main, 1554–1559* (Frankfurt, 1910).

[68] Bauer, *Beziehungen Calvins*, p. 23.

[69] Ebrard, *Französisch-reformierte Gemeinde*, p. 84.

[70] Von Schade, *Westphal und Braubach*, p. 35; Mönckeberg, *Westphal und Calvin*, pp. 52–64.

[71] CO, vol. 16, no. 2401; Bauer, *Beziehungen Calvins*, pp. 26–9.

[72] CO, vol. 16, no. 2422; Bauer, *Beziehungen Calvins*, pp. 30–1.

exiles. The presence of the conciliatory Vauville had done little to satisfy Poullain's critics within the French community, and the election of a new consistory in the summer of 1555 sparked further troubles between the Glastonbury group and the increasingly frustrated and embittered newcomers.[73] An emissary from Geneva (bringing Calvin's dedication to the city council) succeeded in negotiating a fragile settlement, but this was shattered when the newly elected deacons and elders resigned in a demonstrative gesture of no confidence in Poullain and his supporters. Vauville's death in November further exacerbated the situation, and Lasco's authority proved insufficient to the task of reconciling the warring factions. By December 1555 Lasco and Poullain were left with no alternative but to write to Geneva and urge Calvin to intervene in the dispute.[74]

Calvin's reply, written on 26 December, was a magisterial rebuke for Poullain's opponents within the community.[75] Criticizing the main pretext for the continued opposition to Poullain as legalistic and petty (it was alleged that in April 1554 Poullain had simply assumed the role of minister without a proper election), Calvin spelt out in the clearest possible terms the likely consequences of the continued turbulence in the community. It was not impossible, he wrote, that the church's opponents would use these unedifying quarrels as a pretext to destroy the church altogether; certainly the disputes must discourage those who had given the church such stout support hitherto. Calvin had no doubts about the widening implications of the strangers' troubles, and found it incomprehensible that they could not make up their differences at a time when their opponents in the sacramentarian controversy were preparing 'a war of destruction' against them all. As the quarrels in the community continued without abatement through the first months of 1556, Calvin's gloomy prognostication seemed all too likely to be realized. In April Calvin's correspondent John von Glauberg, one of the exiles' most faithful supporters in the Frankfurt patriciate, felt compelled to warn the Genevan reformer that the church could well destroy itself if the dispute continued; indeed it was doubtful if they would find any other town willing to take them.[76] In June Calvin took the opportunity of a letter of recommendation for Vauville's successor to urge the community to make up their differences, but in fact the dispute only escalated further when three of Poullain's opponents absented themselves from

---

[73] Bauer, *Poullain*, pp. 236ff.
[74] Bauer, *Poullain*, pp. 238–41; CO, vol. 15, nos 2352, 2360.
[75] CO, vol. 15, no. 2263; Bauer, *Beziehungen Calvins*, pp. 44–5.
[76] CO, vol. 16, no. 2424.

the Communion and the minister promptly complained to the council.[77] It was by now clear that the only chance of peace lay in a thorough investigation of the accumulated grievances, and the churches at Emden and Antwerp added their powerful voices to those urging Calvin to accept the role of mediator.[78] On 20 August Calvin secured the necessary leave of absence from the council in Geneva and set off on the weary journey towards Germany.

Calvin's personal intervention in the exiles' affairs was the more urgently required as the uneasy peace in Wesel was apparently on the verge of breakdown. Although the French church in Wesel had been functioning smoothly since the Heiliggeistkapelle was made over to them in October 1555, the community still hankered after the freedom to celebrate Communion, and in January 1556 Perussel made a new approach to the council on their behalf.[79] This was peremptorily refused and the depressed minister thought once again of resignation, but as the year wore on it seemed as if this decision might well be taken out of his hands. On 7 August it came to the attention of the town council that a group of the exiles had gone ahead and celebrated their own Communion service against the council's express prohibition. It is not clear from the council minutes whether members of the French community were involved, or whether the report refers to English exiles, but the effect was to precipitate a crisis between the town authorities and both exile groups.[80] Perussel and his English colleagues were summoned to the town hall, and informed that if they were not prepared to conform to the Augsburg Confession they must leave. For Perussel this ultimatum posed a terrible dilemma. His community could ill afford to be deprived of his services at this difficult time, but the unhappy minister could not in good conscience accept the Augsburg Confession as it was interpreted in Wesel. It was with considerable relief that he learnt of Calvin's planned trip to Frankfurt, and in the first days of September he hurried south to consult his opinion.

On his arrival in Frankfurt, then, Calvin faced a complex web of problems. How were the two French exile churches, which now relied heavily on his judgement, to be restored to internal peace and prosperity? On 20 September the commission appointed to settle the dispute in Frankfurt met for the first time. Calvin took the chair, and with the help of Lasco, the English minister Horne and several other

---

[77] CO, vol. 16, no. 2483; Bauer, *Poullain*, pp. 245-7, 251.
[78] CO, vol. 16, nos 2501, 2506.
[79] Neuser, 'Aufnahme der Flüchtlinge', p. 34.
[80] Ibid.

arbitrators including a representative of the elders and a local citizen, the commission worked its way through the 25 articles presented by Poullain's opponents.[81] Both sides were then examined and allowed to put forward further arguments before the commission announced its verdict the following day. When one considers that Calvin was just one member of a commission of which several members were inclined to take a more sympathetic view of Poullain's troubles, the manner in which Calvin achieved his apparent objective was no mean example of his diplomatic skills. The commission's judgement was on the whole favourable to Poullain, but made certain criticisms of the minister's conduct which prompted the sensitive Poullain to offer his resignation. The majority of the community pressed him to remain but Calvin remained demonstratively silent, and the resignation was accepted.[82]

Poullain himself had little doubt that Calvin was responsible for this outcome; the affair caused a rift between the former friends that was not repaired before Poullain's death, but Calvin had clearly reached the conclusion that Poullain's resignation was necessary if the peace of the community was to be restored. Calvin later said as much in a letter to Musculus in Berne,[83] and this conviction seems to have been formed even before the commission met on 20 September. Two days previously, before he turned his attention to the Frankfurt conflict, Calvin had met with Perussel to discuss the problems of the Wesel community. Perussel swiftly convinced the reformer that he could not accept the council's ultimatum, and the letter with which Calvin despatched him back to Wesel was intended to prepare the church for their minister's departure. Calvin's guarded phrases reflect his recognition of the church's reluctance to be deprived of Perussel's services, but it was none the less clear what he had in mind: Perussel should leave Wesel and take Poullain's place in Frankfurt, and thus, he hoped, both communities might be saved.[84]

During the early months of 1556 Calvin had apparently been convinced that Poullain, whom he had previously sturdily supported, bore a large measure of responsibility for the continuous strife within the Frankfurt community. This change of mind may at least partly be attributed to the influence of De Secelles, a close friend of Calvin's who joined the opposition to Poullain at an early stage,[85] but Calvin's

---

[81] Bauer, *Poullain*, pp. 253ff.
[82] Ibid., pp. 257-8.
[83] CO, vol. 16, no. 2548.
[84] CO, vol. 16, no. 2535.
[85] Bauer, *Poullain*, p. 248.

imperative concern was to reduce tension within the community and improve relations with the town at a time when the steadily worsening atmosphere between Lutheran and Reformed made the prospect of continuing toleration for the exile communities increasingly gloomy. Other prominent figures also applied themselves to the delicate task of repairing the relationship between the town and the Reformed community in Frankfurt. In September John a Lasco presented to the Frankfurt council his *Purgatio*, an attempt to demonstrate that the doctrinal tenets of the exile ministers were consistent with the Confession of Augsburg.[86] The council too made its own significant contribution to the restoration of harmony within the town by forbidding the publication of any further tracts of a doctrinal or controversial nature.[87]

To the extent that a new attempt by the Lutheran ministers to persuade the council to order the closure of the foreign churches in October 1556 failed to attract the necessary support, the efforts of Calvin and his allies to improve relations between the exiles and their hosts in Frankfurt must be judged a success.[88] In Wesel, however, the attempt to rescue the church through Perussel's departure had come too late. Immediately after his return from Frankfurt Perussel was called to the council chamber and required to affirm his belief in the Confession of Augsburg. When Perussel, prevaricating, referred to the Confession of Faith that had been accepted two years previously, he was curtly told that much had changed since then, the clearest possible indication of the extent to which the exiles had been caught up in the hardening of confessional divisions which their own conduct had helped to bring about.[89] The most Perussel could achieve was agreement that the exiles' Confession should be submitted to Melanchthon for arbitration. The anxiously awaited judgement was received in Wesel on 25 November, and two days later Perussel and the English minister were summoned to hear their fate. Melanchthon had in fact argued strongly against the foreigners' expulsion, but the council, determined to pursue their own course, read to the ministers only those portions of his letter which identified points of difference between the foreigners' doctrine and the Confession of Augsburg. The exiles were given the choice of accepting the Confession or leaving by 1 March 1557.[90]

---

[86] Kruske, *Sakramentsstreit*, pp. 120–5.
[87] Meinert, *Eingliederung*, pp. 26, 41.
[88] Ebrard, *Französisch-reformierte Gemeinde*, p. 87.
[89] Neuser, 'Aufnahme der Flüchtlinge', p. 34.
[90] Ibid., pp. 35–42.

For Perussel there was little choice but to accept defeat. An invitation from the French church at Frankfurt to take up the place vacated by Poullain arrived a few weeks later, and Perussel accepted with evident relief.[91] His last service to the church at Wesel was to arrange an extension of the 1 March deadline so that the exiles did not have to face another perilous mid-winter journey.[92] Six weeks later, however, the French church was shut up, and those members who did not silently attach themselves to the old Walloon church (which had remained discreetly in the background and was not involved in the quarrel) left the town. The English community quickly followed suit.[93]

The closure of the Wesel church was a bitter blow to Calvin, marking as it did the failure of his attempt to limit the damage done by the steadily escalating conflict with Westphal. In fact, 1557 saw the sacramentarian controversy at its height. The pugnacious Westphal continued to pour out a steady stream of tracts, beginning with an emphatic rebuttal of the letter of dedication published by Lasco with his *Forma ac Ratio*. The *Justa defensio adversus insignia mendicia Ioannis a Lasco* brought the recriminations between Westphal and his opponents to new heights; Westphal stigmatized the exiles as 'the devil's martyrs' and prefaced the tract with his letter to the Frankfurt council of March 1556 in which he had urged the expulsion of the exiles, 'as a sick sheep is driven out of the stall'.[94] A second tract against Lasco, a reply to the *Purgatio ministrorum*, appeared later in the year, along with a response to Valérand Poullain's *Antidotus adversus Joachim Westphal*.[95] Poullain had remained in Frankfurt after his resignation to prepare his own justification of the stranger community, and his *Antidotus* did little to cool the heated atmosphere in the town.[96] Westphal's reply, the *Apologia adversus veneratum antidotu Valerandi Pollani* had like most of his publications in 1557 to be printed in nearby Oberursel, as the Frankfurt council resolutely maintained their ban on the publication of works of religious controversy in the town. The loyal Peter Braubach was happy to meet the

---

[91] Bauer, *Poullain*, p. 261.
[92] Hollweg, 'Calvins Beziehungen', p. 163.
[93] Neuser, 'Aufnahme der Flüchtlinge', p. 44. It is not known how many of the strangers left with their minister. Possibly the number who did so was small. Schilling, *Niederländische Exulanten*, pp. 89–90.
[94] Mönckeberg, *Westphal und Calvin*, pp. 69–71, 74–6; Bauer, *Poullain*, pp. 288–9.
[95] Von Schade, *Westphal und Braubach*, pp. 40–1.
[96] Bauer, *Poullain*, pp. 291–6.

costs of the publication and make the necessary arrangements for distribution and sale.[97]

A further, and from the Reformed point of view alarming, development in this year was the publication of a separate German edition of Westphal's letter to the Frankfurt council, with its explicit call for the exiles' expulsion. The translation was the work of Hartman Beyer, the exiles' most unrelenting critic among the Frankfurt ministers, and its appearance was a clear indication of a growing public interest in the conflict with the exiles. In April 1557 one of Calvin's correspondents in Frankfurt reported the astonishing news that more than a thousand copies of the *Christlicke und treulicke Warnung die Sacramentaer belagend* had been sold at a single fair.[98] Westphal's Latin polemic was proving equally successful among a more educated public: when in 1557 he republished a Eucharistic tract by Melanchthon to combat the impression being given by the reformers that they had Melanchthon's support in the controversy with the orthodox Lutherans, the copies available in Wittenberg sold out within a quarter of an hour. Westphal's works sold so well that by 1560 Peter Braubach's stocks of all the tracts were exhausted, and he was giving serious thought to reprinting them in a collected edition.[99]

It may be noticed that Calvin's contribution at this, the height of the sacramentarian controversy, was extremely modest; to the mass of publications that appeared in 1557 Calvin contributed only one, his *Ultima admonitio*.[100] It is tempting to attribute this reticence to a growing comprehension on the part of the Genevan reformer of the damage being done by the prolonged and bitter struggle with Westphal. The Reformed had from the beginning treated their opponent with an unconcealed contempt. Calvin's initial reluctance to answer Westphal, his dismissal of the *Justa defensio* as a 'silly and poisonous book' and repeated references to 'Luther's apes' are all indications of a serious misjudgement of Westphal's abilities and of the potential appeal of his rallying cry against the Reformed. Calvin confidently expected that moderate Lutherans would take his part in the sacramentarian controversy and reveal Westphal as an isolated extremist; his dedication of the *Secunda defensio* in 1556 to the Saxon Lutheran pastors is a monument to this misapprehension, and up until the summer of 1557 he continued to hope for an expression of support from Melanchthon, who had maintained an uneasy silence in the face

---

[97] Von Schade, *Westphal und Braubach*, p. 43.
[98] Ibid., pp. 39, 40, 42.
[99] Ibid., pp. 42, 126–7.
[100] Mönckeberg, *Westphal und Calvin*, pp. 93–101.

of repeated urgings from Calvin and others to declare himself. In August 1557 Calvin addressed to the Wittenberg reformer a final appeal, enclosing with his letter a copy of the *Ultima admonitio*, in which his conviction that his sacramental beliefs were in full accord with Melanchthon's was quite unambiguously stated.[101]

Calvin urged Melanchthon to speak out before his reputation was irretrievably tarnished, but when Melanchthon did respond it was in a way which could have given Calvin little comfort. As has been made clear, Westphal's protest against the Reformed had evoked a deep response among the German Lutherans, and the timorous Melanchthon was not the man to stand out against such a strong tide of opinion. At the colloquium with the Catholic theologians at Worms in the autumn of 1557, Melanchthon finally bowed to pressure and signed the condemnation of Zwingli's doctrine presented by the orthodox Lutherans, thus effectively barring the way to further dialogue with the Swiss.[102]

Bullinger and his Zurich colleagues felt themselves justified in their low expectations of Melanchthon, but for Calvin this was a bitter rebuff; henceforth his reluctance to engage in further controversy was clearly apparent. When, in the summer of 1558, the indefatigable John a Lasco wrote requesting a foreword to Utenhove's account of the tribulation of the exiles at the hands of the northern Lutherans, which was now almost ready for the press, Calvin was sufficiently weary of the struggle to advise against publication altogether. Little could be gained, he thought, by reopening old wounds at this time.[103] Lasco and Utenhove were not to be deterred, and the *Simplex Narratio* finally appeared in Basle in 1560, together with Lasco's last contribution to the sacramentarian controversy, the *Responsio ad virulentem Joachim Westphal*.[104] This final *Responsio* appeared posthumously as Lasco had died in Poland the previous January, and the sacramentarian controversy itself seems also by this time to have died a natural death. After a final flurry of publications in 1558, Westphal announced in a letter to Hartman Beyer that he did not intend to concern himself further with the 'sacramentarians', and Lasco's final

---

[101] CO, vol. 16, no. 2677; Mönckeberg, *Westphal und Calvin*, pp. 93–4.

[102] W. Neuser: 'Die Versuche Bullingers, Calvins and der Straßburger, Melanchthon zum Fortgang von Wittenberg zu bewegen', in *Heinrich Bullinger, 1505–1574*, ed. U. Gäbler and E. Herkenrath (2 vols, Zürcher Beiträge zur Reformationsgeschichte, 8, 1975), vol. 1, p. 53.

[103] Lasco to Calvin, 5 August 1558, Calvin to Utenhove, 19 Nov 1558: CO 17, nos 2931, 2982.

[104] Kruske, *Sakramentsstreit*, pp. 175–8; *Lasco Opera*, I, pp. 271–344. For the *Simplex Narratio* see n. 9 above.

tract seems not to have moved him from this resolve.[105] Calvin and his colleagues also maintained their silence, although the bitterness of their feelings towards Westphal seems hardly to have abated by the time of his death in 1568.[106] The dispute's sad postscript in 1561, when the Lutheran ministers in Frankfurt finally succeeded in securing the closure of the exile churches and the expulsion of the refugee communities, was hardly able to reignite the passions of the previous decade. The expulsion was largely a result of a change in the balance of power within the Frankfurt ruling elite, which weakened the exiles' faithful patrician allies to the point where they could no longer protect the refugees against the hostility of the ministers and craftsmen.[107] A similar attempt by militant pastors to secure the closure of the remaining Walloon church in Wesel at the same time failed when the Lutherans overreached themselves, and their leader, the theologian Heshuisius, was himself expelled from the town.[108] In both Frankfurt and Wesel, in fact, the exile communities lived on, with or without their churches, a grudging toleration merging into tacit acceptance as the irrefutable economic benefits of the exile presence diluted the effects of Lutheran hostility. From 1559 the restored exile churches in London were once again in a position to cast a benevolent eye over the activities of their Reformed brethren in both Germany and the Netherlands.

If time and the successive waves of skilled and hardworking exiles helped heal the wounds inflicted by the heated conflicts of the 1550s, the controversy that had been triggered by the arrival of the London exiles on the continent in 1553 still left an indelible mark on religious relationships in Germany. In the first place, the sacramentarian controversy of the 1550s gave a decisive impulse to the development of rival confessions within Protestantism. The Peace of Augsburg of 1555 is rightly regarded as a milestone in this respect, but the decisive separation of the confessions after this date should not obscure the much more ambiguous relationships which existed at the beginning of the decade. Several leading reformers believed wholeheartedly that doctrinal reunion between the churches of Germany and Switzerland

---

[105] Von Schade, *Westphal und Braubach*, pp. 42–6, 127; Mönckeberg, *Westphal und Calvin*, pp. 114ff.
[106] Von Schade, *Westphal und Braubach*, p. 48.
[107] Schilling, *Niederländische Exulanten*, pp. 126–31; Ebrard, *Französisch-reformierte Gemeinde*, pp. 96–9.
[108] Wolters, *Reformationsgeschichte*, pp. 236–63; Hollweg, 'Calvins Beziehungen', pp. 163–7.

was a real possibility, and none pursued this aim more fervently than Calvin himself. Calvin had never concealed his hope that the death of Luther in 1546 would make possible a new initiative to bring the leading Protestant churches into agreement, and the accord with Zurich in 1549, the *Consensus Tigurinus*, may be seen in this context as the first step in a more ambitious plan to promote his own interpretation of Protestant Eucharistic doctrine in Luther's homeland.[109] Calvin seems genuinely to have believed that his own sacramental doctrine was entirely compatible with that of the *Confessio Augustana Variata* of 1540, a conviction shared by such decidedly 'Reformed' figures as Lasco and Poullain.[110] The strength of Calvin's conviction helps explain why he was inclined to dismiss Westphal as a marginal figure, an error the extent of which he was only to discover through the bitter experiences of the 1550s.

If the *Consensus Tigurinus* may be seen as the beginning of Calvin's attempt to unite German and Swiss Protestantism, then the dispute with Westphal and its consequences brought it to a decisive halt; to this extent, the campaign which Westphal inaugurated in 1552 with the alarm signal of his *Farrago* was entirely successful. By 1558 Calvin's hopes of a new consensus based on his own interpretation of the Confession of Augsburg had dissolved in acrimony and bitterness, and it was Westphal who had established his claim to be the orthodox interpreter of Lutheran doctrine. In 1557 the obscure northern minister whom Calvin had dismissed as a 'brute barbarian' could marshall to his support doctrinal statements from 25 leading Lutheran reformers and churches, which he published as a single joint exposition of the Lutheran doctrine of the Eucharist.[111] There could be no more emphatic rebuttal of Calvin's claim to be the voice of moderate Lutheran opinion. The dynamic of Calvinist expansion in the Empire had, in fact, been arrested, and at a decisive moment. It is not to underestimate the importance of the Palatinate to note that the gains made by the Reformed in Germany in the second half of the century were extremely modest when compared to the central role played by Calvinism in the religious conflicts of northern Europe.[112]

The *Sakramentsstreit* may then be seen as an important milestone in the development of confessionalism, but it also played its part in a

---

[109]Kruske, *Sakramentsstreit*, pp. 189–92; Mönckeberg, *Westphal und Calvin*, p. 11.
[110]Kruske, *Sakramentsstreit*, pp. 120–5; Bauer, *Poullain*, pp. 292–7.
[111]Von Schade, *Westphal und Braubach*, p. 44; Mönckeberg, *Westphal und Calvin*, p. 91.
[112]Karl Brandi, *Deutsche Geschichte im Zeitalter der Reformation und Gegenreformation* (3rd edn, Leipzig, 1943), pp. 366ff.

more subtle process, and one ultimately much happier from the point of view of Calvin and the Genevan Reformation. The conflict of the 1550s marks a possibly decisive stage in the process by which Geneva replaced Zurich as the leading force within the Reformed church. This was by no means so much a matter of course as general histories of the Reformation seem to assume. Luther died in 1546, yet it was only a decade later that Calvin was finally secure from internal opposition in Geneva; between his return from exile in 1541 and the defeat of the Perrinists in 1555 his international influence grew only slowly, and it was very largely Bullinger and Zurich who carried the candle of the Swiss Reformation into lands where the impact of Lutheranism had been limited. A look back at the circumstances surrounding the foundation of the stranger churches in London during the first years of the Edwardian Reformation is instructive in this respect. The liturgy and institutions of the new independent community clearly reflected the influence of Zurich on Lasco and his fellow ministers. Lasco, Micron, and Utenhove had all visited Zurich and were personally known to Bullinger, to whom they frequently turned for advice and consolation during the churches' early months.[113] Their relationship with Calvin was much more distant and formal. When in 1552 Lasco complained to Calvin that new arrivals in London had compared the practices of the French church unfavourably with those of Geneva, Calvin's response was awkward and evasive; none, he wrote, should make a Jerusalem of Geneva, and he urged his supporters to conform to the church's existing practice.[114] Clearly Calvin did not regard the French church in London as part of his sphere of influence at this time, and the same could be said of the Edwardian Reformation in general.

If by the 1560s and 1570s Geneva had achieved a dominant position amongst the Reformed churches, this is a process which requires explanation rather than an inexorable historical development. The sacramentarian controversy is of interest not least because it shows Calvin at a time when he was beginning to assume a wider European role. Calvin's leading role in the controversy was partly a result of circumstantial factors; it was natural that the French-speaking exiles in Wesel and Frankfurt should turn to Calvin for assistance, but it is indicative of the Genevan reformer's growing stature that Lasco and the Dutch ministers should also have shown such respect for his advice and authority. Lasco in particular had

---

[113] Pettegree, *Foreign Protestant Communities*, pp. 47–54, 68–73.
[114] CO, vol. 14, no. 1653.

enjoyed a rather uneasy relationship with Calvin hitherto,[115] but when in the spring of 1554 he wrote to inform the Swiss churches of his church's trials at the hands of the northern Lutherans it was Calvin, rather than Bullinger, who took up the cudgels on their behalf. Bullinger never shared Calvin's high hopes of the tractability of the German Lutherans and was inclined to view the renewed controversy with a somewhat fatalistic detachment.[116] For Calvin, for whom doctrinal agreement with the Lutherans represented a tangible goal, much more was at stake, and if the zeal with which he pursued the controversy with Westphal was ultimately to prove counter-productive, it did at least play an important role in establishing Calvin as the leading spokesman and defender of the Swiss Reformation.

Significantly, it was about this time that the word 'Calvinist' began to gain currency as a general term to describe the Reformed. The word seems to have been coined during the pamphlet exchange which followed the execution of Servetus in 1553, an incident which also contributed greatly to Calvin's international renown during the decade of the sacramentarian controversy. By 1558 Westphal, who had previously always described his opponents as 'Zwinglians' or 'Sacramentarians', was himself making frequent use of the new epithet.[117] Nowhere was the growth of Calvin's international reputation more clearly signalled than in the London foreign churches after their restoration in 1559. Casting around for a new minister, the French community appealed at once for Calvin's help, and Calvin was sufficiently persuaded of the importance of the post to despatch his friend Nicolas des Gallars to England.[118] Changes in the institutions and practices of the community during the 1560s, from which the more independently minded Dutch churches were not exempt, also reflected the increasingly pervasive influence of Geneva in the emerging Reformed churches of northern Europe.

Such influences were not always so immediately apparent. The Dutch reformers always retained an independent streak, and it would

---

[115] Calvin had expressed misgivings at the extent of Lasco's influence in London. Calvin to Farel, 10 November 1550: CO, vol. 13, no. 1415.

[116] W. Kolfhaus, 'Der Verkehr Calvins mit Bullinger', in *Calvinstudien*, ed. J. Bohatec (Leipzig, 1909), pp. 109–14; Neuser, 'Versuche Bullingers', pp. 45–55. Bullinger contributed only one work to the controversy, his *Apologetia exposito* of February 1556, written to express his solidarity with Calvin. Mönckeberg, *Westphal und Calvin*, pp. 84–7.

[117] Uwe Plath: 'Zur Entstehungsgeschichte des Wortes "Calvinist",' *ARG*, 66 (1975), pp. 213–23.

[118] Pettegree, *Foreign Protestant Communities*, p. 151.

be several decades before Calvinist orthodoxy was securely established in the Netherlands. If the role of Emden as a source of support for the 'churches under the cross' earned it the title of the 'Geneva of the North', it was never simply a pale shadow of its southern counterpart.[119] Nevertheless, the 1550s was a watershed decade for the international Reformed, as it was for the exile churches. Returning to England in 1559, Utenhove, Delenus and their colleagues would give thanks for a second friendly reception in the land of their first exile. They could also reflect that their progress through Denmark and Germany in the intervening years had had repercussions which long outlived the pain and disappointments of their gruelling search for a new home.

[119] W. van 't Spijker 'Stromingen onder de reformatorisch gezinder te Emden', in D. Nauta and J. P. van Dooren (eds), *De Synode van Emden October 1571* (Kampen, 1971), pp. 50–74.

CHAPTER FOUR

Nicodemism and the English Reformation

> And Elijah came unto all the people and said, How long halt ye between two opinions? If the Lord be God, then follow him: but if Baal then follow him.[1]

At several points during the course of the early Reformation, English Protestants faced unpalatable choices. The first fundamental crisis for evangelicals came with the conservative backlash of the 1540s, following the enactment of the doctrinally conservative Six Articles in 1539.[2] With this, and even more with the execution of the evangelical patron Thomas Cromwell in 1540, Catholics at Court appeared clearly in the ascendant and the whole reformist agenda of the 1530s seemed likely to be rolled back. The conservative tide was sufficient to persuade some of the more prominent or vulnerable evangelicals that they should remove themselves to the continent; but most remained, to be rewarded in due course with the triumphant reversal of fortune that followed the death of Henry VIII in 1547.[3]

The death of Edward VI inevitably produced an altogether more drastic crisis. Even though the first religious measures of Mary's reign suggested a desire to proceed by measured and unprovocative steps, committed Protestants could have been in little doubt that the new regime's ultimate purpose would be the full restoration of Catholic worship. The public demonstrations of the Queen's devotion to traditional piety in the first weeks of the regime reinforced what was already well known of her personal religious allegiances; swift measures to induce prominent European Protestants to leave England made clear that the return to Catholicism would not be preceded by

---

[1] Kings 18:21.

[2] For evangelical reactions to the Act and its consequences see particularly Susan Brigden, *London and the Reformation* (Oxford, 1989), pp. 299–377.

[3] Diarmaid MacCulloch, *Thomas Cranmer: A Life* (New Haven and London, 1996), Chapters 7 and 8, now provides a definitive treatment of evangelical responses and attitudes during the last difficult decade of Henry's reign. See also Alec Ryrie, 'Persecution, Survival and Compromise. English Protestantism and the State, 1539–1547' (University of St Andrews, M. Litt. dissertation, 1994).

a lengthy public debate.[4] Over the next 12 months, legislation to restore the Mass and reinstate legal penalties for heresy, combined with the Queen's Spanish marriage and the debacle of Wyatt's rebellion, snuffed out any residual hopes that the destruction of the Edwardian religious settlement might be replaced by a restoration of some sort of Henrician middle way. By early 1555 England was fully reconciled to Rome.[5]

The leaders of English Protestantism were thus faced by stark choices. Either they must reconcile themselves to the new circumstances, and conform, or they must accept one of a limited range of unpalatable options: withdrawing to one of the centres of continental Protestantism or following the yet more perilous course of open witness, risking all the penalties of the revived heresy laws. As is well known, the numbers who opted to follow one or other of these routes was painfully small. Even with the reassessment of the total size of the exile implied by the archival discoveries presented elsewhere in this volume, the total size of the exile could not by much have exceeded 1000. The number who witnessed boldly in England, either in small secret congregations or in the spontaneous acts of defiance which all too frequently led to arrest and execution, was even smaller.[6]

If this was all there was to show for six years of Protestant evangelism in the reign of Edward VI, the harvest would have been meagre indeed. This was something of which those leaders of the Edwardian church who had made the decision to leave England were acutely aware, and which they freely acknowledged in their writings. A sense of the shattering disappointment at this sudden reversal of fortune mingled with despair at the appalling apostasy that had reduced the official state church to such a remnant. For some the thought of this falling off was almost insupportable. When I consider, wrote Thomas Cottisford from the security of Emden in 1555, how idolatry is now sprung up in England, and how an infinite number, who two years past bare a fair face to religion, are now suddenly

---

[4] For the departure of the foreign Protestant leaders see my *Foreign Protestant Communities in Sixteenth Century London* (Oxford, 1986), pp. 113–18.

[5] David Loades, *The Reign of Mary Tudor* (London, 1979).

[6] J. W. Martin, 'The Protestant Underground Congregations of Mary's Reign', in *JEH*, 35 (1984), pp. 519–38; reprinted in his *Religious Radicals in Tudor England* (London, 1989), pp. 125–46. John Foxe, *Acts and Monuments of these latter and perillous Days* [London, John Daye, 1563], pp. 1676–1703. Cited hereafter as *Acts and Monuments, 1563*. The modern edn used here is *The Acts and Monuments of John Foxe*, ed. George Townsend and Stephen Cattley (8 vols, London, 1837–41).

turned back to worship the beast, I can scarce refrain from tears.[7] John Olde was even more blunt: those who favoured the Gospel under Edward VI but had now gone over to the other side, were traitors.[8]

Evangelicals had a term for such fainthearts and fair weather friends: they called them Nicodemites, after Nicodemus, the Pharisee who came to Jesus by night, thus dissembling his sympathy for his teaching.[9] And this was a phenomenon which could truly be said to have obsessed the remnant of English Protestantism gathered in the continental exile churches. Of all the Marian exile writings, perhaps as many as two-thirds of the original tracts addressed themselves to this problem: calling brethren in England to a more faithful witness and defending their own conduct in going abroad.[10] And it is also true that virtually no-one then or since has had much to say in defence of those who compromised in this way. Protestants were virtually united in their condemnation; and historians have mostly followed their lead by making the implicit assumption that the only real manifestation of true faith consisted of faithful witness. True conviction would have led Protestants either into exile or martyrdom.

However, there is more to be said on the subject, and not all of it to the discredit of those who remained in England. There were many reasons, and not all of them ignoble, to hold people in England during Mary's reign, as the more humane of the exile polemicists recognized. Indeed, many of these rationalizations can be reconstructed from the exile pamphlets themselves, where they are seriously addressed if only to be carefully refuted. The fact that arguments of this sort were widely debated suggests that an alternative, Nicodemite strategy was articulated at the time, and found support among many who would do good and faithful service to the Protestant cause in times to come.

---

[7] [Thomas Cottisford], *The accompt, rekenynge and confession of the faith of H. Zwinglius*. Tr. out of latyn by Thomas Cotsforde. Geneva [Emden, Gellius van der Erve], 1555, preface, sig. *5^r. STC 26140. Quoted at greater length in Chapter 1, p. 25.

[8] *A Confession of the most auncient and true catholike olde belefe*. Sothewarke, C. Truthal [i.e. Emden, Gellius van der Erve], 1555, sig. E5^v. STC 18798.

[9] John 3: 1–10. Carlo Ginzburg, *Il Nicodemismo; Simulazione e dissimulazione religiosa nell'Europa del '500* (Turin, 1970). Carlos M. N. Eire, 'Prelude to Sedition? Calvin's Attack on Nicodemism and Religious Compromise', *ARG*, 76 (1985), pp. 120–45. Idem, 'Calvin and Nicodemism: a reappraisal', *SCJ*, 10 (1979), pp. 45–69. Peter Matheson, 'Martyrdom or Mission? A Protestant Debate', *ARG*, 80 (1989), pp. 154–72.

[10] Edward Baskerville, *A Chronological Bibliography of Propaganda and Polemic published in England between 1553 and 1558* (Philadelphia, 1979).

But at bottom the mere fact that this was such a widespread phenomenon is sufficient reason in itself for a more careful examination of the Nicodemite contribution to the English Reformation. English Protestantism owed more to people of this stamp than it has so far been prepared to acknowledge.

The dilemma that faced English Protestants in the 1540s and 1550s – how to witness to their faith in lands where the lay power was determinedly hostile – was not one unique to England: in its origins it was almost as old as the Reformation itself. In Germany the promulgation of the Edict of Worms condemning Luther did not greatly inhibit debate of his teachings, but elsewhere, and especially in Charles V's patrimonial lands, the Netherlands, advocacy of Luther's views carried real dangers. In 1521 Charles V promulgated the first of his placards banning the public dissemination of any of Luther's condemned views, a campaign of repression which culminated in 1523 with the execution of two prominent exponents of the new teachings, Augustinian monks from the house in Antwerp, who were burned at the stake for heresy in Brussels on 1 July.[11] These were the first executions for support of the Gospel anywhere in Europe, and it is clear that the martyrdom of Voes and van der Esschen made a considerable inpact on evangelical circles throughout Europe.[12] The new climate of repression certainly encouraged preachers in the Netherlands who had expressed early public support for the German teachings to become much more guarded in their views. It was in this context that the term Nicodemite seems first to have been coined to describe such timorous fellow-travellers, and more particularly Desiderius Erasmus, whose refusal to offer Luther open support deeply frustrated those friends who had expected more after his first tentative expressions of approval for the evangelical movement. The first known use of the term is found in a letter of Frederik Hondebeke, rector of the Grammar School at Delft, writing to his friend Caspar Hedio in 1522 and commenting sourly on Erasmus's performance:

I am very annoyed that day by day Erasmus is cooling off and, as

---

[11] Alastair Duke, 'The Face of Popular Dissent in the Low Countries', in his *Reformation and Revolt in the Low Countries* (London, 1990), p. 30.

[12] Luther wrote a hymn in their honour, and the story of their suffering became a staple of Protestant martyrologies. For two of the earliest tracts see *Bibliotheca Reformatoria Neerlandica*, ed. S. Cramer and F. Pijper (10 vols, The Hague, 1903–14), vol. 8, pp. 23–114. C.f. *Bibliographie des Martyrologes Protestants Néerlandais* (2 vols, The Hague, 1890), vol. 1, pp. 719–21.

far as I can judge, is secretly reconsidering what he seems once to have said or written more freely, and I recognise a childish fear, which has more respect for the approbation of men than the glory of God. But such Nicodemites among us are in great number.[13]

It is arguable that the use of the term in this way was fair neither to Erasmus, nor indeed to Nicodemus. Nicodemus, after all, would go on to play an honourable part in the Gospel story, coming forward with Joseph of Arimathea to claim Jesus's body when his disciples had fled.[14] And Erasmus, for all his early admiration of the courage of the German reformer, always had real misgivings about the tone of Luther's criticisms of the church authorities, and always made clear that his commitment to church unity took precedence over his genuine desire to see the church reformed.[15] Yet the term once coined would have a long polemical life, even if it was another 15 years before it became common currency among evangelicals.[16] Its re-emergence as a common term of abuse was largely the achievement of one of the century's great polemicists, John Calvin. Calvin left France in 1535 after a period of intellectual development which had seen him increasingly committed to the Parisian humanist/evangelical circle around Nicolas Cop.[17] Yet he had no sooner signalled his own final commitment to the evangelical cause than he rounded on others who remained in France in the first of what became a series of anti-Nicodemite writings, the *De fugiendis impiorum*.[18] As the title suggests Calvin here urged on his readers the stern necessity to fly from the presence of idolatry, a theme to which he returned in the two most famous tracts of this series, the *Petit traité monstrant que c'est doit*

---

[13] D. p. Oosterbaan, 'School en kerk in het Middeleeuwse Delft', *Spiegel der Historie*, 1 (1966), p. 113.

[14] As Calvin indeed recognized; see his *Excuse à Messieurs les Nicodemites* in Francis Higman, *Jean Calvin. Three French Treatises* (London, 1970), pp. 147–8. John 19: 38–39.

[15] Léon-E. Halkin, *Erasmus. A Critical Biography* (Oxford, 1993).

[16] Eire, 'Calvin and Nicodemism', pp. 46–7, cites a number of uses between 1529 and 1535.

[17] Alister McGrath, *A Life of John Calvin* (Oxford, 1990), pp. 21–78, is good on the intellectual atmosphere of Paris during these years. The extent to which Calvin may himself have dissembled his developing evangelical views is one which Calvin scholars have largely preferred not to address. See Alexandre Ganoczy, *The Young Calvin* (Philadelphia, 1987); W. Nijenhuis, 'Calvin's "subita conversio". Notes to a hypothesis', in his *Ecclesia Reformata. Volume II* (Leiden, 1994), pp. 3–23.

[18] CO, vol. 5, cols 237–78. There is an English translation, *On Shunning the Unlawful Rites of the Ungodly*, in *Tracts by John Calvin*, ed. H. Beveridge (3 vols, Edinburgh, 1851), vol. 3, pp. 359–411.

faire un home fidele cognoissant la verité de l'evangile of 1543, and the *Excuse à Messieurs les Nicodemites* of the following year.[19]

These were works of searing power, which brought the debate regarding the obligations of a true evangelical placed in a hostile environment to a new level. Informed by Calvin's close personal acquaintance with the tradition of evangelical agitation for reform from within the French church, the tracts confront such men with what were for Calvin unpalatable truths. Calvin was here writing against an established tradition, now articulated by influential figures such as Gérard Roussel, who argued that a reformist agenda could and should be pursued within the established church. Such arguments gained credence from the evident appeal of the new learning to influential figures at the French Court. Even after the Affair of the Placards had revealed Francis I's own fundamental loyalty to the established church, many in France still clung to the hope of Gallican reform until well into the following decade. In this context Calvin's clear-minded repudiation of such a position was of the greatest importance. The *Petit traité* lays out at length his reasons for rejecting the validity of the Roman church, its sacraments, ceremonies and the deformation of the Mass, and proposes the only satisfactory solution for the true believer: emigration.

Two points are worth making in the light of this initial discussion of Calvin's intervention in the debate. Firstly, the Genevan reformer was turning his formidable mind to what was widely perceived among evangelicals as being *the* burning issue of the day. Most of the leaders of Swiss and exiled French Protestantism contributed writings on the subject at some point, some of them several times over. These included such influential figures as Heinrich Bullinger, Guillaume Farel and Peter Martyr Vermigli, all of whom addressed the question directly and generally offered uncompromising support of Calvin's position.[20] None, however, could equal the productivity of Pierre

---

[19] CO, vol. 6, cols 537–614. A modern edition of the *Excuse* in Higman, *Three French Treatises*, pp. 131–53. An extract from the *Petit traité* (a letter of 1540 in which Calvin lays out his developing attitude) is reprinted in A.-L. Herminjard, *Correspondance des Réformateurs dans les Pays de langue Française* (9 vols, Paris, 1866–97), vol. 6, pp. 297–305 (no. 888).

[20] *Commentarium H. Bullinger in omnes Apostolicas Epistolas* [Zurich, 1537]; *De origine errores circa invocationem et cultum deorum ac simulachronum* [Zurich, 1539]. Joachim Staedtke, *Heinrich Bullinger Bibliographie* (Zurich, 1972), nos 12, 84; Peter Martyr, *Commentary on Judges*. For editions see John P. Donnelly and Robert M. Kingdon (eds), *A Bibliography of the Works of Peter Martyr Vermigli* (Kirksville, MS, 1990), pp. 36–47. For Farel's straightforward views on the question see the letter to Capito in Herminjard, *Correspondance*, vol. 5, pp. 434–44 (no. 630a).

Viret who devoted no fewer than five major writings to the subject between 1541 and 1547.[21] Calvin could rely on some powerful allies in his efforts to persuade French Nicodemites of the error of their ways.

Secondly – and this explains why the reformers' strictures had to be so frequently repeated – the views propounded by Calvin and his colleagues were far from generally accepted. The *Excuse à Messieurs les Nicodemites* was very largely a response to the debate stirred up by the *Petit traité* of 1543, much of it very hostile in tone. Antoine Fumée, a friend of Calvin still resident in Paris, left the Genevan in no doubt as to the hostility his opinions had stirred up: 'A number of people think your assertions are thoroughly wretched. They accuse you of being merciless and very severe to those who are afflicted; and say that it is easy for you to preach and threaten over there, but that if you were here you would perhaps feel differently.'[22] This was to be a common theme of apologists for compromise. The circulation of 200 copies of the *Petit traité* in the French-speaking Netherlands by Calvin's friend and disciple Valérand Poullain stirred a similarly hostile reaction in Valenciennes and Tournai, as Poullain was forced to admit in a review of the state of these troubled small churches.[23] It was typical of Calvin that he gave no ground to his critics in his riposte, but if anything made his criticism more brutal and scathing. Nicodemites were now likened to the cleaners of latrines who after a long time at their work no longer smell the odour of the filth with which they are associated.[24] More importantly, alongside this ritual abuse, Calvin now provides a more precise typology of Nicodemites which incidentally offers a useful insight into the milieux in which Protestant teaching was gaining influence at this time.[25]

But Calvin's critics were right in at least one respect: there were many arguments that could be advanced against Calvin's position, many of them perfectly respectable. The advocates of prevarication found at least one influential sympathizer among the leadership of the German reformers, in the form of the hesitant and somewhat ambiva-

---

[21] Listed in F. G. Higman, 'The Question of Nicodemism', in Wilhelm Neuser (ed.), *Calvinus Ecclesiae Genevensis Custos* (Frankfurt, 1984), p. 169. Extracts from his *Epistre consolataire* (1541) in Herminjard, *Correspondance*, vol. 6, pp. 428–38 (no. 933).

[22] Fumeé to Calvin, CO, vol. 11, col. 646.

[23] Poullain to Calvin, 9 March 1544, CO, vol. 11, cols 683–5 (no. 535). Gérard Moreau, *Histoire du Protestantisme à Tournai jusqu'à la veille de la Révolution des Pays-Bas* (Paris, 1962), pp. 90–1.

[24] Higman, *Three French Treatises*, p. 134.

[25] Ibid., pp. 136 ff.

lent figure of Martin Bucer.[26] In his *Consilium Theologicum Privatim Conscriptum*, a work of 1540–41 which remained (perhaps fortunately for Bucer) in manuscript, Bucer advanced several reasons why the true believer should think carefully before abandoning the universal church. Firstly, and in crucial contradistinction to Calvin, Bucer argued that the Catholic church was a true church, for all its faults, and should not be incontinently rejected. Bucer here expressed the horror of schism which would lead him into many ill-starred efforts to reconcile competing evangelical traditions in the 1530s and 1540s.[27] This argument could hardly be applied in the hardening confessional climate of England in the 1550s, but two other characteristics of Bucer's thinking were definitely relevant to the English situation: his greater stress on the internal beliefs of the individual, a stress on personal piety that gave much less attention to external ceremonies that offended; and a strong sense that too easy a rejection of the church because of offensive external ceremonies was to run the risk of sacrificing the hope of longer term gain.[28]

Bucer was not ashamed to cite appropriate biblical texts in support of his position. He pointed out that the apostles continued to frequent the Temple even after the priests had put Jesus to death, and despite the degeneration of their ceremonies. He also made great play of Paul's assertion of a sort of cohabitation in his first letter to the Corinthians: 'Unto the Jews I became as a Jew, that I might gain the Jews. ... I am made all means to all men, that I might by all means save some. And all this I do for the gospel's sake.'[29] Nor was the Old Testament utterly devoid of helpful texts. Against Elijah's apparently uncompromising rejection of dissimulation cited in the head text of this article, and frequently by the reformers themselves,[30] apologists

---

[26] Matheson, 'Martyrdom or Mission?', pp. 158–71. Francis Higman, 'Bucer et les Nicodemites', in Christian Krieger and Marc Lienhard (eds), *Martin Bucer and Sixteenth Century Europe* (2 vols, Leiden, 1993), vol. 2, pp. 645–58.

[27] Peter Matheson, 'Martin Bucer and the Old Church', and Cornelis Augustijn, 'Bucer's ecclesiology in the colloquies with the Catholics, 1540–41', in D. F. Wright (ed.), *Martin Bucer, Reforming Church and Community* (Cambridge, 1994), pp. 5–16 and 107–21. There is now a modern edn of the Consilium: *Martini Buceri Opera Latina, vol. IV: Consilium Theologicum Privatim Conscriptum*, ed. Pierre Fraenkel (Leiden, 1988).

[28] Higman, 'Bucer et les Nicodemites', pp. 647–53.

[29] I Corinthians 10: 20–23.

[30] For instance, John Philpot: *The Examinations and Writings of John Philpot*, ed. Robert Eden (Parker Society, 1842), p. 219. Cottisford, *Confession of the Faith of Huldrik Zwinglius*, sig. A6^r. Robert Horne, *Whether Christian faith may be kept secret in the heart without confession thereof openly to the world*, Roane [London, Daye?], 1553, uses the text as a title-page epigram. STC 5160.3.

could oppose the apparently contradictory advice of Elisha to Namaan, captain of the host of the king of Syria, who after his miraculous healing at the hands of the prophet asked him whether he could in good conscience continue to serve his master in the Temple of Rimmon. The prophet seemed prepared to condone this: 'And he said unto him, Go in peace.'[31] Something could be made of Abraham's voluntary habitation in Egypt and Cana, after he was commanded to go out from Chaldee.[32] Yet even without specific (if far from unambiguous) texts of this sort apologists for inaction could also derive from the Old Testament a more generalized sense that if one only waited in prayerful anticipation things would turn for the better. Alongside the frequent, almost monotonous condemnations of idolatry which made so deep an impression on Edwardian Protestants and would seem to leave no choice but to flee abroad when idolatrous temples were set up once more, the sacred history of the Jewish peoples was also infused with a strong dialectical rhythm: of sin and repentance, of bad times being inevitably followed by good.[33] One can sense this clearly in the exile literature of Mary's reign; even while they called their fallen brethren to repentance the exiles clearly believed that the reverses they had suffered were only temporary in nature. From this they drew one lesson: of repentance and the rejection of false Gods. But other readers of Scripture could be forgiven for arriving at a different conclusion, that they need only to hold out and wait for better times, for the cycle to turn once more in their favour. Their experiences of the 1540s might have encouraged them in this view, for here the conservative reaction of Henry's last years had indeed been succeeded by the golden age of the young Josiah.

It would, of course, be a gross misrepresentation to suggest that those who remained in England were motivated solely or even primarily by such highly selective readings of Scripture. No doubt in so far as such views were articulated they served mostly to reinforce more strictly practical considerations. But that a debate of some sort was in

---

[31] 2 Kings 5: 17–19. For Bucer's use of Namaan see Matheson, 'Martyrdom or Mission?', p. 169. C.f. also [Peter Martyr Vermigli], *A Treatise of the Cohabitation of the Faithful with the Unfaithful*. [Strasburg, Rihel, 1555], sig. A2ᵛ. STC 24673.5.

[32] Genesis 12. See Martyr Vermigli, *Treatise of the Cohabitation of the Faithful with the Unfaithful*, sig. A2ᵛ for the use of this text.

[33] See here esp. Judges, 2 Kings, Isaiah. For the Edwardian Protestant response to the biblical injunction to destroy idols see Christopher Bradshaw, 'David or Josiah? Old Testament Kings as exemplars in Edwardian Religious polemic', in Bruce Gordon (ed.), *Protestant History and Identity in Sixteenth-Century Europe* (St Andrews Studies in Reformation History, 3, 1996).

progress in evangelical circles is clear enough from the exile literature where certain apologist arguments are frequently presented, if only to be refuted.

The most insidious and corrupting argument apparently advanced to defend Nicodemism was that those who remained true to the Gospel in their hearts could be permitted a degree of outward conformity. Or as John Philpot would put it, writing to encourage Christian friends from his prison cell, 'Some fondly think that the presence of the body is not material, so that the heart do not consent to their wicked doings.'[34] Clearly arguments of this sort were a great temptation to those bound to England by ties of family or property, as the exiles recognized. The exile and future bishop Robert Horne confronted such arguments directly in his tract, *Whether Christian faith may be kept secret in the heart without confession thereof openly to the world.*

> The wisdom of the world doth say: although I do accomplish the desire of my friends, and to the sight of the world am present at the Mass, and with my body do as other men do, or as I may do, yet my heart is clean contrary to their belief, and I do detest such idolatry and believe that the thing that I am present at is no mere idolatry and abomination. Here be fair words for an evil purpose.[35]

The exiles deployed a range of arguments to confute such seductive special pleadings. Bodies were temples of the Holy Ghost, which could only be polluted by contact with the contamination of popish worship; and God had forbidden all contact with idols.[36] Further, the example of outward conformity could only bring weaker brethren into confusion. Here they took their cue from Calvin in quoting St Paul:

> When any one sees him who has knowledge sitting at the idol's feast, will not his conscience, seeing he is doubtful, be encouraged to eat? And by your consciousness shall your weak brother perish, for who Christ died? In this way sinning against the brethren, and wounding the weak consciences, you sin against Christ.[37]

---

[34] *Examinations and Writings of John Philpot*, p. 221.

[35] Robert Horne, *Whether Christian faith may be kept secret in the heart without confession thereof openly to the world*, Roane [London, Daye?], 1553, sig. a3^{r-v}. STC 5160.3.

[36] 1 Corinthians 6. Compare *Examinations and Writings of John Philpot*, pp. 220–1. Horne, *Whether Christian Faith may be kept secret*, sig. a4^r.

[37] 1 Corinthians 8: 7–12. Calvin, *Unlawful Rites of the Ungodly*, p. 375. Horne, *Whether Christian Faith may be kept secret*, sig. a5^r.

Most of all they focused attention on the greatest pollutant of all, the Romish Mass. Thus John Olde:

> Good brethren, be not partakers of the example and faint carnal excuse of those who say, although they go to the church and be present at the Mass, yet they worship none but the living God in their hearts, and hate the Mass as much as we do. Which saying is much unlike to be true, but seemeth rather a vain pretended fantasy, and preposterous wrestling of some texts of scripture, wherewith the Devil deludeth the senses and souls of many tender carpet gospellers, at this present time of trial, to bring them past repentance ... The body goeth not to Mass without the company and consent of the soul.[38]

Here the reformers emphatically followed Calvin and Bullinger, rather than Bucer, in denying that the Roman church might be regarded as the true church. Robert Horne called quite explicitly on the example of the continental reformers:

> I do know that there be many invasions made by men, that teach a man with safeguard of his conscience to be at Mass, but forasmuch as Master Calvin, Master Bullinger and others have thoroughly answered them, such as be in doubt, may read their books.[39]

Horne could speak with authority on this point since it was he who had brought to the press, simultaneously with his own writing on this theme, a translation of Calvin's sermon admonishing all Christians 'to flye the outward idolatry', a partial translation of the *Quatre sermons* of 1552.[40] Thomas Cottisford was at further pains to refute the views of 'a certain great clerk' (probably Bucer?)[41] who in the last five years had written apparently justifying attendance at Mass. But this was written only for 'younglings in the true knowledge and understanding of the mysteries of Christ's religion', not a people who, like the English after the reign of Edward, were fully acquainted with the true religion.[42]

Here the English reformers were drawing on a range of arguments available from the first exchanges of the polemical debate on the continent, ever since Calvin had confronted the arguments for out-

---

[38] Olde, *Confession of the true Catholic Old belief*, sig. E3[r–v].

[39] Horne, *Whether Christian Faith may be kept secret*, sig. a8[r].

[40] *Certain homilies of M. John Calvin containing profitable and necessary admonition for this time* [Wesel?, J. Lambrecht?], 1553. STC 4392. Rodolphe Peter and Jean-François Gilmont, *Bibliotheca Calviniana. I: 1532–1554* (Geneva, 1991), 53/1.

[41] The other possibility is Hooper; see below, p. 97. Bucer's Consilium was certainly circulating in England from an early date: see *Consilium*, ed. Fraenkel, pp. ix–xiv.

[42] Cottisford, *Confession of the faith of H. Zwinglius*, sig. *6[r–v].

ward conformity directly in his *Excuse à Messieurs les Nicodemites* and indeed in the earlier *Against the Unlawful Rites*.[43] But there was also a particular English aspect to the question, which made the reformers' task more difficult, for they were struggling here not only against natural human instincts, but against a tradition of dissembling inherited from Lollardy.[44] Lollardy had a long tradition of evasion and equivocation, which often would extend as far as a bald denial or recantation of alleged heretical views. According to Anne Hudson, in the fifteenth and sixteenth centuries, 'for one suspect persistent and unlucky enough to deserve burning, there are fifty or more who renounced their opinions and practices'.[45] Lollard texts survive which cite Christ's flight from the Temple as an example justifying such behaviour. At least one other gives advice on how to evade questioning, by simply citing Scripture and refusing to elaborate further.[46] Among Lollards, recantation was clearly no badge of shame, and many were prepared to make the further step of justifying outward conformity. A Lollard detected in 1521 stated explicitly that the Mass was 'a holy thing', for all that it was not the body of the Lord. Thomas Boughton of Salisbury, who abjured in 1499, justified his presence at Mass in terms which would be taken up almost word for word by later Protestants: 'I feyned with myn hondys to honour it ... but my mynd and entent was nothyng therto, but to God almyghty aboue in heauen.'

There is plentiful evidence that the intermingling of this Lollard tradition deeply influenced the culture of English Protestantism. This was particularly so in the 1540s, where some quite surprising people were prepared to defend dissembling and outward subterfuge. Tyndale had written that to lie and dissemble is not always a sin, and even in late 1545 a man such as John Hooper was prepared to suggest that it might be permissible to attend Mass, citing the classic Nicodemite text of Elisha and Namaan the Syrian.[47] Complete recantation was practised very widely by early English Protestants, and many of them do not seem to have been troubled by it. When the future Marian

---

[43] Calvin, *De fugiendis*, CO, vol. 5, col. 274; *Unlawful Rites of the Ungodly*, pp. 360–411. Higman, *Three French Treatises*, pp. 133–53. C.f. Calvin's letter of 1540, reproduced in the *Petit traité*. According to Matheson, Calvin had probably developed these arguments first in dialogue with Bucer. Matheson, 'Martyrdom or Mission?'; Herminjard, *Correspondance*, vol. 6, p. 302.

[44] Here I am following the excellent development of this argument in Ryrie, 'Persecution, Survival and Compromise', pp. 48–54.

[45] Anne Hudson, *The Premature Reformation* (Oxford, 1988), p. 158.

[46] Ibid.

[47] Letter to Heinrich Bullinger, *Original Letters*, vol. 1, pp. 38–39.

exile George Constantine was imprisoned in 1529 he recanted quite freely, and even gave away a number of his associates.

The undisputed champion of recantation was Edward Crome, who recanted no fewer than three times between 1531 and 1546.[48] Crome had developed to a fine art the technique of ostensibly renouncing heretical views, according to instruction, while providing a gloss distancing himself from the prescribed words. Protestants were divided as to the legitimacy of such tactics, but dissimulation of this sort was nevertheless widely practised by evangelicals if they found themselves driven into a corner by conservative opponents. In the swirling political and ecclesiastical climate of Henry VIII's last years, the temptation to do what was necessary to live and fight another day must often have been irresistible, and few chose the alternative of outright, open resistance.[49] And Crome could hardly be accused of cowardice, since at moments of crisis he invariably spoke up boldly as a champion of the new faith; in consequence, it is clear that, despite all Crome's slippery cavillations, he never forfeited the respect of other members of the evangelical elite, particularly those who had been forced to chart their own path through the dangerous shoals of Henrician Court politics.

If Crome's case was extreme, few prominent evangelicals had survived Henry's reign without cost to conscience. Nicholas Ridley, for instance, was one of the royal chaplains who had examined Crome in 1546, and urged him to admit his errors without further dissimulation.[50] The beginning of Mary's reign would prove that in this respect at least, old habits died hard. George Constantine was not the only Marian exile to have had an embarrassing prehistory of recantation: Thomas Becon, John Willock and Cranmer's chaplain Robert Watson had also previously succumbed when faced with a crisis of faith; and even some of the movement's leaders, notably Scory, Barlow and Jewel, only departed abroad in 1553–54 after a public and embarrassing flirtation with conformity.[51]

The exiles sought to combat these insidious tendencies in a number of ways. They argued, with Thomas Cottisford, that the achievement

---

[48] Susan Wabuda, 'Equivocation and Recantation during the English reformation: the "Subtle Shadows" of Dr Edward Crome', *JEH*, 44 (1993), pp. 224–42.

[49] Even Barnes, Garrett, and Jerome had signified their willingness to submit before it was decided to make an example of them in 1540.

[50] Wabuda, 'Crome', p. 235–6.

[51] For the identification of Constantine as a Marian exile see Chapter 1. On Watson, ibid., and *DNB*; Jewel, Barlow, and (allegedly) Scory all signed articles of recantation in Oxford in 1554: John Strype, *Ecclesiastical Memorials* (3 vols in 6, Oxford, 1822), vol. 3, i, p. 241.

of a full Reformed polity during Edward's reign meant that circumstances had changed fundamentally since the time of uncertainty in the 1540s; and indeed the changed attitude of men such as Hooper and Constantine suggests that this was widely appreciated. For persistent dissemblers they had an array of biblical texts. First, those texts which seemed to condone cohabitation with the faithful had to be denied. True, Christ went to feasts with publicans and sinners, but there was a necessary distinction between cohabitation where men were not compelled to communicate with ungodly rites, and the situation in England where no such freedom existed.[52] The balance of biblical texts fell clearly on the side of those urging true believers to have no truck with idolatry. 'St Paul to the Philippians affirmeth that we may not have any fellowship with the works of darkness, but in the midst of this wicked and froward generation we ought to shine like lights, upholding the word of truth.'[53] And from the Old Testament, the reformers urged the more inspiring examples of prophets and apostles who had abandoned homes and risked death or disgrace for the cause of truth.[54] Occasionally they would use more homely analogies to ram the point home. For the anonymous author of the *Apologie* attendance at Mass was:

> As if a married woman should submit her body to the use of another man; and when her husband layeth the offence to her charge she answereth: husband, be not angry for my so doing, for although I abandoned my body to that man's use, yet I reserved my heart wholly to you. My friend, I think there is no man, being of any Godly knowledge, could digest that answer of his wife, or take it in good part: but condemning her as an adultress would repudiate and forsake her. And shall we persuade ourselves to please God, being a jealous God (as the Scriptures call him) who requires of us the whole man to serve him withal: when as we give the greater part of his creation to the serving of idols, saying, God knoweth my heart.[55]

---

[52] Peter Martyr Vermigli, *A treatise of the Cohabitation of the Faithful with the Unfaithful*, sig. A2^r, A3^{r-v}.

[53] *Examinations and Writings of John Philpot*, p. 222.

[54] Such as Daniel, Shadrach, Misech and Abednego. Wolfgang Musculus, *The Temporisour, that is to say, the observer of the times*. Trans. by Valérand Poullain, and into English by R.P[ownell]. [Wesel, Singleton?], 1555, sig. A5^v–A6^r. STC 18312. Martyr Vermigli, *Treatise of the Faithful with the Unfaithful*, sig. B6^v–7^r. C.f. Viret's similar use of Daniel in the *Epistre consolataire*, Herminjard, *Correspondance*, vol. 6, pp. 434–5.

[55] *An Apologie or defence against the calumnacion of certain men, which ... do slander those men, which for the better serving of God with a more pure conscience ... have bandoned their livings and vocation, abiding as exiles* [Wesel?, H. Singleton?], 1555, sig. A5^v. STC 23619.

Arguments of this sort were a sensible reinforcement to the more high-minded swopping of biblical texts, for it is clear that in the decisions of those who elected to stay in England practical considerations often loomed as large as the more strictly theological. This is recognized in an illuminating passage in the anonymous *Apologie* defending the exiles against the charge that in retreating abroad they had abandoned other, equally binding obligations. The author here reconstructs a dialogue with a friend evidently bent on remaining in England, who urges on him a number of reasons why he should not join the exile.

> And now to come to the causes which you proposed to me in my house, saying you were sent from many good honest and godly men, which not a little marvelled that I had sent away into Flanders my wife and children, and much more that I myself also deliberated to follow. Wherein, as you alleged, they judged I wrought unwisely and not according to knowledge but rather preferred a will more wilful than godly wise, knowing as well my poor estate and little riches with my great family ... saying, I neither had art, faculty or occupation to live by. More that, if God should turn the impiety of this time, I should never be able to recover the like room or office, and so all my life wander in misery, which they as my very friends much lamented, which many other causes to you alleged, thereby to stay my journey. Which persuasions as to the flesh they seemed hard and uneasy to be borne, and tolerated of any worldly man.[56]

This conversation has the ring of truth, since arguments of this sort must indeed have weighed heavily with those hesitating as to the correct course. The author of the *Apologie*, who reconstructs this dialogue as part of a justification of his own decision for exile, was significantly a soldier by profession, and thus bound to be more mobile than many English Protestants; the same held true of the many scholars and young noblemen who joined the exile. But others were more tightly bound to their homes by family and occupational responsibilities. We have already seen that in the craftsman milieu of the London French church, a high proportion of its members elected to remain during the Marian period, even against their better judgement.[57] And of those Londoners detected for various acts of religious non-observance in the great Easter Visitation of 1554 – a very considerable body of some 400 persons, many of them stalwarts of

---

[56] *An Apologie*, sig. A3[r-v].
[57] See Chapter 2.

the Protestant establishment of Edward's reign – hardly a handful chose to hold fast to their faith when put to the test. Most chose the 'broad pathway' and recanted.[58]

Here, clearly, fear of the obvious consequences of continued resistance was the most tangible factor for those unlucky enough to be denounced and examined by the authorities. But even without the direct stimulus of denunciation to the Catholic authorities there were many other factors which might tip the balance towards conformity. A sense of duty to family and neighbours could weigh very heavily, even against the claims of a tender conscience. Many years after these events the gentlewoman Rose Hickman composed a small treatise in which she described the agonies of conscience she had undergone before she finally, reluctantly, set off abroad. Even so her friends the Lockes refused to follow: Thomas Locke would have done so, but his wife refused to leave home.[59] This was not necessarily an ignoble, self-serving choice. Indeed, a decade earlier Martin Bucer had argued that the true vocation of the pious might be to remain, albeit in a compromised situation, and prepare for the fulless of reformation which could assuredly not be far off. Protestant citizens had an obligation to family, to work and community which could not easily be shrugged off.[60]

In any case, those who remained in England, and reluctantly conformed, could often continue to perform signal service to the cause of the Gospel. Those leaders of English Protestantism rounded up and incarcerated at the beginning of the reign were deeply indebted to those pious friends who brought them food and linen, not without a certain risk to themselves.[61] This was an obligation which the prisoners freely acknowledged, even while they tried to persuade their benefactors to make a more complete commitment to the cause.[62] Others who remained in England formed informal networks, collecting money to sustain the exiles and helping the more vulnerable

---

[58] Brigden, *London and the Reformation*, pp. 562–72.

[59] Joy Shakespeare and Maria Dowling, 'Religion and politics in mid-Tudor England through the eyes of an English Protestant woman: the recollections of Rose Hickman', *BIHR*, 55 (1982), pp. 97–102. And even then Rose Hickman's journey of conscience took her only as far as (still Catholic) Antwerp.

[60] Bucer, 'Consilium', as paraphrased in Matheson, 'Martyrdom or Mission?', p. 159.

[61] Brigden, *London and the Reformation*, pp. 603–4. Prison visitors were sometimes themselves arrested.

[62] See Philpot's letter to Robert Harrington, *Examinations and Writings of John Philpot*, pp. 241–2.

to escape abroad.[63] Clearly activities of this sort carried with them considerable risks and were only for the most committed, but even known Protestants in this category (perhaps particularly these) would have had to accept the necessity of public conformity.[64] Many of those who at some later point in the reign joined the small secret congregations established in southern towns like London and Colchester had been through a period of conformity before their consciences forced them to a total repudiation of the Mass, often with fatal consequences.[65]

The desire to remain in England, even at some cost to the conscience, was not necessarily devoid of a certain highmindedness. Many parish ministers, for instance, may have considered whether their duty to their own consciences was not outweighed by an obligation to continue to minister to their flocks: particularly as any successor was almost certain to be more enthusiastic for the reinstated Mass. Many of the exiles were not entirely comfortable with the decision to abandon their posts, and a number of the tracts written in exile were intended primarily to justify their decision.[66] In London and the towns of East Anglia many of the ministers who took a different decision and remained doggedly at their posts would re-emerge in Elizabeth's reign as committed supporters of the Protestant settlement. A recent study of one such man, William Shepherd, rector of Heydon in Essex, suggests that for him, the duty of service to his congregation was a principal obligation which outweighed all others. Shepherd remained at his post through a long career that stretched from 1541 until deep into Elizabeth's reign. We need not regard this performance entirely cynically. Shepherd was by all accounts a model minister, and entirely comfortable with the new order of Elizabeth's reign.[67] For all that they deplored such behaviour, the leaders of exiled English Protestantism would in fact be deeply indebted to men

---

[63] On these 'sustainers', Strype, *Ecclesiastical Memorials*, vol. 3, i, pp. 227–38. Brigden, *London and the Reformation*, p. 561.

[64] The arrest of a number of these sustainers reported in a letter of John Banks to Heinrich Bullinger, 9 December 1554, *Original Letters Relative to the English Reformation*, ed. H. Robinson (2 vols, Parker Society, 1846–7), vol. 1, pp. 306–7.

[65] For the secret congregations see Foxe, *Acts and Monuments, 1563*, pp. 1676–1703, Brigden, *London and the Reformation*, pp. 600–5. Martin, 'Protestant Underground Congregations of Mary's Reign', pp. 519–38.

[66] Jane E. A. Dawson, 'The Two John Knoxes: England, Scotland and the 1558 Tracts', *JEH*, 42 (1991), p. 557.

[67] Mark Byford, 'The Price of Protestantism. Assessing the Impact of Religious Change on Elizabethan Essex. The Cases of Heydon and Colchester, 1558–1594' (Oxford University D.Phil thesis, 1989).

of this stamp, without whom the implementation of the Elizabethan settlement would have been almost unthinkable.

The exiles reserved some of their bitterest recriminations for those in positions of political influence, who had apparently favoured the Gospel in Edward's reign but now shamelessly abandoned it.[68] Of the Edwardian Privy Council, most made their peace with the new order as best they could, or else returned to their estates to await better times. The exiles, not surprisingly, took a dim view of such conduct, which fitted only too well with the greed and shameless plunder of church lands which had characterized the last years of Northumberland's regime. Some argued directly that the greed for church lands had been the Edwardian councillors' only motivation: the accession of Mary was in this context a wholly comprehensible punishment for endemic sinfulness.[69]

But even here it is not entirely necessary to accept the exiles' strictures wholly on their own estimation. Although the exiles could hardly approve of the conduct of members of the former Protestant elite who remained in England, the fact was that they could still perform useful functions, even while conforming outwardly. Some of those who remained in England were clearly in touch with friends on the continent. Although obviously a marked man after his trial and sensational acquittal in the wake of Wyatt's rebellion, Sir Nicholas Throckmorton maintained an intricate network of friends and allies from the Edwardian period, many of them now in exile abroad.[70] Nicholas Bacon and William Cecil were both, in a similar way, intimately connected with many who had made the decision for exile. Sir William Cecil is perhaps the most interesting case of all. It was hardly likely that the career of a man who had been Secretary of State in Northumberland's Council, and acknowledged as one of the principal lay advocates of reform, would flourish under Mary; but apart from the loss of his principal offices Cecil was in fact able to negotiate the reign largely unscathed. Although not retained in the Privy Council, Cecil was not stripped of his local offices in Lincolnshire,

---

[68] Some of the most vituperative condemnation is in John Ponet, *A short treatise of politike power* [Strasburg, heirs of Köpfel], 1556. STC 20178. As a prominent member of the Edwardian establishment Ponet would have known many of these men personally, and he was not afraid to name names. C.f. sig. I3^r–7^r.

[69] Olde, *Confession of the True Catholic Faith*, sig. E5^r. C.f. the still more vituperative condemnation of the nobility in his *Acquittal and Purgation*, cited Chapter 1, n. 72.

[70] On Throckmorton see Patricia Cole Swensen, 'Noble Hunters of the Roman Fox. Religious Reform at the Tudor Court, 1543–1564' (University of California/Berkeley PhD thesis, 1981), pp. 280–86. For his trial, Brigden, *London and the Reformation*, pp. 551–4.

and he returned the compliment by representing the new regime, albeit in a relatively humble capacity, in several diplomatic missions overseas.[71] The first of these was to meet and accompany to England the papal legate, Cardinal Pole, a mission which may have been envisaged as a public test of Cecil's loyalty. Cecil was sufficiently pragmatic to fulfil this mission and others like it punctiliously, establishing a relationship with Pole of sufficient warmth for him to be left a small bequest in the archbishop's will.

What is interesting about this is that specific criticism of Cecil's conduct among the exiles, then or later, was extremely muted. None of Cecil's correspondents thought fit to rebuke him for his failure to maintain a more defiant stance, and when in 1558 he emerged from his enforced semi-retirement as one of the leaders of the new regime none expressed the slightest doubt that he was wholly committed to the Protestant cause.[72] Cecil's position seems to have been well understood at least among the lay members of the exile community. His remaining in England was in some respects quite convenient to them, particularly to those to whom he was connected by ties of friendship and kinship, whose interests he could watch over during their time abroad.[73]

And on one notable occasion Cecil and others of his stamp were able to do the exiles signal service. In the parliament of 1555 the government attempted to enact a bill which would have prevented religious exiles from continuing to enjoy the income from their English property. After a complicated series of committals and delays, the bill finally foundered in the face of determined opposition in the House of Commons.[74] Although recent writers have been inclined to play down the importance of opposition in Mary's parliaments, it is unthinkable that the Crown's wishes would have been frustrated in this way in other states elsewhere in western Europe. Preventing exiles from receiving financial support from property they had left behind was rightly seen as a fundamental part of any campaign against organized heresy, and both Henry II in France and Charles V

---

[71] On Cecil under Mary see the (largely unsympathetic) account in Conyers Read, *Mr Secretary Cecil and Queen Elizabeth* (London, 1955), pp. 102–16.

[72] See Chapter 6.

[73] Bacon performed similar services for his father-in-law, Sir Anthony Cooke, with whom he kept in close touch, and for whom he carried out several financial transactions during Mary's reign. Robert Tittler, *Nicholas Bacon. The Making of a Tudor Statesman* (London, 1976), p. 54.

[74] Jennifer Loach, *Parliament and the Crown in the Reign of Mary Tudor* (Oxford, 1986), pp. 147–55. C.f. Read, *Mr Secretary Cecil*, pp. 109–12.

in the Netherlands enacted measures to prevent it.[75] That Mary could not get her way on this point was a crucial manifestation of weakness, and a measure of the feelings stirred up when the regime attempted to give its campaign against heresy real teeth. Cecil's involvement with the opposition group active in this parliament was temperate but well-attested, and sufficiently obvious to the government to ensure that they would make no further call on his services until the end of the reign.[76] Cecil remained quietly in the country, the only evidence of his views on the development of current affairs being the diary in which he marked the numbers burned for heresy in each year.[77]

What are we to make of men such as Cecil? It would clearly be absurd to argue that the decision to remain and conform involved a total repudiation of former commitments. In Cecil's case that was clearly not so, and men of his rank and social class had many incentives to remain and hope for a change for the better. Members of the ruling elite would also have been swayed by genuine feelings of loyalty to a legitimate ruler, knowing that to deny this authority was to open the way to anarchy. This was an argument against which the exile polemicists made little headway, at least until the disappointments and hardships of exile bred a more uncompromising strand of thought which explicitly embraced a right of resistance.[78]

It is not necessary for us to judge the legitimacy or highmindedness of any of these arguments. The principal purpose of attempting in this way to explore more sympathetically the mindset of those who remained in England is to demonstrate that there was a variety of reasons holding people in England whose commitment to Protestantism was at bottom wholly genuine; and that it was possible for them to develop a range of plausible rationalizations for their behaviour. Obligations to family, social position and personal prosperity may in truth have been the principal motivations, but theological rationaliza-

---

[75] For the detailed provisions of the Edict of Chateaubriand (1551) inhibiting all contact with Geneva and decreeing confiscation of exile property see E. and E. Haag, *La France Protestante, Pièces Justificatives* (rep. edn, Geneva, 1966), pp. 17–19.

[76] The evidence is reviewed in the brief biography of Cecil in the History of Parliament Trust volumes: S. T. Bindoff, *The House of Commons, 1509–1558* (3 vols, London, 1982), vol. 1, pp. 605–6.

[77] *A Collection of State Papers relating to affairs in the Reign of Queen Elizabeth from the year 1571 to 1596*, ed. William Murdin (London, 1759), pp. 745–7.

[78] For the resistance writings see Gerry Bowler, 'Marian Protestantism and the Idea of Violent Resistance to Tyranny', in Peter Lake and Maria Dowling (eds), *Protestantism and the National Church* (Beckenham, 1987), pp. 124–43.

tions of a sort were also available to the troubled, flexible conscience.

But how important was the phenomenon we have been describing? And what was its long-term importance for the English Reformation? Exiles clearly believed that Nicodemism was very widespread; hence their persistent attention to the problem in their writings. Yet the relationship between exiles and those who remained behind was necessarily somewhat schizophrenic. In all of the north European nations where there was an exile movement of significant size in these years – France, the Netherlands, England – those who had opted for exile spared no efforts to persuade fellow believers to follow their course. Yet without the widespread practice of Nicodemism, the huge surges of support for the evangelical cause which occurred at the crisis points of both the French and Dutch Reformations, in France in 1561–62, in the Netherlands in 1566, would have been unthinkable.[79] The same was true of England in 1559. To a very large extent the Elizabethan settlement was a Nicodemite Reformation.

When the exiles heard the news of Mary's death, many made immediate plans to return to England. But inevitably weeks and sometimes months elapsed before they were back in London and in a position to influence the course of events.[80] In the meantime the key decisions which set England on the road to a new Protestant church settlement had already been taken, under the guiding hand of a triumvirate firmly committed to the restoration of a Protestant order: William Cecil, Matthew Parker, soon to be archbishop of Canterbury, and Elizabeth herself. None of them had retired abroad during Mary's reign, and all indeed had conformed to Catholicism. This was an apostasy which the returning exiles were careful not to throw back in their faces;[81] on the contrary, contemporary commentators, of whatever confessional stamp, harboured no doubts that all were fully committed to the Protestant cause.[82]

In the weeks that followed the new regime faced several formidable hurdles in the restoration of Protestantism, and returning exiles were eagerly embraced as committed and enthusiastic advocates of the new policy. But the Elizabethan settlement would only have been possible if the energies of all who favoured the restoration of an evangelical

---

[79] On the Netherlands see here my *Emden and the Dutch Revolt* (Oxford, 1992), Chapter 5.
[80] Grindal and Sandys arrived in London on 15 Jan 1559. Collinson, *Archbishop Grindal* (London, 1979), p. 82.
[81] With the significant and disastrous exception of John Knox. See Chapter 6.
[82] See Chapter 6.

polity could be harnessed to the task, and these included those who had remained in England during the previous reign. The first generation of leaders of the new regime in fact represented the successful integration of these two strands of English Protestantism. Of the committed Protestant core of the new Elizabethan Privy Council, Sir Francis Knollys and (more ambiguously) Bedford were returning exiles, but more of the other key figures of the new regime were not: Northampton, Sackville, Parry, Cave, Sir Nicholas Bacon and Cecil himself had all remained in England. For Bacon, appointment as Elizabeth's Lord Keeper was a major promotion from the attorneyship of the Court of Wards, the duties of which he had nevertheless continued to perform under Mary.[83] For Parry, Elizabeth's accession represented the restoration of a family fortune apparently damaged beyond repair by his intimate association with Northumberland and Jane Grey.[84] Now restored in rank, Northampton, like Bacon, was one of the intimate circle charged with framing and guiding the new settlement. With men of this stamp performing such key roles in the emerging regime, this was less a cabal of Marian exiles than of excluded Edwardians, for whom Elizabeth's accession represented an opportunity to resume careers if not destroyed by Mary, then at least badly stalled. Many had kept close ties to Elizabeth in what became by the end of Mary's reign an embryonic counter-court. One can understand why Elizabeth would have been more comfortable to have about her men whose experience had quite closely paralleled her own, rather than risk the self-righteous moral superiority of which certain of the exiles were doubtless capable.[85]

The penumbra of public servants outside the Council contained other men of the same stamp. Sir Walter Mildmay, a key financial advisor to the new regime, as he had been under Northumberland, had survived Mary's reign in England with little inconvenience: indeed towards the end of the reign his services had occasionally been called upon by the Privy Council. As Chancellor of the Exchequer and later Privy Councillor under Elizabeth, Mildmay in later life became one of the most influential patrons of advanced Protestant opinions as the founder of Emmanuel College, Cambridge.[86] Mildmay, like Sir Thomas Gresham, was to some extent protected by his specialist expertise, but others who remained included several whose service to

---

[83] Tittler, *Nicholas Bacon*, pp. 52–55, 69 ff.
[84] Northampton had initially been sentenced to death for his part in the setting up of Jane Grey as Queen, before being reprieved. *DNB*, vol. 15, pp. 367–8.
[85] One thinks here of Cecil and Bacon's father-in-law, Sir Anthony Cooke.
[86] *DNB*, vol. 13, pp. 374–6.

Edwardian Protestantism had been both partisan and conspicuous. Sir Thomas Smith, an intimate of Somerset and secretary to the Privy Council, had served on several commissions charged with enforcing the Edwardian settlement of religion, including that to examine Bishop Bonner. Even with such a dangerous enemy, Smith felt it safe to remain in England.[87] Sir Walter Haddon had achieved a certain notoriety when the Edwardian government imposed him on the reluctant fellows of Magdalen College, Oxford, as Master in place of a prominent opponent of religious change. Deprived again under Mary, Haddon returned to the practice of civil law, to re-emerge as a key member of the commissions appointed to enforce the Elizabethan settlement.[88]

The Inns of Court seem to have functioned as a refuge for a considerable number of those who were out of sympathy with the turn of policy under Mary, and who now chose to withdraw from public activity and concentrate on their professional careers. An identifiable group kept terms in the Inner Temple, where in 1555 an apparently foolish prank led to action being taken against four individuals of known Protestant sympathies: Thomas Copley, Thomas Lucas, Richard Onslow and Thomas Norton.[89] All would later sit in Mary's last parliament of 1558, where Copley's partisan enthusiasm for Elizabeth's cause led him into an intemperate outburst for which the Speaker was obliged to put him into custody.[90] Norton, the future 'parliament man' of many Elizabethan ventures, was another whose strong Protestant sympathies had already been revealed in a promising career of service in the inner circles of the Edwardian establishment, inevitably cut short on Mary's accession. Norton is a particularly interesting case, because of the evidence of his considerable personal admiration for John Calvin. As a tutor to the children of the late Duke of Somerset in the reign of Edward VI he had briefly corresponded with the Genevan reformer, and he would occupy much of the first year of Elizabeth's reign preparing the first English translation of Calvin's *Institutes*.[91] Notwithstanding this Norton chose to ignore Calvin's strictures on Nicodemism, of which he could hardly have been unaware, although several close friends and rela-

---

[87] *DNB*, vol. 18, pp. 532–5.

[88] *DNB*, vol. 8, pp. 872–5.

[89] On this incident see Michael Graves, *Thomas Norton, the Parliament Man* (Oxford, 1994), p. 31.

[90] Bindoff, *The House of Commons, 1509–1558*, vol. 1, p. 695. Brief biographies of the other three named in ibid., vol. 2, pp. 555–6, vol. 3, pp. 27, 32.

[91] STC 4415. Graves, *Thomas Norton*, pp. 13–46.

tives were among those who joined the exile.[92] On this issue Norton chose to be guided by the example of his former mentor William Cecil, rather than his new spiritual guide.

Perhaps the most remarkable figure in the group clearly identified with the Edwardian regime was Sir Nicholas Throckmorton, whom even a narrow escape from execution for treason in the wake of Wyatt's rebellion could not persuade of the advisability of withdrawing abroad. Passing the rest of Mary's reign in relative retirement, Throckmorton resurfaced at the beginning of the new reign to offer forthright, and probably unsolicited, advice on the proper course for the new religious settlement.[93] Disappointed in his hopes of immediate preferment (perhaps Cecil recognized in so distinguished a man a potential rival), Throckmorton nevertheless served with distinction in the difficult post of ambassador to France. Throckmorton was in fact one of a number of the members of the new regime who had been heavily involved in the Wyatt rebellion of 1554.[94] Elizabeth's famous aversion to rebels clearly did not extend to veterans of this most serious protest against the religious policies of Mary's reign, an episode which had brought Elizabeth herself perilously close to the block.[95] Throckmorton's escape and metamorphosis was matched only by that of Robert Dudley, who was actually condemned to death with his father, the Duke of Northumberland, before being pardoned and released from the Tower. A career of conspicuous loyalty and military service under Mary was the only sensible strategy for repairing the family fortunes, but Dudley's remarkable rise really began with his appointment as Elizabeth's Master of Horse in the first months of the new reign.[96]

Throckmorton and Dudley were clearly marked as members of the ruling elite, but others prominent in local society would, while conforming, still find occasion to make their continuing allegiance to Protestantism sufficiently clear. These local elites have received less attention in studies of the Elizabethan settlement, but they would play

---

[92] Including his mother-in-law and brother-in-law. Ibid., p. 35.

[93] J. E. Neale, 'Sir Nicholas Throckmorton's Advice to Queen Elizabeth on her accession to the throne', *EHR*, 65 (1950), pp. 91–8.

[94] Including Edward Rogers, Thomas Parr, and the Dudleys. See Hudson, *Cambridge Connection*, p. 25.

[95] Elizabeth's hostility to rebels is frequently argued as a leitmotiv of her foreign policy. See Wallace MacCaffrey, *Elizabeth I* (London, 1993). MacCaffrey recognizes the significance of the Wyatt rebels in Elizabeth's inner circle, without acknowledging the relevance of this fact to his general argument. Ibid., p 41.

[96] Alan Kendall, *Robert Dudley, Earl of Leicester* (London, 1980), pp. 19–25.

a vital role in ensuring the success of the new religious policy in 1559. Here, as in the higher reaches of government, the new regime could rely on the support of many whose conformity under Mary was only a mask for their continued allegiance to the evangelical cause. Several men of this middling rank were, it must be said, bolder in death than they had been in life. In their wills, William Edmundes, a former mayor of Reading, and the Suffolk yeoman John Cossye both used versions of the notorious Protestant preamble of William Tracy, a Gloucestershire gentleman who on his death in 1531 had incorporated into his will a statement of Protestant belief so forthright that it had been brought before Convocation for condemnation.[97] Widely circulated subsequently in both manuscript and print, its inclusion in these Marian testaments was clearly intended as an unambiguous statement of dissent from the restored Catholic order. Tracy's son Henry also left a clearly Protestant will when he died in 1556, apparently undeterred by the posthumous condemnation of his father.[98]

A systematic study of other localities would doubtless reveal many figures of this type, men who while deeply out of sympathy with the turn of events under Mary, chose to bide their time and remain in their posts. Sometimes they may have performed discreet services in protecting known local Protestants, sometimes not. On occasions the local dissenting establishment was sufficiently well-entrenched to risk a calculated act of defiance, as when the commonalty of the Sussex town of Rye elected to parliament one of those summoned for religious non-conformity at the beginning of the reign.[99] This election was immediately overturned by the Lord Warden, but the Rye freemen were undeterred and in the following year chose as their mayor the effective leader of the local Protestant faction.[100] Rye was probably exceptional in the openness of its defiance, and other local elites conducted themselves with more circumspection. The borough leadership in Ipswich made a clear demonstration of its loyalty in Mary's reign through its choice of MPs, for all that the strength of the town's Protestant sympathies were well known. Resistance to the new order was here confined to a discreet footdragging in promoting loyal

---

[97] John Craig and Caroline Litzenberger, 'Wills as Religious Propaganda: The Testament of William Tracy', *JEH*, 44 (1993), pp. 415–31.
[98] Ibid., p. 422.
[99] Graham Mayhew, *Tudor Rye* (Falmer, 1987), p. 73.
[100] Ibid., p. 74.

Catholic clergy to the town's parish churches.[101] But however they conducted themselves, men of this sort were essential to the re-establishment of a Protestant church on Elizabeth's accession. The subtle play of local elite rivalries left considerable scope for those whose conduct during Mary's reign had been circumspect and unheroic.

Nowhere of course was this more important than in London, where reformation and reaction had both produced disproportionately tumultuous consequences in the local community. In her study of London during the Reformation Susan Brigden has made an effective job of identifying the leaders of London's reforming establishment under Edward VI, most of whom would choose, with varying degrees of discomfort, to see out Mary's reign in the capital.[102] It is interesting, but perhaps not surprising when considering London's forward role in promoting reform under Edward VI, how clearly the Godly were known even then. Sir Nicholas Throckmorton clearly owed his life to his subtle understanding of personal religious preference among the potential jurors presented at his trial, exercising his right to peremptory challenge until a sympathetic bench had been empanelled; not perhaps 'heretics to a man' in the Spanish ambassador's angry phrase, but with sufficiently deep connections in the former Protestant establishment to be susceptible to Sir Nicholas's bold and skilful defence.[103] Of course those who exerted themselves in the cause were equally well known to their enemies. London was a bitterly divided city, and many in conforming would be forced to submit to humiliations consciously heaped upon them by vengeful neighbours. Former churchwardens, having presided over the cleansing (or desecration) of churches in the previous reign, were particularly vulnerable.[104] But the former Godly, even in their time of trial, still found ways of expressing some residual evangelical solidarity, even if only by raising money for the evangelical prisoners who now crowded the gaols.[105]

---

[101] Diarmaid MacCulloch, *Suffolk and the Tudors. Politics and Religion in an English County, 1500–1600* (Oxford, 1986), pp. 174–5. Diarmaid MacCulloch and John Blatchly, 'Pastoral Provision in the Parishes of Tudor Ipswich', *SCJ*, 22 (1991), pp. 463–5. According to Foxe, Catholics in Ipswich could in 1556 produce a list of 98 inhabitants of known Protestant sympathies, including five clergy. Foxe, *Acts and Monuments*, vol. 8, pp. 598–600.

[102] The following paragraphs follow Bridgen, *London and the Reformation*, pp. 520–631.

[103] Ibid., pp. 551–5.

[104] Ibid., pp. 567–8.

[105] Ibid., pp. 603–4.

And the less active remnant – those who merely contented themselves with the broad pathway of conformity – performed at least one invaluable service. They survived, often to re-emerge in Elizabeth's reign as the patrons of a religious way of life they had never, in their hearts, abandoned. In the new reign London would once again be conspicuous in its precocious enthusiasm for evangelical reform.[106]

Laymen, inevitably, made compromises. They had a position in society and little in their upbringing would have suggested that abandoning these obligations was the proper course, even to avoid conforming to a deeply distasteful religious regime. But what of the clergy, surely as the principal forwarders of religious change the most susceptible to the heroic lead of the dying martyrs, and the constant urgings of their friends in exile? In 1559 the returning exiles would certainly catch the eye, and their correspondence has done much to frame our understanding of events, but in fact the new Protestant church establishment was characterized by much the same mix and balance as its lay equivalent. The appointment of prominent exiles to the new bench of bishops gave a clear indication of Elizabeth's intended direction in religious policy, and ensured the support of a vital block of advanced opinion. But of the 18 bishops appointed in the first two years of the new regime, only 12 were former exiles: the careers of the other six demonstrate quite neatly the breadth of experience encompassed in Marian Protestantism. Edmund Guest, the new bishop of Rochester, had been a prominent advocate of the new religion in Cambridge during Edward's reign and was said to have spent all of Mary's reign in hiding.[107] Edmund Scambler, nominated to Peterborough, was one of the ministers of the secret Protestant congregation in London.[108] William Downham, now to be bishop of Chester, had occupied an uncomfortably prominent, if protected, position as Elizabeth's chaplain. But the other members of this group mostly survived by making themselves inconspicuous. William Alley had eked out a meagre living as a teacher and scholar in the north of England, a form of internal exile from which he now emerged to secure his appointment as bishop of Exeter.[109] This withdrawal from home to a discreet location elsewhere in England was again a practice with a venerable Lollard tradition and may have

---

[106] Norman L. Jones, *Faith by Statute. Parliament and the Settlement of Religion 1559* (London, 1982), pp. 37–8.
[107] *DNB*, vol. 8, pp. 316–8.
[108] *DNB*, vol. 17, p. 396. Strype, *Ecclesiastical Memorials*, vol. 3, ii, 132, 147.
[109] *DNB*, vol. 1, pp. 326–7.

been quite widely practised under Mary. Foxe suggests that such internal migration was at least comparable in scope to the flight of Protestants abroad.[110] To leave one's home in this way was regarded as clear evidence of malevolent intent by the commissioners established to investigate religious dissent. The inquisition of 1566 which surveyed the state of religion in Essex made no distinction between those who had moved away to some other part of England and those who had gone abroad.[111]

William Alley had been a relatively obscure figure in Edward VI's reign; more remarkable was the case of Richard Cheyney, one of those who had defended the evangelical viewpoint at the first convocation of Mary's reign, but who nevertheless remained in England, retaining his archdeaconry at Hereford until 1557.[112] Although he later claimed not to have functioned as a priest during this period, he was, remarkably enough, still gathering extra preferments towards the end of Mary's reign.[113] Yet there were apparently no hard feelings among those charged with restocking the episcopal bench in Elizabeth's reign, and although he had to wait until 1562 for his appointment to Hooper's old diocese at Gloucester Cecil had clearly had him in mind for high office from early in the reign.[114] The two most prominent of the non-exiles were William May and Matthew Parker, nominated by Elizabeth to the two archbishoprics (though May died before he could take up his post). Both had been leading figures in Edwardian Cambridge, yet both on Mary's accession had been permitted to resign their offices and live out the reign in secluded study.[115] Before his death May performed useful service in the committee of 'apt men' established to discuss the new settlement of religion. His colleagues on this committee were Parker, four returned exiles, and William Bill, the Queen's Almoner, who despite a perilously close identification with Northumberland during the abortive attempt to set up Jane Grey had survived the reign in England. It was

---

[110] *Acts and Monuments*, ed. G. Townsend and S. Cattley (8 vols, London, 1837–41), vol. 8, Appendix 6.
[111] David Loades, 'The Essex Visitation of 1556', BIHR, 35 (1962), pp. 87–97.
[112] *DNB*, vol. 4, pp. 224–6. For the Disputation, *Acts and Monuments*, 1563, pp. 906–16.
[113] Caroline Litzenberger, 'Richard Cheyney, Bishop of Gloucester: An Infidel in Religion?', SCJ, 25 (1994), pp. 567–84.
[114] Ibid.
[115] *DNB*, vol. 13, pp. 146–8 (May), vol. 15, pp. 254–64 (Parker). V. J. K. Brook, *A Life of Archbishop Parker* (Oxford, 1962), pp. 50–4.

Bill who was chosen by Cecil to preach the first sermon at Paul's Cross at the beginning of the reign.[116]

Lower down the hierarchy the conforming element was inevitably much stronger, since even after providing the returning exiles with suitable rewards for their constancy there remained a multitude of positions to be filled. Other notable survivors of the Edwardian period now emerged to play their part in the new settlement. Perhaps as revealing in this regard as the newly constituted bench of bishops is the identity of those men considered for promotion at this time, but who ultimately had to be satisfied with lesser or alternative preferment. At some time in the summer of 1559 William Cecil jotted down a list of 'spiritual men' ripe for promotion, and if the lesser names towards the end of the list do justify Winthrop Hudson's observation that Cecil's checklist becomes 'progressively undistinguished', these lesser figures still had an important part to play in shoring up the new church.[117] Their identities reveal the same strong continuities with the Edwardian church as among the bishops, and potential promotion seems to have been considered regardless of whether they were in England or abroad during Mary's reign. Indeed of those on Cecil's list who failed to achieve episcopal rank the exiles were far outnumbered by individuals who had remained in England during Mary's reign, or even fully conformed.[118] One of these was William Latimer, who had spent an uncomfortable time during the Marian years living secretly with his wife in Ipswich, an internal exile from which he would emerge in the new reign to fill the significant post of dean of Peterborough. But a more representative figure was a man like Robert Banks, a deprived married priest restored to his former benefice in 1559, or Anthony Blake, another deprived married priest, restored in 1556 and then rapidly promoted in the new Protestant establishment of Elizabeth's reign.

These cases offer a partial answer to the question of how far clerical marriage was indicative of enthusiasm for evangelical doctrine; although these men conformed under Mary they were still identifiable to William Cecil as important potential supports for the

---

[116] *DNB*, vol. 2, pp. 29–30.

[117] The list is printed in John Strype, *Annals of the Reformation ... during Queen Elizabeth's happy reign* (4 vols in 7, Oxford, 1824), vol. 1, i, p. 228. Winthrop S. Hudson, *The Cambridge Connection and the Elizabethan Settlement of 1559* (Durham, NC, 1980), p. 108.

[118] My analysis of this portion of Cecil's list has benefited greatly from the opportunity to read an unpublished paper of Brett Usher, 'Sitting on the Old School Bench: the Episcopal Appointments of 1559–62 and the failure of William Cecil'. My thanks to Mr Usher for permission to read this paper.

new clerical regime. Another archetypal figure on this list was Henry Wilslow, an undistinguished Fellow of Queen's College who conformed under Mary and continued in college office until his death in 1592. The nearest in type to William Shepherd of Heydon, Wilslow probably owes his place in this exalted company to the friendship of William May. But the universities were in fact a notable haunt of such survivors of the Edwardian period, who now emerged from semi-retirement to play their part in the new settlement. In Oxford and Cambridge, conforming fellows continued in their posts alongside returning exiles; the absence of any witchhunt in traditionally more advanced Cambridge may have owed something to the fact that the Commission of Visitors appointed in May 1559 included a majority of those who had conformed under Mary, including of course the new Chancellor, William Cecil.[119]

Every new ideological system needs its binding historical myths, and for the Protestantism of the Elizabethan settlement this was rapidly provided by the *Acts and Monuments* of John Foxe. The immense documentation of this literary masterpiece, with its meticulous array of examinations and the poignant nobility of its scenes of execution, offered English Protestants a definitive and immensely satisfying interpretation of their recent past, in which their religion had been tested and purified through the fidelity and heroism of a dogged and by no means inconsiderable band of faithful professors. Who could doubt that some people, such as Matthew Plaice, or Richard Woodman, whose denunciation of a turncoat married priest had brought him to Bonner's attention, were the authentic voice of English Protestantism? The hand of God was visible to all, not only in the patient, untutored eloquence of these simple folk as they laid out their beliefs before petulant and exasperated inquisitors, but also in the horrible deaths so swiftly visited upon many of those who had taken part in the persecution. These too were chronicled by Foxe in a separate appendix.[120] It was a vision of English fidelity to the Protestant faith

---

[119] H. C. Porter, *Reformation and Reaction in Tudor Cambridge* (Cambridge, 1958), pp. 101 ff. James McConica (ed.), *The History of the University of Oxford. III: the Collegiate University* (Oxford, 1986), pp. 380–4, 405–12.

[120] 'The severe punishment of God upon the persecutors of his people and enemies to his Word', in *Acts and Monuments*, pp. 628–64. First in *Acts and Monuments* 1563 as 'Another Chapter or treatise of tyrants and persecutors, and concerning God's scourge and punishments exercised upon the same'. Foxe greatly expanded this section as new information became available to him. All the major Protestant martyrologists included some such cautionary tales, though neither Crespin nor Haemstede matched the copious detail that Foxe brought to this particular enterprise.

behind which many who had behaved less creditably could also shield.

But Foxe, unlike some of the less flexible of his exile colleagues, was also an acute ecclesiastical politician, and he recognized that the contribution of those who had remained in England could not entirely be ignored. More specifically if the reign of the new Queen was to fulfil its allotted role as the period of prophetic deliverance, then Elizabeth's story had to be made part of the heroic tradition of those who had truly witnessed during Mary's reign. Thus the edition of 1563 had appended to its narratives of the martyrs an extended account of Elizabeth's tribulation under Mary: 'The miraculous preservation of the Lady Elizabeth, now Queen of England, from extreme calamity and danger of life.'[121] Here is chronicled in lively detail the extreme peril of Elizabeth's position after Wyatt's rebellion, her imprisonment in the Tower and gradual release to a less severe imprisonment, although one still attended by many indignities and humiliations. The manner of her conformity and attendance at Mass is touched upon only obliquely.

Elizabeth is the only one of those who remained in England honoured in this way, but the inclusion is shrewd.[122] How many of Foxe's readers, even as they marvelled at the constancy of the martyrs, may actually have identified as much with these experiences of Elizabeth: the constant slights at the hands of vengeful Catholic neighbours, the small-minded tyranny of the newly orthodox, and felt that they too had borne a small part of the cross of martyrdom; that, just as with Elizabeth, their uncomfortable conformity had all been part of a faithful waiting and watching for better days. For many, like Elizabeth, the turn towards Catholicism under Mary had indeed brought loss of position, danger of denunciation, and scruples of conscience. To be told by Foxe that this too was all part of God's plan was a comfort indeed.

Nor does this sort of ambivalent witness deserve to be treated with contempt. The heroism we admire in historical figures we seldom practise in our day-to-day dealings with situations of moral complexity; and those who today cut through hesitations and ambiguities by adopting positions of uncompromising moral absolutism are seldom admired by their contemporaries. The terms 'zealot' or 'fanatic' are

---

[121] *Acts and Monuments 1563*, pp. 1708–16. *Acts and Monuments*, pp. 600–25. Reprinted from the 1563 edition in A. F. Pollard, *Tudor Tracts* (London, 1903), pp. 334–64.

[122] *Acts and Monuments 1563*, pp. 1676–94 includes a section of persecutions which stopped short of martyrdom, but all of those involved had refused to hear Mass.

not intended as praise. In this context it ought more frequently to occur to us that to demand of those faced by the religious convulsions of the sixteenth century that sincere commitment should also invariably be attended by moral courage is wholly unrealistic and anachronistic. Many of those who remained in England during Mary's reign did not play a particularly heroic role; but their commitment to Protestantism need not have been any less sincere for all that. And ultimately the contribution of men and women of this sort was vital to the emergence during Elizabeth's reign of a Protestant society in England. It deserves to be treated with greater seriousness and respect than has so far been the case.

CHAPTER FIVE

The Latin Polemic of the Marian Exiles

In a recent number of the *English Historical Review* Dr Jennifer Loach argued for a more positive view of the relationship between the government of Mary Tudor and the printing press. Against a historical tradition which has been persistently critical of the regime's failure to understand the importance of printing, Dr Loach has argued that Mary's government in fact had a very real understanding of the value of printed propaganda, and took positive measures to promote abroad a favourable view of the restoration of Catholic worship in England.[1] The key events of the reign – the Queen's accession and marriage and the ending of the schism – were all marked by the publication abroad of pamphlets in Latin or foreign vernacular languages promoting the government's viewpoint. The speed with which such accounts appeared suggest an official version of events (usually in Latin) was sometimes deliberately circulated to sympathetic printers to ensure wide publicity.[2]

The point is well made, and Dr Loach has certainly identified a substantial body of literature to set alongside the well-known polemical efforts of the Protestant Marian exiles. But her article prompts in turn a further question: how aware were the Protestant exiles of this same international audience? Studies of the exile literature have thus far concentrated almost exclusively on vernacular works, published abroad for clandestine importation and distribution in England. The exiles were extremely diligent in this task, publishing during the six years of the exile more than 120 tracts and pamphlets which found

---

[1] J. Loach, 'The Marian Establishment and the Printing Press', *EHR*, 101 (1986), pp. 135–48. J. W. Martin, 'The Marian Regime's Failure to Understand the Importance of Printing', *Huntington Library Quarterly*, 44 (1980–81), pp. 231–47. I wish to thank Dr Jane Dawson for her help and valuable suggestions which went towards the writing of this paper, and Geoffrey Hargreaves, Bruce Gordon, Scott Dixon and Robert Peberdy for their help with bibliographical references.
[2] Loach, 'Marian Establishment', pp. 143–7.

their way back to England.[3] But this vernacular literature, important and influential though it undoubtedly was at home, would obviously not have had the same impact abroad. To carry their case to an international and scholarly audience the exiles would have had to employ a different medium.

It is with this in mind that I have compiled the list of the Marian exiles' Latin works (see Appendix 4). Latin was by and large the only language which the exiles had in common with their hosts; it was a necessary medium if they were to address a wider court of popular opinion.[4] And on the evidence of this list, this was a more important aspect of the exiles' literary activities than has hitherto been recognized; the 40 different works and 50 editions detailed here represent a considerable body of work. The introduction which follows is intended to do no more than present a brief outline of the works and suggest some of the major issues which the exiles addressed, together with some broad general conclusions as to the scope and purposes of the literature.

The exiles' earliest publications were inevitably largely a reaction to the traumatic events of 1553. These included one very curious work, a Latin narrative of the events surrounding Edward's death and the abortive attempt to set up Jane Grey in his stead.[5] The unknown author is more likely to have been one of the foreign merchants than a theologian, but his hostility towards Northumberland was widely shared among the religious exiles. This little tract has more in common with the popular 'sensation' books than the bulk of the exile writings.[6] More important by far was the account published early in 1554 of the disputation in convocation the previous autumn prior to the restoration of the Mass, where the reformers present had made an

---

[3] E. Baskerville, *A Chronological Bibliography of Propaganda and Polemic Published in English between 1553 and 1558* (Publication of the American Philosophical Society, 1979). Idem, 'Some lost works of Propaganda from the Marian Period', *The Library*, 6th ser., 8 (1986), pp. 47–52.

[4] Grindal taught himself German, but he seems to have been unusual in this. Patrick Collinson, *Archbishop Grindal* (London, 1979), p. 69. See the letter from Aylmer to Foxe, quoted in J. F. Mozley, *John Foxe and his Book* (London, 1940), p. 57.

[5] No 1. Modern edn and trans., *Historical Narration of certain events which took place in the Kingdom of Great Britain*. Written by P. V. (London, 1865).

[6] Not least in giving currency to the rumour that Northumberland had brought about the King's death by poisoning him. There were also two vernacular German editions of this tract: *Warhafftige beschreibung deren ding. die sich in dem loblichen konigreich Engelland, im hew monat dies gegenwertigen 1553. Jars, zugetragen haben. Von kleglichem unzeitigen Tod Edwardi des sechsten, konigs zu Engelland etc. Warhafftiger grundlicher Bericht* (Leipzig, 1554). Copies of both in the British Library.

eloquent last ditch defence of the Edwardian settlement.[7] The account, penned by John Philpot after his arrest, was carried abroad by Valérand Poullain, one of the foreign ministers employed in England in Edward's reign. Poullain rendered it into Latin and published it along with a translation of Archbishop Cranmer's declaration in defence of the Eucharist, publication of which (in September 1553) had effectively sealed his fate.[8] Through Poullain's agency this was now made available to a continental audience.

Valérand Poullain was one of a number of foreign ministers and theologians who had found employment in England during Edward's reign and who were now forced to return to the continent. Their writings made a significant contribution to the literature of the exile. In addition to his translation of Philpot, Poullain was responsible for the publication of two editions of the liturgy used by the Frankfurt exile community. Based on the church order of his former church in Glastonbury and intended primarily for the use of the small French congregation, Poullain's liturgy was endorsed also by representatives of the English congregation.[9] In the same vein the distinguished Polish reformer John a Lasco published in 1555 a Latin version of the church order of the foreign church in London, of which he had been the first superintendent. This model church order would exercise a considerable influence in Reformed Protestant circles. Lasco, an able polemicist, also involved himself in the defence of the troubled Frankfurt community.[10] But the figure of greatest stature among the exiled foreign theologians was undoubtedly Peter Martyr Vermigli, friend of Cranmer and former professor of Divinity at Oxford. Martyr's continuing commitment to defend and elaborate the doctrine of the English church was reflected in several important works. Most influential was the *Defensio ... de Eucharistiae* against Stephen Gardiner, a response to Gardiner's final salvo against Cranmer in

---

[7] No 3. English edn *True report of the disputation*, STC 19890. The revised STC suggests Emden, Mierdman and Gailliart ? as printer, but on typographical grounds this seems improbable. Reprinted in J. Foxe, *Acts and Monuments* ed. G. Townsend and S. Cattley (8 vols, London, 1837–41), vol. 6, pp. 395–411 and *Examinations and Writings of John Philpot* (Parker Society, 1842), pp. 173–214 (with Poullain's preface).

[8] *Purgatio ... adversus infames rumores a quibusdam sparsos de missa restituta*. Printed in J. Strype, *Memorials of Archbishop Cranmer* (3 vols in 4, London, 1848–54), vol. 3, pp. 453–59. Jasper Ridley, *Thomas Cranmer* (Oxford, 1962), pp. 351–53.

[9] Nos 4 & 9. 'Subscripsit etiam Angli ob Evangelium profugi totius Ecclesiae sua nomine' (with five names). *Liturgia Sacra* (1554), sig. f7. Modern edn *Valerandus Pollanus, Liturgia Sacra*, ed. A. C. Honders (Leiden, 1970).

[10] Nos 10, 18, 19. On Lasco see Basil Hall, *John a Lasco. A Pole in Reformation England* (Friends of Dr Williams's Library, 25th Lecture, 1971).

their prolonged controversy over sacramental theology.[11] Writing to Martyr from prison in 1555, Cranmer expressed his regret that no-one had yet answered the book. This task was by common consent consigned to Martyr, who was working on it during his time in Strasbourg, although the book appeared finally only after his removal from Strasbourg to Zurich in 1556.[12] Two other publications also date from this Zurich period: a reply to Richard Smith, who had written against his teaching on clerical celibacy and monastic vows, and an edition of his Oxford lectures on Romans. This latter work Martyr had prepared for publication before he left England, but it was only in 1558 that he had time to see it through the press and Martyr now took the opportunity to add a dedication to Sir Anthony Cooke, in which he expressed the prophetic hope that the church of England might one day be restored.[13] Martyr's continuing commitment to the English church earned him a position of special respect among the English exiles, many of whom attended his lectures in Strasbourg. His stature and reputation ensured that he would be one of the most formidable defenders of the English Protestant settlement during the exile. The foreign theologians' writings in exile served to underline their continuing commitment to the English Protestant polity established with their assistance during Edward's reign. The death of Martin Bucer had deprived the English church of another eloquent advocate, but he too was represented in the publications of the exiles, notably with a posthumous edition of his *De Regno Christi*, his final considered proposals for the organization of a Christian state.[14]

It would be wrong, however, to give the impression that the English

---

[11] No. 46. Marvin Anderson, *Peter Martyr, A Reformer in Exile* (Nieuwkoop, 1975). Idem, 'Rhetoric and Reality: Peter Martyr and the English Reformation', *SCJ*, 19 (1988), pp. 451–69. Gardiner's *Confutio Cavillationem* was published in Paris in 1552 and reprinted in 1554 at Louvain. See M. A. Schaaber, *Checklist of Works by British Authors Printed Abroad in Languages other than English* (New York, 1975), p. 76.

[12] *Original Letters relative to the English Reformation* (2 vols, Parker Society, 1846), vol. 1, pp. 29–30. Anderson, 'Rhetoric and Reality', 464–7.

[13] Nos 37, 47. Anderson, *Reformer in Exile*, pp. 328–55, 497–507.

[14] Nos 7 (including the Commentary on Judges) and 26 (*De Regno Christi*). On the Judges Commentary and its influence on the development on Protestant political thought see Hans Baron, 'Calvinist Republicanism and its political roots', *Church History*, 8 (1939), p. 37. On *De Regno Christi*, C. Hopf, *Martin Bucer and the English Reformation* (Oxford, 1946), pp. 99–126. Bucer's lectures on Ephesians at Cambridge were also later published, ed. by Tremellius. *Praelectiones Doctiss. in Epistolam ad Ephesios* (Basle, Pernam, 1562).

exiles were prepared to leave the defence of their church entirely to their distinguished foreign guests. Several of the English exiles contributed effectively to the doctrinal debate, including John Ponet, former bishop of Winchester and the senior churchman among the exiles.[15] Ponet is best known for his *Short treatise of Politic Power*, a discussion of the right of resistance, which played an influential role in directing the exiles' thoughts into more radical paths, but he also wrote a number of works in Latin, including the *Diallacticon*, a cogent and effective statement of the position of the English church on Eucharistic doctrine. Although not published until after Ponet's death, the work enjoyed considerable success, with several reprints during Elizabeth's reign.[16] Thomas Becon was another exile who alongside his English tracts wrote works aimed at a more scholarly audience, most notably his *Coenae sacrosanctae dominae*, a comparison between the Lord's Supper and the Mass.[17]

The most prolific of the English authors were John Bale and John Foxe, two men whose paths became increasingly intertwined during the years of the exile. Bale, a veteran of the Henrician exile and an energetic pamphleteer since the 1540s, had made his way to the continent from Ireland, whither he had been despatched as bishop of Ossory in the last year of Edward's reign.[18] At Frankfurt he met up with Foxe, before the troubles which afflicted the English congregation in that town caused both men to move on to Basle. Here Foxe (and possibly Bale also) found employment as a proofreader for the printer Oporinus, while both men shared quarters provided by the town for the English exiles in the former *Klarakloster*.[19] The association proved a happy one; over the next three years the two men published more than a dozen Latin works on Oporinus's presses, including arguably the two most important books of the whole exile:

---

[15] Winthrop S. Hudson, *John Ponet, 1516–1556. Advocate of Limited Monarchy* (Chicago, 1942). C. Garrett, *The Marian Exiles* (Cambridge, 1938), pp. 253–8 is useful, though speculative and unsympathetic. See also E. J. Baskerville, 'John Ponet in Exile: a Ponet Letter to John Bale', *JEH*, 37 (1986), pp. 442–7.

[16] No. 28. Hudson, *Ponet*, pp. 79–81. Further edns published 1573, 1576, 1688. On the *Short Treatise* Hudson, *Ponet*, pp. 109–216.

[17] No. 45. D. S. Bailey, *Thomas Becon and the Reformation of the Church in England* (Edinburgh, 1952), pp. 77–91. For Becon's other Latin works see ibid., p. 145 and checklist nos 30, 38.

[18] L. P. Fairfield, *John Bale, Mythmaker for the English Reformation* (Purdue University Press, 1976).

[19] Mozley, *Foxe and his Book*, pp. 37–61. William Haller, *Foxe's Book of Martyrs and the Elect Nation* (1963), pp. 48–81.

Bale's *Scriptorum illustrium maioris Britanniae* and Foxe's *Rerum in ecclesia gestarum*, the Latin prototype of his Book of Martyrs.

Bale's *Scriptorum* was an extraordinarily ambitious undertaking, representing in its final form the fruits of over a decade of research into the history of British authors. Bale's intention was to create a history of the English church and people in the form of a biographical encyclopaedia, and to this end he had collected information on some 900 mythical and historical persons. His catalogue was, however, far from being an impartial work of scholarship; rather Bale offered a scheme of the past which served to validate events in England since 1529 as a return to the pure Christianity of the immediate post-apostolic age, before the Roman pontificate had asserted its tyrannous hold.[20] The biographical sketches were interspersed with appendices dealing with political history and particularly the nefarious activities of papal agents in England. These sections on the papacy were also abstracted and published separately as the *Acta Romanorum Pontificum*, a work similar in style and purpose to Robert Barnes's lives of the Roman pontiffs. Barnes's book, first published in Wittenberg in 1536, was also reprinted by Oporinus during these years.[21]

Bale's historical writings were important too for their influence on John Foxe's intellectual development. Foxe and Bale had known each other in London during Edward's reign, at which time Foxe first began to pursue his historical writing. Foxe's debt to Bale is evident in his first publication abroad, the *Commentarii rerum in ecclesia gestarum*, an account of the life and doctrine of John Wycliffe. This work, published soon after Foxe's arrival in Strasbourg, was probably substantially complete before he departed for the continent.[22] Once settled in Basle, Foxe embarked on a feverish programme of literary activity, writing and translating, in addition to his proofreading and editorial work for Oporinus. From this period date a number of original Latin works, including *Christus triumphans*, an apocolyptical comedy, and *Ad inclytos Angliae proceres*, an appeal to the nobility of England to use their influence with the Queen to stop the

---

[20] Fairfield, *Bale*, pp. 96 ff. See also Katharine Firth, *The Apocalyptic Tradition in Reformation Britain, 1530–1645* (Oxford, 1979), Chapters 2 & 3.

[21] Nos 33, 40 (Bale), 11 (Barnes). Fairfield, *Bale*, pp. 103–5. A. G. Dickens and John Tonkin, *The Reformation in Historical Thought* (Oxford, 1985), pp. 63–5.

[22] No. 5. The *Commentarii* seems not to have sold well, since ten years later Rihel reissued copies with a new title page and dedication. [*Chronicon Ecclesiae*, 1564. Copies Munich SB, Kiel UB.]

persecution, which seems to have been inspired by news of the martyrdom of Cranmer, Ridley and Latimer.[23]

Many of Foxe's energies, however, were devoted to the compilation of a history of the English martyrs, expanding the *Commentarii* of 1554 to take in more recent events. Although Foxe was ultimately to bear the major burdens of authorship, the martyrology was originally conceived as a collaborative venture. The moving spirit behind the project appears to have been Edmund Grindal. Writing to Foxe from Strasbourg, where he was well placed to receive news and materials from England, Grindal suggested that he and his colleagues should compile the English version while Foxe in Basle worked towards a simultaneous Latin edition.[24] In the event the task proved more complicated than he had anticipated. New materials continued to arrive, and Grindal returned to England with the plan for an English martyrology unrealized. Foxe, however, persevered, delaying his return to England to see his Latin work through the press. It was published finally in 1559, a folio of some 700 pages, continuing the story begun with the Lollard martyrs in the *Commentarii* through the reigns of Henry VIII and Mary. Along with accounts of the death of the martyrs furnished from England, Foxe included a number of tracts already published separately, such as Philpot's account of the convocation of 1553 and his own address to the nobility. It was, as far as possible, a full and lasting record of the trials to which the English church had lately been subjected.[25]

Foxe's martyrology was one of a number of ventures on which the exiles collaborated in order to bring the fate of the English martyrs and their works to a wider public. Writing to Ridley in prison in 1555, Grindal recorded that he had received several of his prison writings; he proposed to have his treatise on the Eucharist translated into Latin ready for publication, but would not proceed until Ridley's fate was known, for fear of prejudicing his case. In the event, Ridley

---

[23] Nos 17 and 22. On *Christus Triumphans* see J. H. Smith, *Two Latin Comedies by John Foxe the Martyrologist* (Ithaca, 1973). See also R. Bauckham, *Tudor Apocalypse* (Sutton Courtenay, n.d.), pp. 75–83. Foxe's address to the nobility was reprinted in the martyrology of 1559 (below, n. 25) and in subsequent edns of the *Acts and Monuments*. Mozley, *Foxe and his Book*, pp. 54–5.

[24] Letter of June 1557. *Remains of Archbishop Grindal* (Parker Society, 1843), pp. 226–7. See Mozley, *op. cit.*, pp. 120–3.

[25] No. 39. Mozley, *Foxe and his Book*, pp. 122–8. Disputatio Synodalis Londini, *Rerum*, pp. 215–29; Ad Praepotentes Angliae proceres, pp. 239 ff. See also below, n. 28.

was put to death in October and the treatise on the Eucharist, translated by William Whittingham, published the following year.[26] Other translations were entrusted to John Foxe, including an account of the examinations of John Philpot and Cranmer's second treatise on the Eucharist.[27] Not all of these plans were brought to fruition. John Hooper had despatched a number of his writings to Bullinger in Zurich in the hope that he would see to their publication. But although the works found their way into Foxe's hands, no independent editions seem to have been published, although one was included in the martyrology. Perhaps in this case Foxe was deterred by the misgivings expressed by Grindal (and apparently shared by Bullinger and Martyr) that Hooper had not always expressed himself as carefully as they might have wished.[28] The publication of Cranmer's second Eucharistic treatise, his reply to Gardiner, also ran into difficulties. Foxe completed the translation, despite some problems with obscure passages, but then publication was held up by the delay in finding a printer following a ban on the publication of controversial works imposed as a result of the outbreak of the sacramentarian controversy in Germany. Even Oporinus was reluctant to proceed when advised by the town authorities to hold off, and although the work was passed to Froschover at Zurich he too never seems to have brought it out.[29]

These temporary difficulties in Switzerland may explain why Cranmer's first major writing on the Eucharist was published, unusually, in Emden, far away from the usual centres of Latin printing. Emden was a convenient location for the small vernacular pamphlets smuggled into England, but less so for the distribution of works intended for a

---

[26] No. 13. Grindal to Ridley, 6 May 1555. *Works of Bishop Ridley* (Parker Society, 1843), p. 388.

[27] No. 25 (Philpot). See Strype, *Cranmer*, 3. p. 174. Apparently published separately, Foxe also included this translation in his martyrology. *Rerum* (1559), pp. 543–631. On his Cranmer translation, see below n. 29.

[28] *Later Writings of Bishop Hooper* (Parker Society, 1852), pp. 381–548. Hooper to Bullinger, 11 Dec 1554. *Original Letters*, pp. 105–6. Grindal to Foxe, August 1556. Grindal, *Remains*, p. 223. De sacratissimae coenae Domini included in *Rerum* (1559), pp. 309–403 but omitted in subsequent English edns of the *Acts and Monuments*. The dedicatory epistle to the second tract, 'De vera ratione inveniendae' is reprinted by Strype, *Ecclesiastical Memorials*, vol. 3, ii, pp. 267–73. See ibid., vol. 3, i, pp. 283–4.

[29] Grindal to Foxe, May 1556, Jan and June 1557. Grindal, *Remains*, pp. 220–2, 234–5.

European readership.[30] However the more relaxed attitude displayed by the local authorities at this point was probably the principal motive for entrusting Cranmer's work to an Emden printer. The translation, by Sir John Cheke, was published now with a new preface, extolling the martyrs and the Reformation under Edward for which they died.[31] The appearance of this work in these circumstances was an event of special significance, almost as if the martyred archbishop's writing was being presented as an official testament of the exiled English church. The preface was endorsed by a list of the leading figures of the exile, ranged according to their ecclesiastical rank.[32]

With the accession of Elizabeth in November 1558 the exiles were finally able to contemplate a return home. Not all left off their literary activities immediately. John Foxe, tied to Basle by the need to see his martyrology through the press, rapidly composed a celebratory address expressing the joy felt in Germany at the happy turn of events in England.[33] His friends Laurence Humphrey and John Bale also made their literary response to the new circumstances, Humphrey dedicating his tract *De Religionis conservatione* with its timely reflections on the reforming of religion to the nobility and people of England, while Bale inserted into the latest copies of his *Scriptorum Brytanniae* a new dedication to Queen Elizabeth.[34] By the end of the year all three had returned to England and the literary work of the exile was at an end.

The full significance of this exile literature cannot be explored in detail in a brief introduction of this nature, but it may be appropriate

---

[30] Of the Latin literature only this work and the *Aetiologia* of Robert Watson (nos 14 & 15) were published in Emden. Watson, Cranmer's former steward, had escaped from prison in England only after making a highly equivocal declaration on the Mass. This tract is intended to defend his conduct. The fact that, in contrast, such a high proportion of the vernacular tracts were printed in north Germany (at Emden, Wesel and Strasbourg) must reflect the different markets at which the two classes of literature were aimed.

[31] Nos 20, 21. Reprinted in *Writings and Disputations of Cranmer* (Parker Society, 1844), Appendix, pp. 1–99. Modern edn, including supplementary materials from Emden edn but omitting Preface, *Remains of Archbishop Cranmer*, ed. H. Jenkyns (Oxford, 1833), vol. 2, pp. 275–463.

[32] Cranmer, *Writings*, Appendix, p. 9.

[33] No. 50. See Strype, *Annals of the Reformation* (4 vols in 7, London, 1824), vol. 1, i, pp. 155–61.

[34] Nos 42 (Bale), 49 (Humphrey). Other copies of the *Scriptorum* listed under no. 32. may also contain the new Preface. On Humphrey's tract see Strype, *Annals*, vol. 1, i, pp. 161–2.

to offer a few preliminary reflections. While it would no doubt be stretching a point to make all these works part of a co-ordinated campaign, the authors may be said to have broadly shared a common purpose, that is to present and justify the English Reformation to an international audience. Both the historical and theological works played their part in this scheme, presenting a view of the Reformation in England which both anchored it historically and placed it in the mainstream of the European movement. The exiles often went to some pains to ensure that their writings presented a doctrinally coherent and orthodox face; in this respect Grindal's concern that Hooper and Philpot's prison writings be edited before publication to remove some unguarded expressions seems especially significant.[35] The exile authors were anxious above all to present a positive face of the English Reformation. There is little trace in these writings of the internal debates and divisions which so troubled the exile congregations during their sojourn abroad.[36]

The exiles' works seem to have found a ready audience. It would be rash to draw conclusions about contemporary patterns of dissemination from current locations of surviving copies, but it is clear that some of these works have survived in unusual numbers: these are among the sixteenth century's unrare books.[37] Their success should not surprise us though, because this was a period when European statesmen and church leaders were deeply interested in English affairs. The correspondence of the reformers bears witness to the close attention with which they followed events in England after the death of Edward VI and the progress of the Catholic restoration.[38] Theodore Beza was sufficiently engaged to write a reply to the printed version of Northumberland's recantation, which had circulated widely on the continent.[39] Later in the reign Pole's diplomatic activity as mediator in the Franco-Imperial conflict helped keep English affairs

---

[35] Grindal, *Remains*, 223. See n. 28 above.

[36] Most famously in Frankfurt, but the English communities in Basle and Emden were also troubled by internal dissensions. *A brief discours off the troubles begonne at Franckfort*, ed. J. Petheram (London, 1846).

[37] See Appendix 4. Folio editions are inevitably represented by the greatest number of surviving copies, but many of the smaller books are also preserved in considerable numbers.

[38] See for instance pieces preserved in the Calvin correspondence. CO, vols 14–17, CR, vols 42–45. (1875–7), e.g. nos 1761, 1768, 1778, 1856, 1940, 1953, 1992, etc.

[39] *Response a la confession du feu Jean de Northumbelande, n'agueres decapité en Angléterre* [Geneva], 1554. Index Aureliensis, IV. p. 163. Loach, 'Marian Establishment', p. 144.

to the forefront on the European stage.[40] The role played by the Marian exiles in the wider struggle between Catholic and Protestant in Europe, a struggle which in the 1550s would have appeared particularly tense and delicate, was one which the reformers were not slow to acknowledge. Bullinger dedicated to the exiles his sermons on the Apocalypse published at Basle in 1557, and the hospitality proffered by the Swiss reformers was a further tangible measure of their concern and regard.[41] The exiles responded in kind, both in their dedications and in the sincere expressions of gratitude which followed their return to England.[42]

The middle decades of the sixteenth century were years when, perhaps to an extent never again repeated, the Reformation in England was an integral part of the wider European movement. The reign of Edward VI had been marked by the closest co-operation between the English reformers and their foreign mentors, an association which the exile under Mary served to strengthen and continue. It is within this context that these Latin works should be viewed. For they helped to promote abroad a vision of a reformed Protestant England which, though now temporarily submerged, the exiles never seemed to doubt would one day be restored.

---

[40] Heinrich Lutz, 'Cardinal Reginald Pole and the path to Anglo-Papal Mediation at the Peace Conference of Marcq, 1553–55', in E. I. Kouri and Tom Scott (eds), *Politics and Society in Early Modern Europe* (London, 1987), pp. 329–52. Dermot Fenlon, *Heresy and Obedience in Tridentine Italy* (Cambridge, 1972), pp. 258–69. The polemical campaign waged against Pole by the Italian humanist Pier Paulo Vergerio also forms part of this context. In 1555 he published at Strasbourg a new edn of Pole's *Pro ecclesiasticae unitate*, intending to discredit the religious talks in Germany. See also *Epistolae duae* (no. 12), a short but vituperative polemical work denouncing Pole and contrasting his former policy of moderation with his treatment of the English Protestants.

[41] Bullinger, *In apocalypsim Jesu Christi . . . Conciones centum*, fol. a2: Ad omnes per Germaniam & Helvetiam, Galliae, Angliae, Italiae aliorumque regnorum vel nationum Christi nomine exules . . .

[42] Bale's *Acta Romanorum pontificum* (no. 33) dedicated to the reformers. Foxe dedicated his *Commentarii* (no. 5) to the Duke of Württemberg and his *Locorum Communium* (no. 23) to the students of the university of Basle. Becon's *Coenae sacrosanctae domini* dedicated to William, son of Philip of Hesse. Mozley, *Foxe and his Book*, pp. 42, 53. Firth, *Apocalyptic Tradition*, pp. 79–80. Bailey, *Becon*, p. 90. For the exiles' correspondence with the reformers following their return see *Zurich Letters* (2 vols, Parker Society, 1842), passim.

CHAPTER SIX

The Marian Exiles and the Elizabethan Settlement

When in 1986 Sir Geoffrey Elton published his long gestated study of Elizabethan parliaments, he manfully confessed what many authors undoubtedly feel: that he was heartily glad to be rid of it. 'The completion of a book is always a relief, but I am perhaps exceptionally relieved to be done with the parliaments of Elizabeth.'[1] This is not perhaps the most encouraging recommendation for the intending reader, but Sir Geoffrey had a special reason for turning towards more appetizing projects. For during the course of writing *The Parliament of England, 1559–1581* the reluctant author had gradually persuaded himself that parliament in the sixteenth century was not actually very important. According to Elton the subsequent importance of parliament as an institution of government has led historians to overplay its significance in the sixteenth century. Compare Elton's more jaundiced conclusion: 'I now wonder whether the institution ... ever really mattered all that much in the politics of the nation, except perhaps as a stage sometimes used by the real contenders over government and policy.'[2]

This argument, from one of the greatest scholars of English constitutional history, is not to be taken lightly, but it can hardly be made to apply to the parliament of 1559. For this was a legislative gathering which all writers who have considered the subject agree mattered very much indeed. It was this first crucial parliament of the reign of Elizabeth I which eventually and after some tribulation passed the Acts of Supremacy and Uniformity which defined the course of the Elizabethan religious settlement, and set the pattern of official state religion to the present day. For all the increased historiographical emphasis on informal structures of power in sixteenth-century government it is as well to keep in mind one salient fact: that the Anglican church was created by statute law.

This being the case it is hardly surprising that the obscure and somewhat complicated parliamentary proceedings from which the

---

[1] G. R. Elton, *The Parliament of England, 1559–1581* (Cambridge, 1986), p. ix.
[2] Ibid.

settlement emerged have been the subject of some historical controversy, a controversy to which recent revisionist writing on the English Reformation have added several new twists. For most of the period since the sixteenth century, indeed from the first decades of the Elizabethan period until the 1950s, writers who commented on the settlement were content with a pleasingly obvious explanation, that a Protestant Queen enacted a Protestant settlement over the determined oppostion of those most wedded to Marian Catholicism, principally the bench of bishops. This was the interpretation of most contemporary observers, Catholic and Protestant, as well as of the first historians of the settlement, Foxe, Strype and Burnet; and it was sufficient to content a succession of modern writers down to Maitland and Pollard.[3] In 1950, however, J. E. Neale, the distinguished historian of parliament, proposed an alternative interpretation which effectively stood the received wisdom on its head.[4] According to Neale the settlement which emerged at the conclusion of this troubled parliament was far from what the Queen had originally intended. Elizabeth's personal preference had been for something far more moderate and less decisively Protestant. The Royal Supremacy would be assumed once more, but religious observance would be patterned according to the first, more hesitant (and therefore to Catholics more acceptable) Edwardian Prayer Book of 1549. It was opposition from a determined Protestant pressure group in the House of Commons which eventually drove Elizabeth into accepting a more radical settlement, based on the more fully Protestant second Edwardian Prayer Book of 1552. The final shape of the Elizabethan settlement could, in this reading, be attributed to the effective marshalling of parliamentary force to persuade a reluctant Queen to move beyond her own more conservative inclinations. The House of Commons had come of age.

Perhaps the most surprising aspect of Neale's hypothesis was the speed with which it in turn became the new orthodoxy. For several decades this vision of a conservative Queen badgered by parliament's 'puritan choir' became in effect the orthodox interpretation of the settlement. The vision of a powerful kind of oppositional politics gradually attaining maturity in the century before the decisive confrontation of the English Civil War clearly made good sense to this particular generation of historians; perhaps too the sheer ingenious-

---

[3] For the opinions of contemporary diplomatic observers, see below, notes 12, 27.
[4] J. E. Neale, 'The Elizabethan Acts of Supremacy and Uniformity', *EHR*, 65 (1950), pp. 304–32. C.f. his *Elizabeth I and her Parliaments, 1559–1581* (London, 1953).

ness of Neale's hypothesis, and his own great authority as a historian, contributed to its attractiveness. In the last few years, however, Neale's thesis has not fared so well. The work of Elton, Neale's most distinguished student, has dealt some heavy blows, not least in dismantling the notion of an organized oppositional lobby in the first decade of the reign, Neale's cherished 'puritan choir'.[5] Even if an identifiable group of this sort had coalesced by the end of the first decade of Elizabeth's reign, it is extremely unlikely that an effective opposition faction could have been marshalled by the time parliament met in 1559. Certainly such a faction could not have been created from returning religious exiles. The writ for the parliament went out on 5 December, just 18 days after the late Queen's death, leaving little time for returning exiles to secure seats. Consequently fewer exiles sat in the parliament of 1559 than would do so in 1563, and most who secured seats were gentlemen clients of leading figures of the new regime.[6]

The most sustained rebuttal of Neale's thesis has been provided by an Elton pupil, Norman Jones. In his own painstaking reconstruction of the work of the first Elizabethan parliament, Jones in effect reinstates the received view: that the settlement of 1559 which emerged from the parliamentary process was by and large that which the Queen and her close advisors intended. The most troublesome opposition came, as one might expect, not from the House of Commons but from the entrenched Catholic group in the House of Lords.[7]

Given the care and (in the view of this author) authority with which Jones marshalled his evidence, it is somewhat of a surprise that his interpretation of the settlement has not yet found general acceptance.[8] This is all the more the case since Jones's thesis received strong corroboration from a simultaneous though independent study by W. S. Hudson, who approaches the issues of the settlement from an entirely different direction and yet reaches essentially identical conclusions.[9] Although it is now generally recognized that the Neale

---

[5] Elton, *Parliament of England*, pp. 205–16, 351–4.
[6] Kenneth Bartlett, 'The Role of the Marian Exiles', in P. W. Hasler (ed.), *The Commons, 1558–1603* (3 vols, London, 1981), vol. 1, pp. 102–10.
[7] N. L. Jones, *Faith by Statute. Parliament and the Settlement of Religion, 1559* (London, 1982).
[8] See, for instance, the review of Jones and Hudson (n. 9, below) in *Heythrop Journal*, 25 (1984), pp. 228–32.
[9] W. S. Hudson, *The Cambridge Connection and the Elizabethan Settlement of 1559* (Durham, NC, 1980), pp. 110, 145.

hypothesis in all its intricacy cannot be made to stand up, elements of his interpretation still survive in recent survey treatments of Elizabeth's reign. Perhaps the key to its survival lies in a largely fortuitous congruity between Neale's picture of a Queen with essentially conservative religious inclinations and recent revisionist writings on the English Reformation. Thus the view of the Elizabethan church as a *via media* lives on, even if the evidential base on which Neale constructed his original hypothesis looks increasingly threadbare. In his recent survey of the English Reformation Christopher Haigh presents a picture of a half-hearted Reformation, which introduced an ambiguous Book of Common Prayer; 'a liturgical compromise which allowed priests to perform the Church of England communion in Catholic regalia, standing in the Catholic position and using words capable of Catholic interpretation'.[10]

The publication of so emphatic a restatement of a view of the Elizabethan settlement as a tepid, tentative return to a less than full-hearted Protestantism, suggests that the controversial events of 1559 will still bear further re-examination. The present essay will not attempt a full reconstruction of the making of the settlement, but rather focus on those crucial points where the Queen is deemed to have pulled back from a fully Protestant settlement. I intend here to pay particular attention to contemporary comment, particularly the remarks of those English and foreign exiles who in 1559 returned to England after time spent on the continent. Here it is possible to adduce some new evidence which may help square the circle of why the Queen enacted what was in all essentials a fully Protestant settlement, and then stepped back from following the full preferences of those who had been to this point her principal supporters and advisors, thus setting the pattern for some of the most serious collisions of the Elizabethan period.

That Elizabeth ultimately disappointed many of those who had entered into the discussions over the settlement of religion in 1559 is beyond question. Many of those who returned from exile in 1559 would later reflect, often more in sorrow than in anger, on the ways in which their initially bright hopes had been dashed. But there are two important qualifications to be made here. Firstly, it is important not to read back into the initial discussion of the events of 1559 divisions which only became apparent in subsequent years, as posi-

---

[10] Christopher Haigh, *English Reformations. Religion, Politics and Society under the Tudors* (Oxford, 1993), p. 241.

tions hardened and the difficulties of remaking England as a Protestant country took their toll. The fact that Elizabeth and Cecil would later find themselves seriously at odds with many of the more ardent evangelicals does not justify the further inference that in 1559 they did not share the basic aims of those lobbying for the restoration of Protestantism.

This is an important point, because for Neale and others who have followed his lead it was an article of faith that Elizabeth never aimed at much more than a tepid Protestantism, possibly even the Henrician Catholicism that he believed would have reflected best her own personal religious and political predilections.[11] Given that, in the political context of 1559, this was never a realistic option, Elizabeth's favoured option would, according to Neale, have been the retention of the first Edwardian Prayer Book of 1549, a moderate solution which would indeed, in the context of this later decade, have had the appearance of restoring a sort of half-way house.

Yet the evidence that the 1549 Prayer Book was ever even raised as a possibility in 1559 — still less discussed — is remarkably flimsy for what would become such an important cornerstone of Neale's argument. Neale in fact depends for this crucial aspect of his hypothesis on an entirely spurious identification between the 1549 Prayer Book and the Lutheran Augsburg Confession, for which Elizabeth sometimes expressed a vague and quite unspecific preference in conversations with foreign ambassadors and in diplomatic correspondence. On the day that the Bill of Uniformity finally passed through the House of Lords the Queen apparently mused to Feria, the Spanish ambassador, 'that she wished the Augusteanean [sic] confession to be maintained in her realm', or at least something very like it.[12] Earlier in the year she had made a similar if more enigmatic declaration of her general approval for the Lutheran Confession in correspondence with the Duke of Württemberg.[13]

Two observations are relevant here. Firstly, there is no real justification for equating the first Edwardian Prayer Book with the Augsburg Confession, an entirely different type of document with quite different theological underpinnings. The only evidence Neale cites in support is in fact astonishingly trivial: the remark of a Protestant layman in 1549 likening the 1549 Prayer Book to 'the manner of the

---

[11] Neale, 'Elizabethan Acts of Supremacy and Uniformity', p. 328.

[12] Ibid. *Calendar of State Papers Spanish, 1558–1567*, ed. Martin Hume (London, 1892), pp. 61–2.

[13] Neale, 'Elizabethan Acts of Supremacy and Uniformity', p. 218. *Calendar of State Papers Foreign, Elizabeth*, vol. 1, pp. 115–6.

Nuremberg churches and some of those in Saxony'.[14] It might also seem extremely unwise to read any great significance into Elizabeth's genial endorsement of the Augsburg Confession in conversation with ambassadors. Such observations can as easily be seen as part of the developing pattern for Elizabeth to use audiences of this sort as a means of laying a false trail; a technique which, as most of her biographers have recognized, Elizabeth developed to a fine art.

Nor is it clear, when the Queen spoke in this way, that she had anything very specific in mind in theological terms. True, Elizabeth must have been aware that the Augsburg Confession was the core document of the German Lutheran churches, and thus could appropriately be praised in necessary attempts to establish a sound relationship with the German Lutheran princes. But the Augsburg Confession was also beginning at this time to take on a life of its own in negotiations which had little to do with any real attempt to establish Lutheran doctrines or church orders. By the mid-sixteenth century the Augsburg Confession was functioning frequently, if rather curiously, as a sort of representative ecumenical religious formula, which might be proposed as a means of bringing together warring religious factions in a wide variety of situations. Thus in 1561 at the Colloquy of Poissy, the leader of the French Catholic delegates, the Cardinal of Lorraine, proposed that the Calvinist representatives might endorse the Confession of Augsburg as a means of breaking the religious deadlock.[15] Similarly in 1566, during the first stages of the Dutch Revolt, William of Orange attempted to unite the different groups among the Antwerp Protestants by proposing the Augsburg Confession as an acceptable middle way.[16] Neither of these efforts came to much, nor, arguably, were they ever intended to. Rather they took advantage of a certain unclarity which attached to the Confession, a general sense that it offered some sort of middle way.

Diplomatic initiatives of this sort were greatly assisted by the fact that there were two versions of the Augsburg Confession: the original document of 1530, which adopted a straightforwardly Lutheran

---

[14] Neale, 'Elizabethan Acts of Supremacy and Uniformity', p. 318. *Original Letters Relative to the English Reformation* (2 vols, Parker Society, 1846), vol. 1, p. 266.

[15] Donald Nugent, *Ecumenism in the Age of the Reformation. The Colloquy of Poissy* (Cambridge, MA, 1974), pp. 142–3, 208–18. C.f. Wolfhart Pannenberg, *Die ökumenische Bedeutung der 'Confessio Augustana'* (Munich, 1981); Wolfgang Reinhard (ed.), *Bekenntnis und Geschichte: die Confessio Augustana in historischen Zusammenhang* (Munich, 1981).

[16] Felix Rachfahl, *Wilhelm von Orangien und die niederländische Aufstand* (3 vols, The Hague, 1906–24), vol. 2, pp. 770 ff.

formula on the central question of Eucharistic doctrine, and the so-called *Variata* of 1540, a revision of Philip Melanchthon intended to facilitate bridge-building initiatives with other German churches through a more subtly modulated Eucharistic formula.[17] This historical accident had the undoubtedly beneficial result that later generations could express general sympathy for the Augsburg Confession without making clear which version they intended: circumstances which undoubtedly increased its ecumenical potential. This was the spirit in which the Confession was generally cited at the beginning of religious negotiations; when matters moved on to specifics its ambiguities became less helpful, and the Lutheran Confession was generally abandoned. It is in precisely this context that one may interpret Elizabeth's remarks in 1559. A statement of support for the Augsburg Confession in this context made her no more a 'Lutheran' than others who sought to exploit its symbolic potential, such as Theodore Beza or the Cardinal of Lorraine.

This sort of contextualizing is also helpful if one turns to the other allegedly moderating feature of the eventual settlement, the change to the words of institution in the 1552 Prayer Book. In 1559 the austerely memorialist form of words used at the dispensing of the sacraments in 1552, 'Take and eat this, in remembrance that Christ died for you, and feed on him in thy heart by faith, with thanksgiving', was placed alongside the 1549 form, 'The body of our Lord Jesus Christ which was given for thee, preserve thy body and soul unto everlasting life.' According to Haigh, 'The words of administration were changed to allow a Catholic understanding of the real presence of Christ.'[18]

This, however, is an unnecessary overinterpretation of a change which, had it borne the implications that Haigh and others have drawn from it, would certainly have been more controversial at the time. In fact the alteration of the words of administration drew no comment, hostile or otherwise, from the supporters of the settlement. For in the context of contemporary continental theology the words of institution adopted in 1552 were anachronistic even as they were formulated. Almost certainly the brutal, uncompromising memorialism was a reaction to the debate which had followed the first book, and in particular Stephen Gardiner's declaration from prison that he

---

[17] W. H. Neuser, *Bibliographie der Confessio Augustana und Apologie, 1530–1580* (Nieuwkoop, 1987).
[18] Haigh, *English Reformations*, p. 240.

found in the 1549 formula sufficient to bear a Catholic interpretation of the Real Presence.[19] It is doubtful if even as subtly compromising a spirit as Gardiner's could actually have found such a position sustainable, and his motive may simply have been to sow discord in the ranks of his opponents. Be that as it may, the revisers of the book left nothing to chance, and the new formula acted as a tangible demonstration that transubstantiation (and Gardiner) had been utterly repudiated. But in doing so Cranmer and his colleagues adopted a forthright and somewhat clumsy statement of a Zwinglian memorialism which even in terms of Swiss theology was already in 1552 outdated and anachronistic. For by this time Zwingli's heirs in the Zurich church had moved towards a more subtle understanding of the central Communion rite, a change reflected in the adoption in 1549 of the *Consensus Tigurinus*, a common doctrinal statement agreed between the churches of Zurich and Geneva after long negotiations between Heinrich Bullinger and John Calvin. The Eucharistic articles of the *Consensus* affirmed a doctrine of real, spiritual presence more usually associated with Calvin; it was a significant shift for Bullinger and the basis of a single unitary position in the Swiss Reformed churches.[20]

Unpublished at this time, the *Consensus* in fact first became a public document when it was published in England in 1552, as an appendix to a set of lectures by John a Lasco.[21] By the time of the exiles' return in 1559, the doctrine of the *Consensus* represented the leading position of all the major Swiss churches, and the Eucharistic statement created for the Elizabethan Prayer Book by the linking of the two earlier formulations essentially encapsulates this development. In this respect the change of 1559 should be seen as a corrective adjustment rather than a weakening of the doctrine of 1552.

Shorn of these two elements the Neale case is weak indeed; where then rests the continued stress on the 'moderation' or tepidity of the principal architects of the settlement? In part the conviction that Elizabeth and Cecil were but half-hearted reformers in 1559 rests on a back projection of their distaste for Protestant radicalism later in

---

[19] W. K. Jordan, *Edward VI. The Threshold of Power* (London, 1970), pp. 242–3. Glyn Redworth, *In Defence of the Church Catholic* (Oxford, 1990), pp. 286–7.

[20] Paul Rorem, *Calvin and Bullinger on the Lord's Supper* (Grove Liturgical Study, 60, 1989).

[21] John a Lasco, *Brevis et dilucida de sacramentis ecclesiae tractatio* [London, 1552]. STC 15259. Modern edn, *Joannis a Lasco Opera*, ed. A. Kuyper (2 vols, Amsterdam, 1866), vol. 1, pp. 99–232.

the reign. The fact of their conformity under Mary is also sometimes taken as evidence of a less than whole-hearted commitment to Protestantism. This is certainly the case for Conyers Read, whose assessment of Cecil as a straightforward politique had continued to be the definitive judgement of his conduct in 1559.[22]

Yet these sceptical judgements would have been a considerable surprise to contemporary observers, none of whom seemed to have any doubt that both Elizabeth and Cecil were fully committed to Protestantism. 'Our pious Queen', as Richard Cox described her, was generally commended by the returning exiles for her efforts on behalf of the true religion. 'We have a wise and religious queen, and one too who is favourably and propitiously disposed towards us', was John Jewel's fairly representative judgement.[23]

Part of the key here is that contemporaries judged far less harshly the conduct of those who, like Elizabeth and Cecil, had remained in England during Mary's reign. That this did not necessarily imply any less of a commitment to the Protestant cause is a case made elsewhere in this volume, and seems to have been generally accepted at the time. Returning exiles co-operated easily with friends and former allies who re-emerged from the shadows on Mary's demise, and even the continental reformers most critical of such behaviour in their writings rejoiced at the influence in the new reign exercised by men such as Cecil.[24] Viewed dispassionately, all the ties of history, family and affinity made Protestants of Elizabeth and Cecil, as contemporaries had no difficulty in discerning.

Contemporary observers on both sides of the religious divide quickly assessed Elizabeth's accession as a golden opportunity for Protestantism, and a disaster for Catholicism. From Zurich, Peter Martyr Vermigli expressed the joy and expectation of all continental Protestants in an effusive congratulatory message. His expectation and confidence were echoed by other leading figures such as Rudolph Gualter and John Calvin.[25] Meanwhile Catholics were appalled, and gloomily foretold disaster for their religion. The conservative Thomas Thirlby warned the agent of Cardinal Granvelle against the new Queen's councillors, and predicted the fall of true religion in Eng-

---

[22] Conyers Read, *Mr Secretary Cecil and Queen Elizabeth* (London, 1955), p. 134: 'Being a pragmatist like the Queen he probably favoured the middle of the road.'
[23] *Zurich Letters*, vol. 2, pp. 27 (Cooke), 32–3 (Jewel).
[24] See the letters of Calvin cited below, notes 44, 45.
[25] Jones, *Faith by Statute*, pp. 12, 15. *Zurich Letters*, vol. 2, p. 5.

land.[26] The Spanish and Venetian ambassadors had few illusions about the likely turn of events.[27]

Were all of these contemporary observers deceived? Elizabeth's personal religious convictions have been the subject of endless speculation, and admit of no certain analysis.[28] Hers was not a personality marked by particular religious enthusiasm. As the reign wore on she enjoyed exercising the prerogatives of Supreme Governor, the defence of which she came to see as a fundamental part of her regality. But at the beginning of the reign there was no hint that this would lead to a clash of fundamental principles with the Protestants who lauded and celebrated her accession. Protestant writers such as Aylmer and Foxe may have exaggerated her personal commitment when they celebrated the accession of a new Deborah, but they discerned at least one central truth: that Elizabeth's personal history and political circumstances bound her closely to those who wished the speedy destruction of Mary's Catholic regime. It was, after all, for her alleged complicity in Wyatt's rebellion that Elizabeth had been in most serious peril during Mary's reign, and she had no reason to view with affection those who had harassed and humiliated her through her years of subsequent enforced retirement from Court. Those who gathered around her or retained discreet contact through these difficult years were of much the same stamp: generally men who had prospered in the Edwardian period, and whose careers had been blighted or stalled by the restoration of Catholicism under Mary. There was little doubt that on Elizabeth's accession this reversionary interest would form the Queen's strongest support.

In this respect William Cecil was entirely typical of the new men of 1559. In later years he would be outstripped as a patron of forward Protestantism by rivals on the Privy Council, and the zealous advocates of further reform certainly tried his patience. But by background, affinity and personal religious conviction, in 1559 Cecil was strongly Protestant.

Cecil's conformity under Mary could not disguise the closeness of his association with policy-making under Edward VI. Although he had made the transition from Somerset to Northumberland with

---

[26] Jones, *Faith by Statute*, pp. 10–11.

[27] See, for instance, the report of the Duke of Feria to Philip II, 14 December 1558: 'The kingdom is now entirely in the hands of young folks, heretics and traitors, and the Queen does not favour a single man whom Her Majesty, who is now in heaven, would have received.' *Calendar of State Papers Spanish, 1558–1567*, p. 7.

[28] See John Guy, *Tudor England* (Oxford, 1988), pp. 250–1. Wallace MacCaffrey, *Elizabeth I* (London, 1993), pp. 48–52.

remarkable facility in 1549, Cecil was already closely associated with the inner policy-making circle, and clearly identified by foreign and native theologians as one of the lay councillors most wholly committed to the achievement of a Protestant settlement.[29] As relations with Northumberland deteriorated towards the end of the reign the leading Protestant bishops and theologians had looked increasingly to Cecil to facilitate necessary business.[30] Given his proximity to the leaders of the regime, Cecil was lucky to survive in 1553; perhaps his outstanding administrative talent made him too valuable to sacrifice at a time when Northumberland's more rough-hewn henchmen joined him on the scaffold.[31] During Mary's reign Cecil took refuge in scholarship, philosophy and provincial life, but he never severed his ties with other dispossessed members of the former Edwardian establishment.[32] In 1559 Cecil, acting as Elizabeth's agent, could move with remarkable speed to put together a skeleton administration which signalled an unambiguous break with Mary's Catholic clique. No-one should have been in any doubt that supporters of a Protestant settlement were in control, and that change would be swift and decisive.

If they had any doubts on the question, they would have been quickly dispelled by the Queen's actions at the beginning of the reign. The initial signals of the new regime were unambiguously Protestant, whether it be the appointment of William Bill to preach the first sermon of the new reign at Paul's Cross, three days after Mary's death, or the imprisonment of the traditionalist Bishop Christopherson when he preached against the changes in religion one week later.[33] As in Edward's reign, the capital was soon witnessing unauthorized attacks on Catholic images, the sort of iconoclasm which was often the harbinger of radical change. Significantly those who

---

[29] Bucer and others to Cecil, August 1549. Strype, *Memorials of Archbishop Cranmer*, vol. 3, p. 697. W. K. Jordan, *Threshold of Power*, p. 319. In 1551 Cecil took the lead in organizing debates on the Eucharist at his London home, as part of the discussions preceding the Prayer Book revision of 1552. John Strype, *The Life of the learned Sir John Cheke* (Oxford, 1821), pp. 69–86.

[30] Lasco to Cecil, Nov 1552; Martyr to Cecil, March 1552, April 1553; Strype, *Memorials of Cranmer*, vol. 2, p. 641, vol. 3, pp. 659–61.

[31] According to John Guy, Cecil also received a degree of protection from his friendship with Paget. Guy, *Tudor England*, p. 229. On Cecil and Northumberland, Jordan, *Threshold of Power*, pp. 500–1.

[32] Read, *Mr Secretary Cecil*, pp. 105, 114–6 for Cecil's contacts and scholarly pursuits under Mary.

[33] Jones, *Faith by Statute*, p. 36. On Bill, one of the leading Protestant clerics who had remained in England during Mary's reign, see Chapter 4.

perpetrated these attacks went unmolested. Further straws in the wind came on the eve of the Queen's coronation, when the City of London presented her with a triumphant entry with a tableau showing True Religion treading Ignorance and Superstition underfoot. London's susceptibility to advanced religious views could be taken for granted, but it is hardly possible that the Queen would have signalled such evident approval, lingering at every display, had she not wished to give the clearest signal that decisive religious change was in the offing.[34]

It was therefore hardly necessary for an organized exile pressure group to press for further change. The initiative came, as one would have expected, from the heart of government, and was essentially in tune with the wishes and aspirations of those returning from the continent. If returning exiles and divines had any doubt on the matter they should have been stilled by Lord Keeper Bacon's speech to the Commons at the opening of parliament in which he inveighed against idolatry, superstition and irreligion. And it was the government, of course, which brought forward the bills which would form the basis of the new religious settlement.[35] The long drawn-out process of enacting the reform statute in parliament certainly led to misgivings and on occasions a temporary collapse of confidence on the part of the regime's supporters; but generally the anxieties of Protestant commentators were focused on the obstructive potential of conservative forces.[36] It was not until later that they began to doubt their former friends in the regime.

Where then lay the seeds of later discords? The first signs that all would not go smoothly between the new regime and the supporters of the Protestant settlement came with the introduction, late in the session, of the government's Bill of Exchanges. Up until this point the Protestant churchmen had had little cause to argue with the personnel proposed to man the new Protestant church hierarchy. Cecil's lists of recommendations made shrewd use of the best available talent, drawing on capable and experienced hands from among both returning exiles and those who had remained in England.[37] Less satisfactory was the dawning realization that the new bishops might come to their

---

[34] *The Passage of Queen Elizabeth through the City of London*, in *Tudor Tracts, 1532–1588*, ed. A. F. Pollard (London, 1903), p. 376. S. Anglo, *Spectacle, Pageantry and Early Tudor Policy* (Oxford, 1969), pp. 344–59.

[35] Jones, *Faith by Statute*, pp. 83 ff.

[36] See, for instance, the letters of John Jewel and Sir Anthony Cooke to Peter Martyr: *Zurich Letters*, vol. 1, p. 10, vol. 2, pp. 13–14.

[37] See Chapter 4.

offices shorn of a large part of their income. Doubtless the regime's main motive in proposing a wholesale resumption of church property, from which bishops would then be granted sufficient if moderate income, was opportunistic – the new administration had already shown an alert sense of how the reversal in religion could be turned to financial advantage.[38] At the same time the proposed bill was also in tune with a more radical vision of reformed episcopacy, to which Cecil at least may have been attracted.[39] Be that as it may, the scheme caused considerable disquiet in the House of Commons, and foundered on the nominated bishops' adamant refusal to take up their new burdens on such penurious terms. But the conflict, though quickly resolved, was important, if only because it sowed seeds of distrust between the administration and their natural supporters at a time when other issues were bound to arise as the regime moved from the enactment to the implementation of the settlement.

This applies particularly to the troubles which blew up in the autumn over the Queen's insistence on retaining a crucifix on her private altar. In November 1559 leading churchmen observed with alarm that the Queen had installed on the altar of her private chapel a crucifix and two candles. They respectfully protested, and when this elicited no response, quietly had them removed. Returning to the Court the Queen promptly restored the crucifix and stubbornly ignored all further representations on the subject from friend and critic alike. Those who favour a view of Elizabeth's personal religious preference as essentially conservative and traditional have seized upon this incident as one pregnant with significance. And certainly the Queen's intransigence was both puzzling and wounding for those in the church who had previously had no reason to doubt that Elizabeth shared their agenda and inclinations. But was this as Christopher Haigh would have us believe, 'a hint to conservatives that she was really one of them'?[40]

In fact it seems more likely, given all that we now know about the settlement, that the Queen was making a rather different point, one more concerned with authority than theology. That the discord over ornaments grew from a relatively minor incident into a major source of division and discord is perhaps only possible to comprehend if one takes into account the potency of such Catholic survivals for Protestants in all the continental churches, and the prior history of disputes over clerical dress and ornamentation within the English church.

---

[38] Jones, *Faith by Statute*, pp. 160–1.
[39] See Chapter 1.
[40] Haigh, *English Reformations*, p. 244.

Although the issue of the Queen's chapel was in itself trivial, the underlying issue was of considerable importance, not least for its echoes of an earlier dispute which had similarly blown up over an apparently trivial cause in the reign of Edward VI, and yet had attained a degree of constitutional and ecclesiological significance. In 1550, it will be recalled, John Hooper, then the acknowledged leader of those pressing for a complete reform of the English church according to the pattern of the Swiss Reformed churches, had been appointed bishop of Gloucester. Hooper accepted the appointment, but refused to be consecrated in the prescribed vestments, which he and many others regarded as a popish remnant. At first Hooper seemed to have prevailed. The Privy Council accepted his arguments, and gave permission for a consecration which fell outside the prescriptions of the new ordinal. But this decision was reversed after a sustained lobbying of the council by other leading churchmen, notably Nicholas Ridley, who saw the dangers of such a disorderly procedure. The dispute became bitter; Hooper at first refused to conform to the council's new decision, and complied only after he had for a time been committed to the Fleet prison for his recalcitrance.[41]

Hooper's imprisonment and eventual conformity was one of the most sensational, and in many senses defining, moments of the Edwardian Reformation. The strong feelings expressed on both sides were indicative of the fundamental principles at stake: on Hooper's side the imperative need to proceed with all speed towards a complete Reformation, removing all vestige of popery from the English church; on the side of Ridley and Cranmer the right of the church in England to establish its own sense of what was seemly and proper in a Reformed church, particularly in matters which were not regarded as fundamentals of faith (*adiaphora*, in Philip Melanchthon's influential characterization). Different churchmen might take a different view as to what precisely constituted *adiaphora* – Ridley, for instance, was no less zealous in his determination to secure the removal of altars – but for those charged with the establishment of an orderly and uniform church settlement the necessity to establish due order was paramount.

The issues which stirred feelings so strongly in 1559 were in essence not much different. In her stubborn insistence on the crucifix in her chapel, as in the later ornaments rubric and in her infinitely more destructive insistence on uniformity in the wearing of prescribed

---

[41] Pettegree, *Foreign Protestant Communities*, pp. 30–45. J. H. Primus, *The Vestments Controversy* (Kampen, 1960), pp. 5–12.

vestments, Elizabeth was in effect reasserting the independence of the English church in matters of organization and ceremony; the points which had been so painfully established in 1550 in the conflict between Hooper and his later fellow martyrs Cranmer and Ridley. And there were, in 1559, good reasons for Elizabeth and her council to believe that these were principles which needed to be established again quickly and forcibly. In the making of the Elizabethan settlement, Elizabeth and her advisors had co-operated easily enough with those who had been abroad, and now returned to offer their services to the re-established church. Many were soon functioning as preachers or advisors, and the leading exiles were inevitably candidates for leading positions in the church as they became available. But the Queen would have been acutely aware that many of these men had enjoyed first-hand experience of the Swiss Reformed churches, whose organization and doctrine Hooper and his allies had sought to make prescriptive in the earlier reign. More so even than in the Edwardian period, the ecclesiology of the 'best Reformed churches' was to be a powerful and potentially irresistible model for England's reformers.

It still remains to be seen why Elizabeth should have seen this as in some way threatening. True, there is every indication that the Queen would have seen the integrity and independence of the English church as worthy of defence in its own right. But in the context of 1559 there was a particular issue which was, unluckily for the leaders of the Swiss churches, at the forefront of the Queen's concerns, and may have played a disproportionate part in the Queen's determination to keep them at arms' length. We see something of this if we observe Calvin's own reaction to the unfolding of events in England.

In company with all other continental Protestant reformers Calvin had welcomed Elizabeth's accession as a providential liberation from the Roman tyranny of her sister; one of a sequence of providential events in this remarkable year which undoubtedly proved God's favour for the Protestant cause.[42] And the Genevan reformer did not neglect necessary practical steps to encourage the new Queen along the paths of righteousness. On 15 January 1559 (the date of Elizabeth's coronation), he sent her a copy of his Isaiah commentary, together with a letter dedicating the work to her. Reminding her of the excellent work accomplished in the reign of her brother Edward VI, Calvin urged Elizabeth to raise up the poor persecuted flock of Christ, to receive back the exiles scattered abroad, and ultimately to

---

[42] Jean-Daniel Benoit, 'L'année 1559 dans les annales calviniennes', *Revue d'Histoire et de philosophie religieuses*, 39 (1959), pp. 103–16.

ensure that true religion was quickly restored to its former splendour.[43] Two weeks later a further letter to William Cecil, Elizabeth's new first minister, reinforced this message with a new admonition to unflinching pursuit of the paths of righteousness.[44]

Calvin was due a rude awakening. A second letter to Cecil later in this crucial spring period is very different in tone: at once aggrieved, defensive and conciliating. It is worth quoting here at some length, for it suggests quite clearly what was the main point of difficulty which militated against an easy acceptance of the Genevan reform in England:

> The messenger to whom I gave in charge my commentaries upon Isaiah to be presented to the most serene Queen brought me word that my homage was not kindly received by her Majesty, because she had been offended with me by reason of some writings published in this place. He also repeated to me, most illustrious sir, the substance of a conversation held by you, in which you seemed to me more severe than was consistent with your courtesy, especially when you had been already assured by my letter how much I promised myself from your regard towards me.[45]

The point at issue here, as Calvin's letter goes on to acknowledge, was John Knox's notorious *First Blast of the Trumpet against the Monstrous Regiment of Women*, published in Geneva, with ghastly and quite unprovidential timing, just before Elizabeth's accession.[46] Calvin denied having any knowledge of its publication, but for Elizabeth the name of the Genevan reformer was indelibly associated with this most unfortunate production of the Genevan press.

How damaging this might be for exponents of the Genevan reform, Calvin was immediately aware; hence his hurried (and rather unconvincing) attempts to distance himself from Knox's book. But the scale of Elizabeth's anger may be further illustrated if one introduces here the evidence of another contemporary source, a pair of letters buried away in the church archives at Emden and therefore not known to other scholars who have worked on the Elizabethan settlement.[47] The author, Anthony Ashe, was a former member of the Edwardian

---

[43] *Joannis Calvini commentarii in Isaiam prophetam* (Geneva, Jean Crespin, 1559). The dedication to Elizabeth is on sig. *1ʳ⁻ᵛ, and was clearly added at the last moment. Rodolphe Peter and Jean-François Gilmont (eds), *Bibliotheca Calviniana. II: 1555–1564* (Geneva, 1994), 59/1.

[44] CO, vol. 17, cols 418–20 (no. 3003). *Letters of John Calvin*, ed. Jules Bonnet (4 vols, Edinburgh and Philadelphia), vol. 4, no. 522.

[45] CO, vol. 17, cols 490–92 (no. 3036). *Letters of John Calvin*, vol. 4, no. 538.

[46] [Geneva, J. Poullain and A. Rebul], 1558. STC 15070.

[47] Emden, Archiv der Evangelische-Reformierte Kirche, rep. 320 varia, 14, 51. Published in English translation in this book as Appendix 5.

stranger church, and at the time of writing he had recently returned to London as the delegate of the refugee congregation in Emden, charged with negotiating the return of the church's privileges. The foreigners hoped this would be a fairly smooth process. After all, the foreign congregations had been established with a generous royal charter in 1550, and there was no reason to believe that the new government would be any less well disposed. But in fact Ashe's negotiations did not run smoothly. By May 1559 little had been achieved, and Ashe's gloomy foreboding for the prospects of the foreigners' churches was matched by a general sense that all was not well: the settlement appeared momentarily to be stalled on the brink of success, and conservatives had taken renewed courage. Furthermore, there were worrying indications that the Godly were drifting out of favour. The hoped-for preferment had not yet materialized, and John Scory had been charged to draw up a register of the returning or not yet returned exile scholars. Whether this was to assist Cecil in his attempts to allocate available preferment, or whether there was a more sinister motive, is not clear.

Ashe's inference (and in other respects he is a canny and experienced observer of the English scene) was that this sudden cooling of relations was the result of the publication of John Knox's book and its unhappy reception in England. 'They [the exiles] believe that it has been done on account of some who have written a book against the regiment of women, and that women have no place in the office of the magistrate.' More sensationally, Ashe goes on to report that Elizabeth had apparently been so exercised by the whole issue of Knox's book, that a house to house search had been ordered and three arrested. This active pursuit of Knox's work is not attested in any other source known to me, but it underscores just how damaging was the association with Knox for any of those closely connected with the Genevan reform. This is re-emphasized by Ashe's second, shorter, letter, written three days later, this time to Wouter Delenus, the aged former minister of the London foreign church now settled in Emden. By this time Ashe had had occasion to visit the prisoners in the Marshalsea, who had no doubt in their own minds that the cause of their discomfiture was, as they put it, 'the extreme predestinarians'.

Ashe's letter confirms what is in fact well known from other sources, that any association with Knox, and by association of guilt, Calvin, could be extremely dangerous in English government circles at this stage. Calvin, persisting in his efforts to guide and assist in the rebuilding of Protestantism in England, would soon despatch Nicolas des Gallars, one of his principal Genevan lieutenants, to take over the leadership of the London French church. But although welcomed by

Bishop Grindal, the church's new superintendent, Des Gallars was soon embroiled in a troublesome dispute with a portion of his own congregation which required the sympathetic intervention of the English authorities. Reporting these events to Calvin, Des Gallars was forced to admit, painfully but candidly, that any mention of the Genevan reformer's name was more likely to impede than to help his cause, so much had Calvin's perceived role in Knox's book been resented.[48]

Elizabeth's aversion to Knox proved to be deep-seated and enduring. Knox did not help his cause by being forthright enough to point out to the Queen her ambiguous conduct during Mary's reign. In contrast to the English exiles, who preferred to gloss Elizabeth's Nicodemism as a tale of divine deliverance, Knox, alone of the returning exiles, called the Queen bluntly to account for her conduct. Urging help for the Protestant rebels in Scotland, Knox presented this as a way of making amends for her conduct under Mary, when she did 'decline from God and bow till idolatrie'.[49] It is little wonder, in view of this, that Knox's presence among the Scottish delegates attempting to find the basis for English intervention in the Scottish insurrection was regarded on the English side as highly provocative. Negotiations made progress only when Knox was replaced in the Scottish delegation by professionals such as Maitland, who soon found common ground with William Cecil, himself fully committed to the maintenance of a Scottish Protestant party.[50] Cecil had been under no illusions how damaging had been Knox's participation in these negotiations. Confiding to a correspondent in October 1559 his fears at the lack of a suitable ambassador for the Lords of the Congregation, Cecil expressed the matter quite starkly: 'Of all others Knox's name, if it be not Goodman's, is most odious here.'[51] The coupling with Christopher Goodman, the author of *How Superior Powers ought to be Obeyed*, the other influential radical exile work justifying deposition of a legitimate monarch, is significant, reinforc-

---

[48] Pettegree, *Foreign Protestant Communities*, pp. 150–62. Patrick Collinson, *Archbishop Grindal* (London, 1979), p. 132.

[49] John Knox to Elizabeth, 20 July 1559. *Calendar of the State Papers relating to Scotland and to Mary, Queen of Scots, 1547–1603*, ed. J. Bain (Edinburgh), vol. 1, p. 222.

[50] Mark Loughlin, 'The Career of Maitland of Lethington, c. 1526–1573' (University of Edinburgh, PhD thesis, 1991). An important reinterpretation of Cecil's role in the decision to intervene in Scotland will be available in Stephen Alford's forthcoming St Andrews PhD thesis. C.f. Jane E. A. Dawson, 'William Cecil and the British dimension of early Elizabethan foreign policy', *History*, 74 (1989), pp. 196–216.

[51] *Calendar of State Papers Foreign, 1559–60*, p. 73.

ing the point that it was specifically Knox's *First Blast* which made him *persona non grata* at the English Court.

Goodman at least had the grace and political acumen to recognize the disastrous effect of his writing and offer a humiliating apology, but the damage was already done.[52] Goodman's intervention was if anything even more disastrous, for the development of his argument on the right of resistance had been accompanied by an emphatic denunciation of those Protestants who had connived at the accession of Mary. Furthermore, in the case of Goodman's *Superior Powers*, the connection with Geneva was all too obvious. Whereas Knox's *First Blast* had at least concealed its place of publication on the title page, Goodman's book was openly acknowledged as the work of Jean Crespin's Geneva press.[53] The text of the book had originally been a sermon preached in the English church in Geneva, and it was published with a commendatory preface by William Whittingham.

Not surprisingly, none of those connected with Goodman or Knox's book flourished in the changed climate of Elizabethan England. Goodman himself is thought to have visited England briefly in 1559, but he could not risk appearing in public and left England for Scotland very quickly.[54] It would be six years before he would judge it safe to return to his native land. William Whittingham's career was similarly blighted, and it needed the energetic patronage of the Earls of Warwick and Leicester to secure for him a post commensurate with his status as one of the leading authors and organizers of the exile. Even so it was not until 1563, after uncomfortable service as chaplain to the plague-ridden Newhaven expedition, that Whittingham was collated to the deanery of Durham.[55] The Geneva connection also helps explain the otherwise mysterious neglect of Miles Coverdale, most venerable and saintly of the returned exiles. Even the friendship of Cecil seems to have secured nothing for him, and it was not until 1564 that Grindal was able to promote him to a City living. It is unlikely, despite Coverdale's later association with the vestiarian

---

[52] Strype, *Annals*, vol. 1, pp. 184–5.

[53] Jean-François Gilmont, *Bibliographie des Editions de Jean Crespin, 1550–1572* (2 vols, Verviers, 1981), vol. 1, pp. 98–9 (no. 58/10). On Goodman's book, Jane E. A. Dawson, 'Resistance and Revolution in Sixteenth-Century Thought: the case of Christopher Goodman', in J. van den Berg and P. G. Hoftijzer (eds), *Church, Change and Revolution* (Leiden, 1991), pp. 69–79. Dan Danner, 'Christopher Goodman and the English Protestant Tradition of Civil Disobedience', *SCJ*, 8, no. 3 (1977), pp. 60–73.

[54] Danner, 'Goodman', p. 64. Jewel told Martyr in August 1559 that he had heard that Goodman was in England, 'but he dare not shew his face'. *Zurich Letters*, vol. 1, p. 21.

[55] *DNB*, vol. 21, pp. 150–3.

nonconformists, that he would have refused an earlier offer; his apparent destitution, dependent on the charity of the Duchess of Suffolk, makes this plain.[56] More significant is his clear association with Geneva, and in particular an inopportune act of kindness in acting as godfather to the child of John Knox.[57]

It says much for Calvin's towering status as writer and theologian that his reputation in England could recover from this unfortunate beginning. Although efforts on the part of the English Protestants to move England towards the adoption of forms of church organization derived directly from those of the Swiss never made progress, Calvin swiftly attained a pre-eminent position as a religious writer. A study of the numerous translations of his works during the Elizabethan period demonstrates that he was, uniquely, the theologian of choice of both radical critics of the church and members of the mainstream Protestant establishment.[58]

But the reverberations from the publication of Knox's book, the strength of which are fully revealed by Ashe's letters published here, were profound and far-reaching. These circumstances help explain why Calvin was never in a position to exercise a close influence over the shape of the religious settlement in 1559, notwithstanding the fact that in its essentials it adopted statements and positions that put it in the mainstream of the international Reformed movement. Even a natural friend and ally like William Cecil was forced to distance himself from the Genevan reformer, a tactical choice dictated by Calvin's perceived association with Knox rather than any lack of theological affinity, for the evidence is rather that at this stage of his career Cecil was a committed supporter of both mainstream Reformed theology and a forward, aggressive Protestant foreign policy.[59]

Yet thanks to Knox, Calvin's name swiftly became associated in England in 1559 with a complex of radical ideas potentially damaging to the health of an independent English church. Hence Ashe's remark that the prisoners in the Marshalsea blamed 'the extreme predestinarians' for their tribulation; and similarly an observation of

---

[56] *DNB*, vol. 4, p. 1293.

[57] Celia Hughes, 'Coverdale's *Alter Ego*', *Bulletin of the John Rylands Library*, 65 (1982), p. 120.

[58] Francis Higman, 'Calvin's Works in Translation', in Andrew Pettegree, Alastair Duke and Gillian Lewis (eds), *Calvinism in Europe, 1540–1620* (Cambridge, 1994), pp. 82–99.

[59] Cecil's library, catalogued in 1568, contained books by both Calvin and Beza. For this piece of information I am grateful to Stephen Alford, who is preparing an edited version of Cecil's library list for publication.

Thomas Early, vicar of St Mildred Bread Street, that the end of the Latin Mass 'was to all mens' comfort except a few of Calvin's church', and peevish obstinate papists.[60]

This association was misleading and unhelpful, because Calvin with other reformers rejoiced at what had been achieved in England, and continued to think well of England's new Protestant establishment. But the specific circumstances of these events occurring as and when they did certainly provides a key to understanding why Elizabeth, having set in train an essentially mainstream Protestant settlement, nevertheless made a point of insisting on a more conservative rubric on ceremonies and ecclesiastical accoutrements. For all that she was clearly committed to some sort of Protestant settlement in England, and surrounded herself with an intimate circle who shared this commitment, Elizabeth was also determined to preserve a certain independence and freedom of action in matters of church government. Her perverse insistence on items of ecclesiastical furniture which gave pain to her loyal Protestant admirers was one way of emphasizing that she would not be dictated to by the continental centres of reform; that their practice should not be prescriptive for England. The attempt to bully her into removing her crucifix set off unfortunate resonances of earlier quarrels, and the simultaneous furore over Knox's book underscored the potential peril of allowing Genevan dictation. For a brief but fatal moment Geneva was indelibly associated in the mind of the Queen with political subversion as well as religious prescription. The ornaments rubric was a useful weapon as a means of making the point that the English church would preserve its independence.

This was something which the Godly, consumed as they were by a zeal to complete a work so well begun, were not well equipped to grasp. Their failure to understand that the Queen's attachment to the ceremonial of which they disapproved was more symbolic than theological was in some senses a tragedy for the English church, since it drove them into a premature opposition and alienation. The Vestments Controversy of 1565–66 represented the first decisive clash, and once again divided those who strove for complete reformation against those who accepted, sometimes reluctantly, that the authorities had the right to establish uniform practice even when this led to the enforcement of distasteful measures.[61] Significantly the

---

[60] Norman Jones, *The Birth of the Elizabethan Age* (Oxford, 1993), p. 13.
[61] Patrick Collinson, *The Elizabethan Puritan Movement* (London, 1967), pp. 71–83.

upholders of the official view in this instance included several prominent former exiles, such as Grindal, now divided from their former friends who held to the straighter path. But their presence in the official church was a recognition that, for all its faults, the English church was a full member of the international Reformed community; and this was the essential, and inevitable, consequence of the Elizabethan settlement.

Conclusion: Marian Protestantism

Scholars writing on the English Reformation frequently comment on the difficult choices facing Englishmen and women in the mid-sixteenth century, confronted as they were with repeated and bewildering changes in religion. But England was not the only country where the religious and political perspective changed with astonishing rapidity at about this time.

The restoration of Mary in 1553 was a great success for Catholicism in Europe, but in fact the whole international perspective was generally more encouraging for followers of traditional religion in these years. The two other major powers of north-western Europe also had loyal Catholic regimes, with little sign of any Protestant resurgence. Indeed, in the case of both France and the Netherlands, Catholicism had begun to regain ground after early worrying flirtations with evangelism. In France, Henry II had now decisively abandoned that hint of equivocation which had always characterized the policy of his father Francis I, and which had given evangelicals (if not necessarily Protestants), cause for hope. His renewed campaign against dissent had been assisted by a reorganization of heresy prosecutions which considerably increased the pressure on evangelicals and claimed some prominent victims.[1] These were some of the toughest and most depressing years for French Protestantism. In the Netherlands, Charles V had never had any truck with Protestant dissent, an aversion he passed – along with one of the best organized and most persistent apparatuses of perescution anywhere in Europe – to his son Philip II in 1554–55.[2] All of this time the Council of Trent was gradually moving towards the doctrinal definitions of orthodox which gave cause for hope that the Protestant tide would finally be

---

[1] For instance the five students of Lyon, young protégés of Calvin travelling from Geneva arrested and executed in 1553. *Histoire Ecclésiastique*, ed. G. Baum (3 vols, Paris, 1883–89), vol. I, pp. 108–9. For the persecution apparatus under Henry II see Fred Baumgartner, *Henry II, King of France* (Durham, NC, 1988), pp. 128–32. Nathaniel Weiss, *La Chambre Ardente* (Paris, 1889).

[2] Alastair Duke, 'Building Heaven in Hell's Despite. The Early History of the Reformation in the Towns of the Low Countries', in his *Reformation and Revolt in the Low Countries* (London, 1990), pp. 71–100. Mia Rodriguez-Salgado, *The Changing Face of Empire. Charles V, Philip II and Habsburg Authority, 1551–1559* (Cambridge, 1988).

pushed back. For Catholics in Europe the early 1550s must have been years of optimism and hope.

And yet within a decade, all of this was radically altered. By 1562, the rise of Calvinism, coupled with calamitously ill-timed royal deaths, had plunged France into a religious crisis from which it only emerged two generations later, and then only at the price of conceding protected status to a hated Calvinist minority.[3] Four years after the onset of religious war in France, the Netherlands followed the same path, as the regency regime of Margaret of Parma finally lost control of a complex of political and religious difficulties which had been building up since 1559. Here the eventual resolution would be the establishment of a free Protestant state, a situation almost inconceivable to members of the small harassed Protestant communities of earlier decades.[4] Even leaving aside the changes in England and Scotland, and the confessional freedom now guaranteed to Germany's Lutherans under the Peace of Augsburg, the balance between the two religions in northern Europe had shifted decisively.

Reflecting on the speed with which apparently healthy Catholic societies could collapse – as in both these instances – should be a sobering experience for students of the English Reformation. For it is sometimes claimed, and perhaps too easily conceded by those wishing to give some ground to revisionist writers, that had Mary lived, England would almost certainly have remained a Catholic country. As usual the most succinct statement of this view is provided by Christopher Haigh: 'And then Mary made her only serious – her fatal – error: she died on 17 November 1558.'[5]

But would England have remained Catholic? The experience of both France and the Netherlands, where the central power remained unblinkingly loyal to Catholicism and yet could not prevent a major religious crisis, should caution against too glib an assumption of this sort. There is no assurance that Mary's regime would have ridden out the challenge posed by the rise of Calvinism in the early 1560s any better than these other regimes. It can of course be argued that the governments in both France and the Netherlands were in some sense

---

[3] The best survey is now Mack Holt, *The French Wars of Religion, 1562–1629* (Cambridge, 1995). On the settlement of religion in 1598, the Edict of Nantes, see also the perceptive remarks in Mark Greengrass, *France in the Age of Henry IV* (London, 1984), pp. 68–87.

[4] The growing crisis in the Netherlands is described in Geoffrey Parker, *The Dutch Revolt* (London, 1977). On the early Calvinist communities, Duke, *Reformation and Revolt in the Low Countries*, Andrew Pettegree, *Emden and the Dutch Revolt* (Oxford, 1992), Chapter 3.

[5] Christopher Haigh, *English Reformations*, p. 236.

CONCLUSION 153

structurally weak. Philip's regency government was hampered by his frequent absence and lack of sympathy for local concerns; the French monarchy plunged into crisis brought on by a sequence of young monarchs and competing Court factions.[6] But by the same token how secure could Mary's regime ever have been, dependent as it was on the health of an ageing, childless Queen for the continuance of Catholic rule? For all that Englishmen and women may have accepted the changes in religion sponsored by Mary with complacency, even contentment, it was asking too much that they should return immediately to patterns of devotion, and, perhaps more importantly, devotional giving, which had been interrupted by the reigns of Henry and Edward. A realistic sense that what had been abolished once could easily be swept away a second time, coupled with a cold assessment of the Queen's likely life expectancy, militated against the rapid restoration of the elaborate fabric of traditional worship. Faced with uncertainty, people reacted pragmatically. There is considerable evidence to confirm a sense that having been surprised once by the rapid dismantling of traditional religion under Henry VIII and Edward, lay people required more than royal assurances and statutory changes to reinvest substantially in the old ways.[7] The wills of London citizens dying during Mary's reign reveal hardly any return to the practice of leaving legacies for prayers for their departing souls, for all that purgatory was officially reinstated.[8] And while the capital threw itself with vigour into the restored religious processions, there was only one successful attempt to refound a religious fraternity, an institution which had played an absolutely critical role in the vitality of pre-Reformation religion.[9] The reason for this is not difficult to imagine. While processions were an eye-catching demonstration of loyalty to the present regime, the investment of large sums in restored religious institutions required a belief that this regime had a long-term future. The Marian administration could offer piety, goodwill, even religious zeal. But it could not offer that assurance of survival that was fundamental to consolidate the conservative reaction.

These remarks are offered not to reinstate a determinist 'Protestant' view of the English Reformation, but to challenge too easy an

---

[6] Though the conventional view that Philip neglected the Netherlands is challenged by Rodriguez-Salgado, *Changing Face of Empire*.

[7] Robert Whiting, *The Blind Devotion of the People* (Cambridge, 1988).

[8] Susan Brigden, *London and the Reformation* (Oxford, 1989), p. 581.

[9] Ibid., pp. 582–3. Eamon Duffy, *The Stripping of the Altars. Traditional Religion in England, 1400–1580* (New Haven and London, 1992); J. J. Scarisbrick, *The Reformation and the English People* (Oxford, 1984), pp. 19–39.

acceptance of the reverse case: that it was *only* accidents of succession that made England a Protestant country. For, as the studies here have attempted to show, Protestantism had by 1553 made sufficient progress in England to leave a robust residue; indeed, a far more robust and numerous remnant than has often been recognized.

In seeking to make this case I have argued here for a more generous and broader view of Protestant survival than has generally been the case. In particular I have made a plea for recognizing the importance in the wider scheme of things of Protestants who remained in England during Mary's reign, and yet despite their conforming remained essentially committed to the Gospel cause. It was an unheroic experience, but one vital for the future re-emergence of English Protestantism. And this Nicodemism seems to have been a widespread phenomenon, both numerically and socially. This latter point is important, because previous studies of Nicodemism, essentially dealing with France and Italy, have treated Nicodemism almost wholly in the context of groups within the social elite.[10] Men of this stamp had both a substantial social position which they were reluctant to put at risk and the education to intellectualize the decision to compromise; it must be said that their superior social station also gave them a degree of protection against denunciation to the authorities.[11] It was men of this type that continued the tradition of the *spirituali* in mid-century Italy, and they were the sort whom Calvin had in mind when he wrote his tracts denouncing evangelical conformists in the Paris humanist milieu of which he himself had been part.[12] But as we have seen from our analysis of the English evidence, a whole range of motives might persuade or compel well-meaning evangelical sympathizers to remain in England. By no means all of these were reducible to a pleasing philosophical system or even clearly articulated, and considerations of a more pragmatic nature weighed as heavily, perhaps more so, among members of the broad artisan strand in society as with scholars and intellectuals. As we have seen in Chapter 2, many of the members of the French church who decided to stay in England in 1553, despite an unambiguous commitment to their church, were relatively simple workmen. The records of the

---

[10] Delio Cantimori, 'Submission and Conformity: "Nicodemism" and the expectation of a conciliar solution to the religious question', in Eric Cochrane (ed.), *The Late Italian Renaissance, 1525–1630* (London, 1970), pp. 244–65. Perez Zagorin, *Ways of Lying. Dissimulation, Persecution and Conformity in Early Modern Europe* (Cambridge, MA, 1990).

[11] Equally in England: see below, n. 22.

[12] See Chapter 4.

London French church allow us to document their experience rather better than English contemporaries in the same social milieu, but much the same pressures and considerations would have applied in the indigenous population. We simply have no way of knowing how many of those who conformed in 1553 did so with reluctance.

But that they were sufficiently numerous is suggested by the incidents of iconoclasm perpetrated in the capital in the first months of Elizabeth's reign; once again London was giving at least the appearance of radicalism. And the broad importance of this phenomenon of Nicodemism can once again be suggested by the analogy of France and the Netherlands. The rapid exponential growth of evangelical communities in the years before their respective religious wars – in France in 1561, in the Netherlands in the spring of 1566 – is only really explicable if one accepts that there were many sympathetic to the evangelical cause who had not previously declared themselves, but now in the time of opportunity did so. The broad mass of the vastly increasing congregations was provided by enthusiasts in the artisan classes, but such secret sympathizers stretched up into the magistracy of Antwerp, or the judges of the Parlement of Paris.[13] The reluctance of such men to commit themselves had in previous years, as in English Protestantism, caused a degree of friction between themselves and those who did join the secret congregations.[14] But now in the Reformation's moment of opportunity they were quite indispensable.[15]

It is interesting to speculate how far the Marian regime was aware of this potential fifth column in England; or whether the more obvious Protestant irreconcilables, in England or on the continent, consumed the bulk of their energies. Certainly reading the contemporary documentation one has the impression that Protestant dissidence and survival, in one form or other, was and remained a leading preoccupation of the regime throughout Mary's reign. How effectively, in fact, did Mary's government deal with this Protestant

---

[13] L. van der Essen, 'Les progrès du luthéranisme et du calvinisme dans le monde commercial d'Anvers', *Vierteljahrschrift für Sozial- und Wirtschaftsgeschichte*, 12 (1914), pp. 152–234. Linda Taber, 'Royal Policy and Religious Dissent within the Parlement of Paris, 1559–1563' (Stanford University PhD thesis, 1982), pp. 43–5.

[14] For the disputes which divided the important Calvinist church in Antwerp on this issue see A. J. Jelsma, *Adriaan van Haemstede en Zijn Martelaarsboek* (The Hague, 1970), pp. 36–60.

[15] Mack Holt, *French Wars of Religion*, pp. 53–4, comments on the leading role played by members of the municipal magistracy in the internal coups which turned many towns over to Protestantism in 1562. C.f. Philip Benedict, *Rouen during the Wars of Religion* (Cambridge, 1981), p. 98.

residium? It is now customary to argue that the Marian government pursued a coherent and generally well-thought-out strategy for the restoration of Catholicism.[16] This was certainly not a passive or inert regime; a number of significant and well-targeted initiatives laid the basis for what might, in time, have been a well-rooted and broad-ranging renewal of Catholic culture, albeit of a rather more intellectual nature than was recognizable as the traditional religion of the pre-Reformation period. But allowing that this was the case (and that time was not on the regime's side) it is still arguable that this sureness of touch deserted Mary and her intimate advisors when it came to dealing with the problem of Protestantism. Mary personally had no empathetic understanding of dissent, and attempts to root out and obliterate surviving Protestant cells spoke more of the Queen's sense of personal outrage than a subtle strategy of control. Having secured the restoration of the Roman obedience, albeit without restoration of the alienated property of the church, the government turned its attention to the destruction on Protestantism, a campaign which swiftly moved beyond the restoration of the Mass to the destruction of any individuals who maintained a public profession of the new faith.

But this campaign, made possible by the restoration of the traditional statutes against heresy in Mary's second parliament of 1554, and pursued doggedly until the dying days of the reign, was conducted with a clumsy heavy-handedness which took little account of the experiences of other European regimes which had similarly endeavoured to eliminate dissent through a campaign of repression. Even accepting that it was inevitable that Mary's government would proceed to trials and executions of defiant evangelicals, the campaign which created the Marian martyrs took several false directions. Arguably the first was the initial strategy of attempting to terrorize evangelicals into conformity through the execution of a small number of high-profile preachers and bishops. In the first weeks of the burnings John Rogers, Rowland Taylor and John Hooper went to their deaths, to be followed in the summer by bishops Ridley and Latimer. But the execution of well-educated and respectable citizens by such a barbaric means was never popular, as Calvin found to his cost when the Genevan magistracy proceeded to the execution of Servetus in 1551. Even fellow Protestants who respected the rights of

---

[16] Rex Pogson, 'The Legacy of the Schism: Confusion, Continuity and Change in the Marian Clergy', in J. Loach and R. Tittler (eds), *The Mid-Tudor Polity, c. 1540–1560* (London, 1980), pp. 116–36.

the Genevan city state to defend its religious polity balked at the sight of the destruction of a gifted and broadly educated author, even one of admittedly scandalous and eccentric views, by such a painful method. Calvin clearly had some sense of this when he appealed for Servetus to be beheaded rather than burned alive.[17] The execution of Anne de Bourg, justice of the Paris Parlement, in France in 1559 created a similar sensation, for here again heresy proceedings were touching social groups who would normally have expected to be safe from such a fate.[18]

There is a sense that the social consensus that generally supported the execution of witches or heretics, at least when they were found among the categories of social outsiders who were the normal victims of the law in the early modern period, tended to collapse when those put to death were persons of high respect and generally acknowledged decency. When Bishop John Hooper was returned to his diocesan city of Gloucester to be put to death in February 1555 he was met outside the gates of the city by a large and sympathetic crowd. They were not there to demonstrate their approval of this particular aspect of Marian policy. Even Charles V, a diligent pursuer of heretics, but of all sixteenth-century rulers perhaps the one with the greatest sense of how to court popular approval without compromising his regality, recognized the folly of burning respected local figures in their communities, not least because town regimes would seldom deliver up popular preachers or prominent local laymen to the heresy administration.[19] In consequence, after the very first years, most victims of the persecution in the Netherlands were comparatively humble folk.

A second crucial error was to proceed with the execution of Thomas Cranmer even after he had signalled his willingness to recant. This was an act of revenge rather than policy, and it backfired badly when Cranmer summoned the courage to repudiate his recantation and make a dramatic demonstration of his Protestant faith. The

---

[17] On the Servetus affair Alister McGrath, *A Life of John Calvin* (Oxford, 1990), pp. 114–20; William Naphy, *Calvin and the Consolidation of the Genevan Reformation* (Manchester, 1994), pp. 182–5.

[18] On de Bourg see now Tabor, 'Royal Policy'; Nancy Roelker, *One King, One Faith: the Parlement of Paris and the Religious Reformations of the Sixteenth Century* (Berkeley, 1995). Jean Crespin, *Histoire des vrais tesmoins de la Verité de l'evangile* (Geneva, 1570), pp. 525–36. Significantly of the five councillors arrested in the parlement only de Bourg was ultimately condemned, and he positively courted martyrdom.

[19] James D. Tracy, *Holland under Habsburg Rule, 1506–1566* (Berkeley, 1990), pp. 147–75.

decision to proceed with his execution thus provided English Protestantism with one of its most dramatic and moving martyr stories, and it deprived the regime of an enormously prestigious propaganda success.[20] Cranmer was the last major victim of the campaign of burnings. Hereafter the continuing pursuit of heresy resolved itself into a series of investigations, delations and trials at a local level, a context which provided plentiful opportunity for acts of vengeance and the settling of old scores.[21] But on the whole, in the social context of the English local community, the victims of this phase of the persecution were more likely to be relatively humble people, since the well connected could generally rely on a degree of protection contingent on their social status.[22] Even allowing that this phase of the persecution was not closely directed from the centre, these circumstances did provide the regime with one further opportunity which they manifestly failed to seize. For it was in the nature of things that these humbler folk, whose unwisely and inarticulately expressed views had brought them unluckily to the attention of the local magistrates, would include many whose beliefs strayed far from the orthodox.[23] Other continental regimes experienced in the pursuit of heresy exploited this opportunity quite cannily. For mainstream Protestants any association with the outer reaches of dissent was deeply offensive and embarrassing, so the Netherlands regime of Charles V was at some pains to label any of its victims as anabaptists, to the acute irritation of those members of mainstream reform groups who fell foul of the heresy laws. This tactic extended as far as executing anabaptists and Calvinists in batches together – even in the same fire.[24] The English government hardly seemed to have realized the propaganda potential of this strategy. Perhaps any dissent was so deeply abhorrent, that shades of perdition were hardly a concern; in

---

[20] Though the regime did still attempt to exploit his recantations through wide publication. See Jennifer Loach, 'The Marian establishment and the Printing Press', *EHR*, 101 (1986), pp. 135–48.

[21] P. E. Hughes, *The Reformation in England* (3 vols, London, 1954), vol. II, pp. 264–74. Diarmaid MacCulloch, *Suffolk and the Tudors: politics and religion in an English County, 1500–1600* (Oxford, 1986), pp. 172–3.

[22] In Norwich, a diocese with pockets of conspicuous support for Protestantism, not a single gentleman or merchant was arraigned for heresy during Mary's reign. Ralph Houlbrooke, *Church Courts and the People during the English Reformation, 1520–1570* (Oxford, 1979), p. 236. C.f. James Oxley, *The Reformation in Essex to the death of Mary* (Manchester, 1965), pp. 221–37.

[23] Brigden, *London and the Reformation*, pp. 614–6.

[24] Pettegree, *Emden and the Dutch Revolt*, p. 237.

any case the failure to exploit divisions within Protestantism was a critical lost opportunity.

The authorities' negligence in this regard would in turn give John Foxe – himself an able and nimble propagandist – the opportunity to present the English martyrs as if they were one group united by a holy witness to the truth, even if this meant concealing some of the more troubling views expressed during their interrogations. The extent of Foxe's selectivity in this regard is only now becoming apparent as scholars trawl more systematically the surviving manuscript sources of the *Acts and Monuments*. What they reveal is that Foxe, while a compiler and researcher of extraordinary diligence, was also concerned to a very significant degree to preserve a façade of Protestant unity among those who suffered for the faith under Mary.[25] Examination records, personal testimonies and oral evidence were all carefully edited to ensure that the sympathies of Foxe's readers were not jeopardized by expressions of troubling unorthodoxy.[26] Yet even before Foxe's sleight of hand had been demonstrated by archival investigation, the sheer implausibility that the doctrinal coherence of Edwardian Protestantism would survive the experience of disintegration characteristic of any period of persecution would be immediately apparent to any scholar of comparative European countries. In both France and the Netherlands the removal of the first generation of educated leadership resulting from a period of persecution opened the way for a comparative doctrinal anarchy which in both cases left a troubled and unsettling legacy for the later Calvinist churches.[27] The exiled leadership of English Protestantism struggled mightily to preserve the doctrinal coherence of a movement where local leadership now often fell into relatively untutored lay hands.[28] Foxe's artistry has to some degree concealed the full extent to which Elizabethan

---

[25] Particularly remarkable is the fact that Foxe virtually ignores the famous disputes between different evangelical groups in the London prisons, although these are well documented from other sources. Andrew Penny, *Freewill or Predestination. The Battle over Saving Grace in Mid-Tudor England* (Woodbridge, 1990).

[26] A strategy exposed by Patrick Collinson, 'Truth and Legend: the Veracity of John Foxe's Book of Martyrs', in A. C. Duke and C. A. Tamse (eds), *Clio's Mirror: historiography in Britain and the Netherlands* (Zutphen, 1985), pp. 31–54. C.f. Susan Wabuda, 'Henry Bull, Miles Coverdale, and the making of Foxe's *Book of Martyrs*', in Diana Wood (ed.), *Martyrs and Martyrologies* (Studies in Church History, 30, 1993), pp. 245–58. T. Freeman, 'Notes on a source for John Foxe's account of the Marian persecution in Kent and Sussex', *Historical Research*, 67 (1994), pp. 203–11.

[27] David Nichols, 'The Nature of popular heresy in France', *HJ*, 26 (183), pp. 261–75. Alastair Duke, *Reformation and Revolt in the Low Countries*.

[28] Oxley, *Reformation in Essex*, pp. 210–37.

nonconformity was incubated in the shadowy conventicles where artisan leaders held sway.[29]

But this was for the future. In the meantime Foxe could seize, eagerly and effectively, on the salient truth that simple people were being put to death for a courageous affirmation of evangelical belief, and sealing thereby the identification of Protestantism with English nationhood to which his literary masterpiece would contribute so largely. And even at the time, the strategic merit of the government's pursuit of heresy by these methods was increasingly questionable. For Mary and Pole there seemed little alternative but to root out religious dissent by whatever means; but on a wider European front it was clear that opinion was now turning against the execution even of the more humble folk who were the characteristic victims of heresy prosecutions. Here the climate of opinion had changed significantly since the first evangelical decades. The regime in the Netherlands had executed several hundred anabaptists at the high point of its campaign against radical dissent in the 1530s, a campaign fuelled by a general abhorrence of the anabaptist kingdom of Münster. But by the 1550s European regimes were beginning to move away from such wholesale persecution, not least because local opinion was increasingly hostile to executions for dissident religious beliefs. In Rotterdam in 1558 the city authorities proceeded with the execution of two anabaptists, only to have the occasion degenerate into chaos when a sympathetic crowd tried to rescue the victims from the stake. Although in no way sympathetic to heresy the town authorities of Rotterdam never again attempted to pursue a heretic to destruction in the period before the Dutch revolt.[30] Even at the height of Henry II's campaign to snuff out the incipient Calvinist communities in France,

---

[29] Brigden, *London and the Reformation*, p. 615 for five deeply unorthodox victims of the persecution whom Foxe simply omitted. J. W. Martin, 'The Protestant Underground Congregations of Mary's Reign', in his *Religious Radicals in Tudor England* (London, 1989), pp. 124–46. Even while now recognizing Foxe's selectivity in his use of sources, Foxe scholarship has still to recognize the extent to which his accounts were elaborated and embroidered according to established prototypes and martyr paradigms. For comment on these issues in relation to the major continental martyrologists see David Watson, 'Jean Crespin and the writing of history in the French Reformation' and Andrew Pettegree, 'Adriaan van Haemstede: the heretic as historian', in Bruce Gordon (ed.), *Protestant History and Identity in Sixteenth-Century Europe* (St Andrews Studies in Reformation History, 3, 1996). For further comment on this issue see my 'Haemstede and Foxe', forthcoming in David Loades (ed.), *John Foxe and the English Reformation* (St Andrews Studies in Reformation History, 1996).

[30] H. ten Boom, *De Reformatie in Rotterdam, 1530–1585* (The Hague, 1987), pp. 54–5. Tracy, *Holland under Habsburg Rule*, pp. 160–75.

a survey of opinion in the Parlement of Paris revealed considerable opposition to the *principle* of capital punishment for heresy.[31]

In contrast the English government in 1555 embarked on a campaign of persecution which was by contemporary European standards now both intense and somewhat anachronistic. Three hundred victims in four years was a very high number even by the standards of famous persecuting regimes on the continent: the infamous persecuting chamber of the Paris Parlement initiated by Henry II to make heresy trials more effective in France, the *Chambre Ardente*, for instance, passed only 37 capital sentences in the period 1547–1551.[32] The famous and scandalous incident at the Rue St Jacques in 1557, where a Calvinist service in Paris was surprised and 130 worshippers arrested, resulted in only eight executions, and none of these touched the higher reaches of Parisian society.[33]

By 1558 the English government, doggedly pursuing its campaign of conversion by execution, would have seemed decidedly old-fashioned as well as brutal. In London and other southern centres of heresy the authorities began to look increasingly harassed and fraught as executions became the occasions for public expressions of support for the victims: an alarming and potentially extremely dangerous manifestation in an age when the police powers available to the state were extremely limited.[34] By 1557 England was experiencing all the manifestations which in other countries would indicate that the social consensus underpinning support for the regime's religious policies was dangerously weak: open dissent at the place of execution, the need for heavily armed guards to prevent tumult and protect those charged with executing the sentence, even daring prison raids to liberate imprisoned evangelicals.[35]

The contrast here between the beginning and end of the reign was quite stark. Some of the early victims of the heresy campaign do not seem to have attracted much sympathy. John Bland, pastor of Adi-

---

[31] Taber, 'Royal Policy', pp. 49–62.

[32] Weiss, *Chambre Ardente*; David Watson, 'The Chambre Ardente and its portrayal in the Martyrology of Jean Crespin, 1547–1550', unpub. paper, St Andrews Reformation Studies Institute, 8 Dec 1994.

[33] Jean Crespin, *Histoire des Martyrs*, ed. D. Benoit and M. Lelievre (3 vols, Toulouse, 1885–9), vol. 2, pp. 563–70. Taber, 'Royal Policy', pp. 26–31.

[34] Brigden, *London and the Reformation*, p. 605. Orders issued to restrict the numbers who attended the burnings in 1556 and 1557 were an implicit recognition that the policy no longer commanded public support. *Acts of the Privy Council of England*, ed. J. R. Dasent (11 vols, London, 1890–93), vol. 5, p. 224.

[35] Brigden, *London and the Reformation*, p. 605. For an example of a demonstration at the place of execution, Foxe, *Acts and Monuments*, vol. 8, p. 559.

sham, was a man who might be said to have quite consciously courted martyrdom, provoking the conservatives in his parish by taking down the rood screen and re-erecting a communion table in defiance of the Queen's command. In this case it was enraged parishioners who denounced Bland to the heresy commissioners and ensured his arrest.[36] Here it was clearly the minister who was the disturber of the peace. But by 1557–58 it seems to have been the local officials who officiously sought out surreptitious religious dissidents who were regarded as the greater threat to communal harmony. A fine illustration of this changing sentiment is provided by a remarkable act of communal solidarity in the Suffolk village of Layfield, in protest at the execution of John Noyes. Noyes, a local man, was returned from the county prison in Eye to be burned in his home village, but when the sheriff's officer went in search of flame to kindle the pyre they found that every household in the village had extinguished their fire.[37] Gestures of this sort could not in themselves put an end to the policy of burnings; but they could reinforce a sense that the local officials who zealously sought out heretics could no longer expect the support from within the community which was necessary for the execution of justice in the early modern period. In many places their activities left a legacy of bitterness which lasted long into Elizabeth's reign.[38]

In pursuing its campaign against heresy with such stubborn determination the Marian regime signally failed to profit by the advice of those who had experienced the campaign against heresy on the continent at first hand. Significantly Philip II's Spanish advisors were among those who urged caution in the policy of executions.[39] When Mary proceeded nonetheless Philip's reward was to have his Spanish coterie demonized as the evil spirit behind what Foxe would effectively characterize as a foreign tradition of vengeance and retribution; a poor reward for the characteristically prudent King.

If the persecution of Protestants may in this way be characterized as clumsy and ill-thought-out, what then was the best strategy for dealing with heresy? Perhaps it was the policy which the regime did in fact pursue simultaneously with the persecution, of attempting to

---

[36] Foxe, *Acts and Monuments*, vol. 7, pp. 287–306.
[37] Ibid., vol. 8, pp. 424–7. Hughes, *Reformation in England*, vol. 2, pp. 272–3.
[38] Patrick Collinson, 'Cranbrook and the Fletchers', in Peter Newman Brooks (ed.), *Reformation Principle and Practice* (London, 1980), pp. 179 ff. MacCulloch, *Suffolk and the Tudors*, pp. 190–1.
[39] David Loades, 'Philip II and the government of England', in Loades, Scarisbrick and Cross (eds), *Law and Government under the Tudors* (Cambridge, 1988), pp. 177–94. Philip's confessor, Alphonsus, actually preached against the burnings. Brigden, *London and the Reformation*, p. 607.

isolate the leaders of English Protestantism, particularly those who had gone abroad, from their potential followers. This was a tried and tested strategy for countries which were faced by the threat posed by communities of evangelicals in exile in the middle decades of the century; the authorities in both France and the Netherlands gave a great deal of attention both to restricting the flow of literature from the exile centres back into their lands, and to cutting the exiles off from their potential sources of support and finance at home.[40]

But even in these basic tasks the Marian regime experienced significant reverses. The failure to pass into law a bill confiscating exile property emasculated the campaign against the exiles, and the lines of communication between the exiles and their friends at home continued to function effectively.[41] One may legitimately ask why, after such a promising beginning, the Marian regime had to suffer these humiliations (for such they must have been in the context of a culture where parliament seldom pressed opposition to the point of causing government legislation to fall).[42] The general trend of comment on the Marian regime in recent years has been to suggest that it continued robust and vibrant, at least until the major influenza epidemic of 1557–58 and the loss of Calais caused a serious lowering of morale. But the regime's religious policy had suffered serious blows even before this. The first was the decision, early in the reign, not to execute Elizabeth in the aftermath of Wyatt's rebellion. It was certainly Elizabeth's moment of greatest peril, and arguably the new regime's greatest strategic mistake. For, following the abandonment of any official hope that the Queen would conceive a child some time in 1556, Elizabeth's survival created an automatic – and Protestant – reversionary interest: perhaps the greatest single barrier to the long-term acceptance of the return to Catholicism. With the options for succession so limited and so obvious the abandonment of the Queen's official pregnancy was an ominous augury for the future; for those who wished to read such signs, it was a public recognition that Mary's regime was living on borrowed time.

Certainly in respect of the campaign against heretical books there is a clear sense of diminished vitality as the reign wears on. The failure to stem the flow of heretical literature was probably one of the Marian regime's most damaging reverses; but the necessity for such

---

[40] See here the text of the Edict of Chateaubriand, 1551, in E. and E. Haag, *La France Protestante. Pièces Justificatives* (rep. edn, Geneva, 1966), pp. 17–29.
[41] Indicated, for instance, by the correspondence between Cecil and Sir Anthony Cooke. See Chapter 4.
[42] Jennifer Loach, *Parliament under the Tudors* (Oxford, 1991).

controls was certainly recognized. Although Protestant books seem to have been freely available in the capital for most of the first year of the reign,[43] in October 1554 the government did take decisive measures to bring this to an end. In the space of a fortnight over 60 persons involved in the trade in Protestant books were arrested, including John Daye, who had boldly continued to print Protestant books in England, albeit under a pseudonym.[44] The following year a proclamation banned the reading or possession of books by a long list of Protestant authors and made provision for the inspection of booksellers' stocks for forbidden titles.[45] These measures seem to have had some immediate effect. The leading Protestant printers of Edward's reign either ceased trading or took refuge abroad, and little overtly Protestant material was printed in England for the rest of Mary's reign.[46] But this pressure was not effectively sustained. Protestant books continued to be almost freely available, smuggled in from abroad and distributed among the underground Protestant networks.[47] Perhaps there was never any real chance of cutting off the flow of heretical literature through ports as busy as those of London and East Anglia. Even Protestants held in the London prisons seem to have had free access to the latest products of the Protestant exile presses.[48] And those caught in possession of heretical literature were dealt with remarkably leniently. Possession of forbidden books only became a capital crime by a proclamation of June 1558, in the dog days of the regime.[49] The contrast with Charles V's Netherlands regime, where the possession of heretical books had been treated as *prima facie* evidence of heresy since the first decade of the Reformation, is instructive.[50]

---

[43] John N. King, 'The Account Book of a Marian Bookseller, 1553–4', *British Library Journal*, 13 (1987), pp. 33–57.

[44] Foxe, *Acts and Monuments*, vol. 6, p. 561. L. P. Fairfield, 'The mysterious press of "Michael Wood" (1553–1554)', *The Library*, 5th ser., 27 (1972), pp. 220–32.

[45] *Tudor Royal Proclamations*, ed. P. L. Hughes and J. F. Larkin (3 vols, New Haven, 1964–69), vol. 2, pp. 57–60. Foxe, *Acts and Monuments*, vol. 7, p. 128.

[46] Daye, Whitchurch and Grafton all went into virtual retirement; printers who joined the exile included Singleton, as well as the Dutchmen Hill, Mierdman and van der Erve.

[47] Philippa Tudor, 'Protestant Books in London in Mary Tudor's reign', *London Journal*, 15 (1990), pp. 19–28.

[48] Brigden, *London and the Reformation*, p. 603.

[49] D. M. Loades, *The Oxford Martyrs* (London, 1970), pp. 239–40.

[50] *Corpus documentorum inquisitionis haeteticae pravatatis Neelandicae*, ed. P. Fredericq (5 vols, Ghent and the Hague, 1889–1902), vol. 5, pp. 1–5. It is instructive also to contrast the fate of printers arrested for printing heretical books. In the Netherlands several were executed; John Daye was merely released on caution.

This was all the more extraordinary because Mary's government clearly did understand the need to take effective action to combat the effect of Protestant propaganda. Jennifer Loach has demonstrated that the Marian government devoted considerable attention to publicizing its actions abroad, sponsoring Latin and foreign vernacular accounts of several of the key events which marked England's return to the Catholic fold.[51] But this attempt to influence opinion at home and abroad seems to have been fitful, and was barely sustained. Philippa Tudor points out the surprising absence of any attempt to put pressure on friendly regimes on the continent to limit the production of heretical English literature, as had been very successfully orchestrated in the later years of Henry VIII's reign.[52] The overall result was that English Protestants working from the exile towns, unmolested by English government agents and subject only to the normal domestic regulations of their hosts, managed to out-produce the Catholic presses active in England in both Latin and vernacular works. With much of the established talent of the London printing trade still at their disposal, and access to the superior European book distribution network, this is perhaps less surprising that it might appear. But it is still a considerable tribute to the evangelical faith in the power of the printed word, and to the irrepressible optimism of the exiles themselves.

In all the circumstances the achievement of Mary and her government was extraordinary. The attention they devoted to the restoration of Catholicism bore prolific fruit: a fine bench of bishops, some modest repair of parish incomes, a renewal of vocations to the priesthood, the restoration of some of the apparatus of traditional worship. But any attempts at restoration were forced to confront the iron law of nature as it applied to religious change: that it was easier to destroy than to rebuild a culture which depended so much on richness of fabric and church decoration. This was a major advantage of Protestantism, which went a long way to compensate for the fact that those who pursued evangelical change were seldom more than small minorities. The sheer destructiveness of the first stages of evangelical reform was in fact one of its most potent weapons.

This is the context in which one should really try to understand Protestant iconoclasm. This is perhaps one of the hardest aspects for

---

[51] Jennifer Loach, 'The Marian Establishment and the Printing Press', *EHR*, 101 (1986), pp. 135–48.
[52] Tudor, 'Protestant Books', p. 20.

even sympathetic analysts of sixteenth-century reform to observe with charity, sensitive as we are to the great aesthetic loss as a result of the assault on images, altars and church decoration.[53] But for Protestants the destruction of idolatry was the primary imperative in the creation of Godly worship; it was, furthermore, an initiative that should *precede* the reorganization of worship and liturgy. This was the order prescribed in the Old Testament, where Godly kings are applauded mostly for their assaults on the altars of Baal; and we now know how closely English Protestants allowed themselves to be tutored by these biblical prototypes in their agenda of reform.[54] In this sense iconoclasm was not sheer vandalism – the spirit in which it is approached by some recent historians – but a form of worship. And it was immensely effective as a means of forcing the issue in towns or countries hesitating on the brink of Reformation.[55]

This sense that even parts of English Protestant culture that we find uncongenial proceeded to a clearly biblical prototype should remind us that English Protestantism, though young, was by the middle decades of the century both articulate and intellectually mature. The astonishing achievement of the exile writers, both in Latin and the vernacular, is celebrated in this volume; the Latin achievement certainly demands more serious attention, of the sort that the loyal and effective Catholic writings of the earlier decades of the reign of Henry VIII have now begun to receive.[56] But if the exiles were intellectually sophisticated they were also opinionated and quarrelsome; the years abroad were hardly happy ones, as almost all of their congregations were at some time riven by dissent. Perhaps the Elizabethan regime was aware of this as it declined to have its church order thrust into a rigidly Swiss mould in 1559. Be that as it may, the exiles and those who had remained behind during Mary's reign collaborated quite

---

[53] Even Margaret Aston, *England's Iconoclasts* (Oxford, 1988), never really conquers her distaste for the destructive nature of the attack on church art.

[54] Christopher Bradshaw, 'David or Josiah? Old Testament Kings as exemplars in Edwardian Religious Polemic', in Bruce Gordon (ed.), *Protestant History and Identity in Sixteenth-Century Europe* (St Andrews Studies in Reformation History 3, 1996).

[55] From the 1520s onwards, iconoclasm remained a standard Protestant tactic for forcing the issue in towns and countries hesitating on the brink of decisive religious change. For Switzerland, see Lee Parmer Wandel, *Voracious Idols and Violent Hands. Iconoclasm in Reformation Zurich, Strasbourg and Basel* (Cambridge, 1995). On France and the Netherlands, Pettegree, *Emden and the Dutch Revolt*, pp. 115–32, 197. Benedict, *Rouen*, p. 98. Denis Crouzet, *Les guerriers de Dieu: La violence au temps des troubles de religion, vers 1525–vers 1610* (2 vols, Paris, 1990).

[56] See here the fine book of Richard Rex, *The Theology of John Fisher* (Cambridge, 1991).

easily in the formation of the Elizabethan settlement. And they created a church which was in some respects a celebration of the best of mid-Tudor English Protestantism – from its growing to maturity under Edward VI to its defiant survival under Mary.

APPENDIX ONE

Books Published for the English Exile Community in Emden, 1554–1558

Author	Title	STC	Date
John a Lasco	*Confessio*		*c.*1554
John Knox	*Faithful Admonition*	15069	1554
William Turner	*Hunting of the Romish Fox*	24356	*c.*1554
William Turner	*New Book of Spiritual Physic*	24361	1555
Girolamo Savonarola	*Meditation on 80th Psalm*	21799.2	*c.*1555
Ulrich Zwingli trans. Thomas Cottisford	*Confession of Faith*	26140	1555
Marten Micron trans. Thomas Cottisford	*Antitheses*		*c.*1555
Marten Micron trans. Thomas Cottisford	*Short and Faithful Instruction*	17864	*c.*1555
John Scory	*Epistle unto the Faithful*	21854	1555
John Olde	*Acquittal of Edward VI*	18797	1555
Anonymous	*A Warning for England*	11024	1555
Nicholas Ridley	*Brief Declaration*	21046	1555
John a Lasco	*Forma ac Ratio*	16571	1555
John Scory	*Two books of St Augustine*	921	1556
Thomas Cranmer	*Copy of certain letters*	5999	1556
John Olde	*Confession of Belief*	18798	1556
Michael Throckmorton	*Witty Letter*	15693	1556
John Scory	*Works of Ciprian*	6152	1556
Nicholas Ridley ed. John Olde	*Comfortable dialogues*	21047.3	1556

Rudolf Gualter trans. John Olde	*Antichrist*	25009	1556
John a Lasco	*Toute la Forme et manière*	16574	1556
Robert Watson	*Aetiologia*	25111	1556
John Philpot	*Examination*	19892	1557
John Philpot	*Apology*	19892	1557
Anonymous	*Description of Antichrist*	673	1557
Thomas Cranmer	*Defensio Doctrinae*	6005	1557
Thomas Cranmer	*Defensio Doctrinae*	6005(var)	1557
Marten Micron	*Apologeticum Scriptorum*		1557

APPENDIX TWO

English and Scottish Newcomers Enrolled as Citizens of Emden, 1554–1558

Source: Emden Stadtarchiv, Bürgerbücher, vols 1 & 2.

Those names which also appear in Garrett's *Marian Exiles* are printed in bold type.

Vol. 1
fol. 99ᵛ   (20 June 1554)
               Dr Joannes Scory
               David Sympson
               John Willock
               Robertus Roningh
               Balfredus Josus

Vol. 2
fol. 6ʳ   (11 January 1555)
               Christopher Colman
fol. 12ʳ   (5 November 1555)
               Henrik Jacobson
               Nicholas Burthaen[1]
               Thomas Young
               Stephen Green
fol. 14ᵛ   (6 May 1556)
               John Bruem
               Willem Ratheby
               George Constantinus
               John Rowe
               John Olde
               John Hill
               William Haell
fol. 16ᵛ   (19 January 1557)
               Robert Anderson

---

[1] Nicholas Bullingham?

fol. 21ᵛ	(19 January 1557)
	John Applebens
fol. 25ᵛ	(8 March 1558)
	Edmund Willum
	Thomas Keck
	Michael Merrill
	Thomas Bind
	Robert Miller
fol. 30ʳ	(9 June 1558)
	Edward Brokelsbeij
	John Dowley
	Humphrey Palmer
	John Payne[2]
	Thomas Dawberry
	Benedict Alread
	Marmaduke Fulnebey
fol. 30ᵛ	Thomas Heenwch
	William Howe
fol. 32ᵛ	(6 July 1558)
	Christopher Dickenson
fol. 33ʳ	(18 August 1558)
	Thomas Thomason

---

[2] Possibly identical with the John Payne presented as having departed for religion in the Essex inquisition of 1556. David Loades, 'The Essex Inquisition of 1556', *BIHR*, 35 (1962), p. 96.

APPENDIX THREE

John Dowley's Submission to the French and Dutch Churches

Emden, Archiv der Evangelische-Reformierte Kirche, Rep. 320A, no. 6. (Translation by William Naphy.)

My most respected and charitable fathers and brothers in the Lord. May the grace and peace of Jesus Christ be with you.

    I assume that you are aware of the importance of this matter as you have already been told the beginning and progress of our controversy. I am a brother of the English church at Emden. I heard we were going to abandon the normal place for our prayers and assemblies. We had held our prayers and assemblies in a certain house which was very near to a house contaminated by plague. I and a few others were offended that we would abandon our usual place for prayers and assemblies to God in this manner because of a visitation from God.[1] With a gentle disposition and meek spirit, I left my house and met alone with our pastor. I hoped to explain to him why many of us were upset that we were to abandon our usual place for praying and meeting. He said he could show us from God's Word and common sense, why we ought to do this. He began to make his case but his arguments were less than convincing. However, I accepted them as satisfactory as I am a lover of quiet. I did ask, as one ought, that he would satisfy the church, as it was the Lord's day. We met at our usual place for prayers and assembly. While in the assembly he tried to convince everyone. Those who were still not satisfied, he admonished to see him there or at home, after the service. I remained there with a few others after the greater part of the congregation had left. I asked him whether those who struggled with the plague ought to be avoided more than lepers. (He had said this during the assembly.) And, as the Israelites were warned to expel the lepers from the camp, and the same was commanded by God to us Christians, as he had also said in the assembly, why it was that the magistrates had not expelled those persons affected with plague from the city as if they were lepers? He

---

[1] This reflected the widespread perception in the sixteenth century of plague as a divine scourge. In Dutch, it was commonly known as God's gift, *De gave Gods*. See Nordegraaf and Valk, *De Gave Gods*.

answered that the magistrates (so he claimed) had ordered the sign 'tau' to be placed over the doors of plague-ridden homes as a warning to everyone. Next, I asked, after I had sought permission to ask, whether the pastor was obliged to visit his sick sheep if he knew they were plague victims? He responded that if it were necessary and they were *in extremis* because of the sickness. I added, 'I believe, as my conscience directs, that this is most necessary as the plague rages in the city and Christ's flock was smitten with the sickness.' Meanwhile another brother asked him politely (?) whether we would have the usual prayers on Wednesday and Friday of that week. He said, in front of me, that we would not. We left there assuming we would not meet again until the following Lord's day. In the afternoon, I visited a sick brother, whose wife and servant were also sick. After a greeting, he indicated that he had heard that we would not have prayers or assembly until the following Lord's day. I said that I had heard that same thing that day when the pastor said to a certain brother that we would not have prayers that week. We both lamented the sad state of the church. He charged me sternly to come along to his house the next day. Giving thanks to him and his family, I agreed to visit the next day. That day, I found that a number of other brothers and sisters were also there. A short exhortation was given and we knelt in prayer. As the names of the sick were read, we prayed. We then left although we had decided to do the same thing the next day at the home of another sick person. I call God to witness that no evil was intended. The next day at dawn a certain brother came to me. He said the pastor and elders of the church were furious about what I had done the day before. However, later when he was questioned about it, he changed his story and said that he had only said some members were upset. Meanwhile, I marvelled to myself that they could be so outraged by this good deed. However, I said to that brother that I would cease what I was doing in the meantime until I could find out what was the reason they were upset. I hoped thereby to explain the reason for my act. Thus I could remove the cause for their outrage when it was known to me. They did not summon me and in the interim my conscience was being tormented.

Obviously they were outraged by the Godly act. Especially as they all refused to visit the sick brothers and sisters in person every day in obedience to God's Word. And this in a time of plague! Also, the pastor was heard to speak of me in a very ill-tempered manner to a certain brother. I wrote a single brief note to the pastors and elders telling how they, and especially the pastor, had offended me. I complained that they, personally, did not visit daily the brothers and sisters of the church in this time of plague, which they were obliged to do by God's Word. Also, they had lessened the times of public prayers as the pastor had said that we ought not to have any prayers on Wednesday or Friday of this week. Then [About these things],[2] I asked them to satisfy my conscience out of God's Word. Secretly, I gave this letter to one of the elders by hand asking that they might all read it. In a spirit of gentleness, I was asking that my conscience might be put at ease. We had that day the usual prayers as a result of the persuasion of a certain brother, a deacon of the church, as he told me. When the service was over they took up my letter by hand.

Then they said to the whole church, 'Brothers, there are certain persons among us, deceitful wolves in sheep's clothing, hypocrites, liars, disturbers of the peace and unity of this church. They desire to rend this church asunder. Not long ago, a letter was given into our hands which scandalously blasphemed against you, your pastor and your elders.'

Moreover, the pastor said, 'I have ministered God's Word among you now for three or four years. In that entire time one or another of you has always been shooting barbs at me (this was well shot) and now I am made, as well as you, the object of just such an arrow (well shot).'[3]

All three elders added their unanimous consent, 'We have decided to bring this whole matter to you (although the whole church was not present) on the Lord's day.'

Therefore, we all left and met again on the Lord's day. After the prayers and a short sermon they began this tragedy when we ought to have been celebrating the Lord's Supper. (For it was the normal day for the Lord's Supper in our church.)[4] They read my letter to the whole assembly and the whole assembly was astonished when they heard my name. On the previous day they had concealed my name.[5] After reading my letter to the assembly, Doctors Schore and Young both took in hand their own letters co-written against me. The pastor read his reply to the 'deceitful (as he said) questions of John Dowley'. I remained seated in a corner room. Then Dr Young called me by name after these letters were read and cast even greater charges and

---

[2] Scored out.

[3] Demonstrating, incidentally, that Scory, notwithstanding his visits to other exile centres in Germany, had remained pastor of the church in Emden all this time.

[4] 7 August 1558. Unfortunately this reference does not make clear whether Communion in the English church was monthly or quarterly. If the church followed the rule established in John a Lasco's *Forma ac Ratio*, they would have celebrated a monthly Communion.

[5] This was the normal procedure in churches where congregational discipline was practised, that the name would have been kept secret in a first public denunciation.

crimes upon me. Thus they cast me down both before the whole church and laid up on me in heaven these crimes. Before this the elder had ordered the man to be called so that he might stand to respond to the charges. I stepped nearer. He then began to read out his letters against me written after the custom of an English judicial enquiry. He was well-trained in English jurisprudence.[6] He read. I listened. Finally, I was called upon to respond.

Therefore I began to speak but to the whole church not to them, 'Brothers and sisters, you all know that I have no desire to offend all the elders of this church except those present here with the pastor. Indeed, three of the elders and four of the deacons are absent.[7] As I have spoken to some other brothers I ask that you allow this case of ours to be judged by two pious and just men although I would not at all name the men to be chosen from our fraternity.'[8]

Everyone was silent. I took the silence as a sign of consent.[9] So I pressed the matter. I took a document from my bosom. It was my defence and apology against all the insults and crimes hurled at me on Wednesday. (This is as you have heard.) For, by God's will, a pretext had been given for writing from Wednesday to Sunday. I asked the church as well as the pastor and elders to listen patiently to my response to the charges against me. The church readily agreed but the pastor and elders were reluctant. I began, but after I had read only eight or ten lines the accusers cried out that I had not observed the required form as I had not responded to the charges directly. The church was patient for me to continue, able to reject later whatever they wanted. I continued another twelve or sixteen lines.

The accusers cried out, 'He distorts the scriptures blasphemously.'

The church again asked them to allow me to read on. Again I read a little and again the accusers cried out. The church was greatly offended by their constant interruptions. They even dared to reprimand the interrupters.

---

[6] Young, according to the brief bibliographical note in the Parker Society edition of Philpot's *Examinations* had studied civil law for some years before entering holy orders. *Examinations and Writings of John Philpot*, ed. Robert Eden (Parker Society, 1842), p. 171.

[7] Along with the three elders mentioned above, this makes six in all.

[8] Again, this practice of proposing mediators to settle a quarrel was borrowed from the London stranger church. See Pettegree, *Foreign Protestant Communities*, pp. 195–6.

[9] This was perhaps presumptuous, but it mirrored the normal practice where a decision was presented to the congregation for approval. In Geneva, for instance, on the election of a new minister the congregation signified their consent by silence.

Meanwhile, I myself said to the interrupters, 'Unless you desire to effect a tyranny allow the reading to continue as you agreed.'

Thus I read my defence and apology against all the charges. Whether these were the charges levelled the previous Wednesday, when my name was suppressed, or those that day as the same accusations were made both times. That was the end of the defence. They said my short treatise was infamous and false and they would raise many objections against me and would prove many things were in it against me.

'Let them prove it,' I said.

Then Dr Young said, 'This man is duplicitous. I can prove that this very moment. I know that in this affair you had confederates with you at dinner, instigators and counsellors.'

I replied, 'I call God to witness, that no man, by word or deed, instigated, counselled, or knew anything about this. I do not understand how you, Dr Young, can so harshly injure these men with scandal whom ... '

One of the brothers broke in whom Dr Young rounded on contemptuously, saying, 'You are a wretch in league with evil, Sancy.'[10]

Thus he ordered the whole church, over which he reigned, to be silent. And another elder gave the same order to the man.

I said to them, 'You have no right to order or command a brother this way without the consent of the church.'

They said they were so able [After these things were done the accusers sought consent].[11] After this Dr Young told the church the story from Matt. 22 about the disciple sent by the Pharisees to test Christ.[12] By various analogies he applied the story to me, thereby implying that I did not know the difference between a pious and simple man and godless ones sent by someone to do the things which I did.

Consider well, O fathers, my plight. This man, by accusing me and others in this way, blasphemously distorted the scriptures. The accusers sought me no less after these things were done. I refused to give them the apology I had written and gave it to the church instead. I handed it over to a certain brother to keep until a copy could be written out for me. Then everyone went home to his house. A copy was subsequently made for me at that brother's house.

Then two brothers came to me saying, 'If you are a lover of peace

---

[10] This supporter of Dowley has not been identified. From the name he may be a member of the small French community in Emden.

[11] Scored out.

[12] Matthew 15: 15–22.

and unity you ought to commit all of this quarrel to four or six brothers of the church for judging and deciding, provided that pastor and elders agree to the same.'

An elder came by as well. He wanted to know what I had against him.

I said, 'I have nothing against you personally. What offended me about you and the rest, I wrote in my first letter. Also, later, you all castigated a brother in public with godless scandal.'

He argued maliciously with me. He said that the other brother was contentious and that I was a schismatic. I then called upon the two brothers to bear witness. But immediately he asked for forgiveness which I happily gave. I would never have mentioned this injury except that he repeated it later openly before the church while accusing me when he was overcome with his emotions. Meanwhile the two brothers urged me to peace, as was said above. I said that although this was a serious matter to me for the sake of the church's unity, peace and quiet, as well as mine, I agreed. We all immediately went to the house of the pastor. The brothers explained the reason for the visit. He said that he would do no more but that the whole affair should be referred to the elders. This was necessary, he said, because I had brought a formal accusation in my letter.

I said, 'I did not accuse anyone in particular by name. But as my conscience has been offended, I wrote to all three of you equally and fairly.'

He produced the letter and read it. He questioned certain words in the letter. I explained and interpreted my meaning. He was reluctant to choose two brothers, while I would do the same, to judge this affair.

He said, 'Either the elders judge or no one does.'

'I understood that one party of a dispute was not supposed to act as a judge to the entire dispute,' I replied.

Turning on me, he said, 'I see you are well versed in the law.'

Then his wife came in and began to hurl all sorts of abuse at me in front of her husband and all of us. Her husband did not even reprove her. Nevertheless I went with them then to Dr Young's house. When we saw him we greeted him and we suggested the same solution to him as we had to the pastor previously. He gave a long, boring reply which managed to say nothing. Moreover he asked to know the names of the two brothers I proposed to speak for my side. He asked for the names specifically.

He then attacked them and said, 'They will not judge this affair. There can be no decision unless it is made by the elders of the church.'

'This must not happen and it will not,' I replied.

Realising that I was being mocked and vainly disappointed by him, I asked for a copy of my initial letter. He promised a copy would be available in two days. After the two days the promised document did not appear. So again, on the third day, I asked for a copy in the presence of the pastor, another elder, and a deacon.

'I am not your slave,' he said.

'That is not a very charitable thing to say,' I answered.

I left. I then made my request another day. He then gave me a copy so poorly written that even I could not read it. I asked to see the actual letter so that I myself could make a copy of it there.

He replied peevishly, 'You will get what you want and all those deceitful wolves who are of counsel as well. You will see your letter. But before I hand it over to you I will prove that you are the most godless member of Christ's church.'

He said this to me in front of two brothers in his own house. After this was said by the man the church met on the following Lord's day, 14 August. When the prayers and the assembly were finished I stood up in the middle.

I said, 'Let the church hear me. This is profitable to everyone.'

I read to them a brief speech as I am of a weak constitution. Thus I kept my statement short.

'Brothers,' I said, 'we have already had the godly prayers and assembly. But if, as on the previous Lord's day, I am obliged to contend and there is still a mutual quarrel among us, is it not better to have nothing at all be it prayers or assembly until this need to argue is settled and finished.'

At this point I began to say what I was willing to do about the events of the past week for the sake of the church's unity and peace.

Then I said, 'As I was concerned about nothing for myself, therefore I would have united all the adversaries in peace. But then the quarrel became greater and greater. I affirm every truth of the church,' I continued. 'Let them show themselves to be peaceable men of God. Moreover, they assume for themselves, in the case of our controversy, and they assert the authority handed to them by Christ. Also, the pastor and elders, who are themselves parties to the case, contrary to God and all honest laws, whether divine or human, desire to judge and determine the case themselves. This whether the church wills it or no! If this is not the height of tyranny and arrogance, I do not know what tyranny is.'

After I had read my opinion, I gave this document to a deacon of the church as a testimony that I wished to commit my case wholeheartedly to the entire church, but that my opponents did not; even though, all three of them accused me of all sorts of evil before the whole church. They especially said that I had attacked and scandalised them in my letters. I said that they should prove what they said since I, for my part, was quite ready to stand by my letters.

'The whole church would see that in no way whatsoever did I attack or scandalise any of you,' I said. 'In my first letter I humbly showed all of you, privately and equally, why my conscience was troubled by you. I said that I wanted my conscience to be put at ease in a spirit of gentleness according to God's Word. As to the charges that in my third letter I accuse you of overthrowing your wisdom and reason and all of the other good gifts of God, I commit this to the church as I said. Your accusations alone show the degree to which human emotion and affection have abounded in all of you.'

Dr Young then began to recite a long parable to the church, 'Once there was an evil citizen who intended to commit a crime. First he gathered together several criminal types to be his conspirators. Together, they all committed the crime. Later, when he realised that the magistrate had discovered his crime he was afraid of the punishment he might face. Therefore to conceal and hide his evil under the form and substance of some good, he wrote to the city Senate. Lying, he told the Senate that in some way the magistrates had upset his conscience. He hoped thereby to keep the citizens from doing their jobs efficiently. Now, just because of what he said, is there any way it would be right for the man to escape the punishment he deserved at the hand of the magistrates?'

As you might imagine, after this and the previous story, the elder, who was puffed up with his own ingenuity, triumphed. Then the church was asked whether we ought not to follow the things which led to peace and to submit to the voice of edification. Also, they said the pastor and elders were freely willing to commit the case to the whole church. They said that the church had already heard enough, and more, from both sides. They managed to wrap everything in ambiguity. We all left with nothing decided for certain. Yesterday, 17 August, we met again. After the prayers during the assembly, the pastor attacked me from the passage of scripture in Acts 13. There the apostles discovered a certain man, a magician, a false prophet, a Jew, etc. He used the text in such a way that the whole church could see that the false prophet meant me. He then added the text in II Tim. 4, 'there will come a time when they will not tolerate sound doctrine, but they will collect teachers to themselves with ears itching to their desires.'[13] Moreover he listed the evil deeds of some members of the church whom I did not know, saying some were schismatics and heretics. He cautioned the church to beware of these. Now I was sure that he meant these things to apply to me although he said them of some others. This was especially so as since the previous Lord's day when the contention, which was previously related, occurred with another elder in the house of a certain brother. However, he tried to conceal that at the time he had called me a schismatic.

Therefore, I responded to him before everyone, 'Behold, it is obvious that you, an elder of this church, were totally overcome by your emotions. This was known only to a few and had been forgiven by me. Since you have been open and forthcoming about this affair I am compelled to be as forthcoming. At that previous discussion you called me a schismatic. And now you force me to tell what I never would have.'

That Wednesday, yesterday, after the meeting when the prayers were finished I stood before the church. I asked the pastor whether he would indicate if the things he said about the false prophet were meant of me. Was he implying that I was such a person?

He answered, 'If your conscience tells you that you are such a one then consider that these things were said of you.'

'I call God to witness,' I said, 'before this whole church that my conscience witnesses that as touching the things that were said, I am innocent and pure. Also, if there were anything which would be said against me it has already been said before Christ's church.'

I also questioned him about his remarks on Paul's epistle to Timothy. I asked if he meant me or some other member of the church when he used the words heretic and schismatic and cautioned the church against such persons. He answered that if my conscience or someone else's witnessed against me or him then the sermon should be received as directed against that person whether it were me or another. I answered that I dared anyone to claim that I or any other member of this church was a heretic, especially as the church was careful, at all cost, to avoid heresy or schism. Indeed, I said there was no one in the whole world able to prove that I was a heretic or a schismatic. Then in front of the whole church I asked whether the pastor and elders would indicate clearly and plainly if they intended to submit this controversy to the whole church or not. They would not indicate anything clearly since they hoped that by delaying and prolonging the case I would be seen as guilty. I daily saw more and

---

[13] In the original Latin Scory is here quoting from the Vulgate.

more evil arising from the quarrel and contention. The church began to take sides. The majority was also offended by Dr Young's stories and saw that he clearly intended to call my supporters conspirators and cunning wolves, and to assert that I had gathered an evil group together when I had done an evil deed. By which of course, he meant the saying of public prayers in the house of a sick brother. Therefore as the church knew me I asked that it please them that after all of this that it was necessary for me to be compelled to seek the advice of pious men and to request visitors (mediators) from the godly German and French churches to decide this matter. This said, we all departed.

Behold, most respected and most charitable of my fathers and brothers in the Lord how easily I was able to recount these things from the beginning of the controversy even to its present state. I ask and beseech you, most honest of men, to attend to the peace and unity of our church. The authority and supreme rule is given to you, as I confess, most worthy and likewise pious teachers of the ministry of the church, in all Christ's churches of East Friesland by the supreme Lord. Thus you are empowered according to Ezekiel 34, 'to feed the flock, to console those who were ailing, to heal those who were ill, to gather those who were lost, etc.' Finally I beg and beseech you that you realise that it was the farthest thing from my mind to attack any good pastors or pious elders who labour hard by word and doctrine. They are worthy of double honour. Rather, I accused those who were neglecting their office but who would not make a godly change when they were admonished. Instead their insane and arrogant spirits drove them into admonishing in return to the point that they scandalised a brother publicly. They threw many charges and accusations on him. Thus he was forced to seek out pious and learned men. He sought those, not the least, who were mortified in the mind by Christ and circumcised in the heart and who continually put off the old man entirely and put on the new man in Christ Jesus as was commanded by the Holy Ghost through the apostle in Ephesians 4. Farewell.

Note appended:

The first point is that:

if the brother was upset in his conscience by the pastor and a couple of elders and he wrote the reason in a short letter to one of the elders requesting the letter be made available to all of them and afterwards they satisfied his mind, the pastor and elders ought not then to have opened and read his letter before the whole church. Also, they should not have insulted this brother by calling him 'a wolf in sheep's clothing', 'a hypocrite', 'a liar', 'a disturber of Christian peace and unity'. Nor should they have said that he was going around trying to destroy Christ's church without first speaking to the brother.

The second point is that:

since the pastor and elders published and declared this matter and case before the whole church, which was also asserted, the same pastor and elders ought not to judge or determine the case rather the whole church ought to judge and determine the matter.

The third point is that:

Although the pastor and elders wish to judge and determine the case themselves and will not suffer the church to judge and determine the matter, this must be done by the church.

APPENDIX FOUR

Checklist of Latin Polemic Published by the Marian Exiles Abroad, 1553–1559*

1553

1. *Narratio/ historica vi/cissitudinis, rerum/* quae in inclyto Britanniæ Regno/ acciderunt, Anno Domini/ 1553. Mense Iulio.// Scripta a P.V.// 1553.
   1553.
   8o.   Col: A1–B8.
   Copies: London BL*.

2. John Ponet. De ecclesia ad regem Edwardum.
   Zurich, 1553.
   No copies known. Noted in *DNB* (art. Ponet), vol. 46, p. 79.

1554

3. John Philpot. *Vera/ exposi/tio disputa/tionis/ institu/tæ mandato D. Mariae Reginae/* Angl. Franc. & Hibern. &c. in Synodo/ Ecclesiastica, Londini in Comitijs re/gni ad 18. Octob. Anno/ 1553.// His accessit Reverendiss. in Christo patris ac Domini./ D. Archiepiscopi Cantuariens. epistola apologetica/ ex Anglico autographo latino facta. ... 1554.//

---

* I have included all works by English exiles on religious themes, along with works by foreign theologians who were part of the exile movement. Latin works by English authors have been omitted where they appear purely literary in character (works by Cheke, Becon), as have works by the foreign exiles which relate to new controversies on the continent, and thus have no relevance to the English context (such as Marten Micron's writings against Menno Simons).
   Italic type indicates that this part of the title is capitalized in the original. An asterisk (*) indicates that I have inspected that copy.
   In compiling the checklist of copies I have made use of Schaaber's *Checklist of Books by English Authors Published Abroad*, along with published library catalogues and, where possible, personal visits. But it is recognized that this list will be by no means complete.

Impressum Romae Coram castro S. Angeli [i.e. Cologne], 1554.
STC 19891. Translated from the English by Valérand Poullain.
8o. Col: A1–8, a1–d8.
Copies: London BL, Lam*, Oxford Bod (2), Mert, Queens, Cambridge UL, Emma, Berlin SB.

4. Valérand Poullain. *Liturgia/ sacra, seu ritus/* Ministerii in Ecclesia peregrinorum/ Francofordiæ ad Moe/num.// Addita est summa doctrinæ seu fidei pro/fessio eiusdem Ecclesiæ.// Francofordiæ/ 1554.//
[Peter Brubach], Frankfort, 1554.
8o. Col: a1–f8 (f8 blank).
Copies: London BL*, Oxford BNC, Glasgow UL, Stuttgart LB, Zurich ZB.

5. John Foxe. *Commentarii/ rerum in ecclesia ge/*starum, maximarumque, per/ totam Europam, persecutio/num, a Vuicleui temporibus/ ad hanc usque aetate descripto./ Liber primus.// Autore Ionne Foxo Anglo.// ... Argentorati/ Excudebat Vuendelinus Rihelius/ Anno M.D.LIIII.
Rihel, Strasburg, 1554.
8o. Col: a1–8, A1–Z8, Aa1–Dd8, Ee1–3.
Copies: London BL, Oxford Bod, BNC, Cambridge UL, St Andrews UL*, Munich SB, Wolfenbüttel HAB, Colmar CAC, Paris BN; Harvard, Yale, Ohio UL, Williamstown CL.

6. John Bale. *Nova prae/fatio Anglica, in/ veterum librum Vintonien/*sis, ante 20. annos de vera obedientia/ scriptum, & editam Hamburgi, an/no 36. Latino sermone, missa in hoc/ mercatu Lypsico verno ex Anglia, & bo/na fide conversa in Latinum spacio trium/ horarum// ... *Lipsiae,/* In officina typographica/ Georgij Hanzsch.// *1554.//*
8o. 15 pp.
Copies: Berlin SB, Wolfenbüttel HAB.

7. Martin Bucer. Psalmorum libri quinque ad He/*braicam veritatem traducti, et/* summa fide, parique diligentia a Martino Bucero enarrati.// *Eiusdem commentarii/* In librum Iudicum,/ &/ In Sophoniam Prophetam.// Oliva Roberti Stephani./ M.D. LIIII.
R. Stephanus, [Geneva], 1554 (May).
fo. Col: *1–8, a1–z8, A1–P8.
Copies: London BL, Lam, Oxford Bod, AS, Bal, BNC, Cor (imp), Ch Ch, Mert, Queens, Trin, Cambridge UL (2), Trin,

APPENDIX FOUR 185

Clare, Queens, Emma, Pemb, Magd, Caius, Edinburgh UL, St Andrews UL*, Dublin Trin, Augsburg SB, Berlin SB, Erlangen UB, Nuremberg StB, Regensburg SB, Dresden LB, Zurich ZB, Vienna NB, Paris BN, Basle OB, Geneva BP, Lausanne BCan, Sibiu (Romania) BM, Stockholm KB; Brown UL.

8. [An acquittal of the Church of England]. Latin version recorded in preface to translation by John Olde (Emden, 1555). 1554? No copies found.

1555

9. Valérand Poullain. *Liturgia/ sacra, seu ritus Mini/sterii in ecclesia peregri/norum Francofordiae/ ad Moenum.// Addita est summa doctrinæ, seu fidei pro/fessio eiusdem Ecclesiæ.// Editio Secunda.// Francofordiæ./ 1555.//*
   [Peter Brubach], Frankfort, 1555.
   8o.   Col: A1–H8.
   Copies: London BL* (2), Oxford Bod, Dublin Trin, Munich SB, Wolfenbüttel HAB.

10. *Forma/ ac ratio tota eccle/siastici Ministerij, in peregrinorum, po/tissimum vero Germanorum Ecclesia: in/stituta Londini in Anglia, per Pientissi/mum Principem Angliæ &c. Regem E/duardum, eius nominis Sextu' : An/no post Christum natum 1550. Addito/ ad calcem libelli Privilegio/ suæ Maiestatis.// Autore Ioanne a La/sco Poloniæ Barone.// ...*
    [Ctematius, Emden & Egenolff, Frankfort, 1555]. STC 16571.
    8o.   Col: α1–Σ8, μ1–4, A1–Z8, Aa1–Pp8. 348 ff.
    Copies: London BL (2)*, Dutch Church, Lambeth*, Oxford Bod, Cambridge UL (imp), Caius, Emma*, West, Edinburgh NL, UL (2), Dublin Trin, Brussels KB*, Groningen UB, Utrecht UB, Paris BN, Strasburg BNU, Geneva BPU, Bonn UL, Dillingen StUB, Göttingen UB, Munich SB*, Tübingen UB*, Wolfenbüttel HAB, Copenhagen KB (2); Folger, Huntingdon.

11. Robert Barnes. *Vitae/ Romanorum ponti/ficum, quos Papas vocamus, summa/ diligentia ac fide collectæ, per D./ Robertum Barns, S. Theo/logiæ Doctorem Anglum, Londini/ Anno abhinc XV pro Chri/sti nomine com/bustum.// Eiusdem sententiae,/ sive præcipui Christianæ religionis articuli ... // Basileae.//*
    [Oporinus], Basle, [1555].
    8o.   Col: α1–8, μ1–4, a1–z8, A1–B8, C1–4, D1–8, E1–4.

Copies: London BL (2)*, Lam (misf)*, Oxford Bod, Cambridge UL, Dublin Trin, Berlin SB, Cologne SUB, Gotha LB, Halle UB, Leipzig UB, Münster UB, Munich SB, Wolfenbüttel HAB, Zurich ZB, Paris BN, Vienna NB; Harvard UL, New York Union.

12. *Episto/læ duæ, duorum/ amicorum, ex quibus/* vana, flagitiosaque Pontificum Pau/li tertij, & Iulii tertij, & Cardinalis Po/li, & Stephani Gardineri pseudoepiscopi Vuintoniensis/ Angli, eorumque adulatorum sectatorumque/ ratio, magna ex parte potest/ intelligi.// *Cum Papae Privilegio/* ad momentum horæ.// 1555.
   8o. Col: A1–8, B1–4.
   Copies: London BL*, Cambridge St J, Florence BN.

1556

13. Nicholas Ridley. *D. Nicolai/ Ridleii episcopi Lon/dinensis De Coena/* Dominica assertio,// *contra/ scelaratam illam trans/* substa'tiationis hæresim, quam e carcere author/ scripserat: unde etiam paulo post, id est XVI./ Octobr. die. M.D.LV. igni comburendus ex/trahebatur.// *Genevae./ Apud Ioannem Crispinum,/* M.D.LVI.//
    Jean Crespin, Geneva, 1556. Translated from the English by William Whittingham.
    8o. Col: A1–G8, *1–**8.
    Copies: London BL, Lam (2)*, Oxford Bod, Bal, BNC, Ch Ch (2), Corp, Jesus, Queens, St J, Univ, Worc, Cambridge UL (2), Trin, Caius, Emma, St J, Pemb, Jesus, Edinburgh NL, UL (2), Dublin Trin, York Min, Paris BN, Geneva NP, Maldon PL; Chicago New.

14. *Aetiologi/a Roberti Vvatsoni/* Angli, in qua explicatur, quare depre/hensus annum unum & menses pene/quatuor, propter Evangeliu' incarce/ratus fuit: quena' inter ipsu' & eius An/ tagonistas in carcere habita fuit disce/ptatio, de Transubstantiatione & reali/ Christi præsentia in Sacramento: &/ quo pacto corpore incolumi &/ illibata conscientia tandem/ expediuit eum/ Dominus.// ... // Anno. M.D.LVI.
    [Ctematius, Emden], 1556. STC 25111.
    8o. Col: A1–H8, I1–4. 68ff.
    Copies: London BL* (2), Cambridge UL*, Edinburgh UL, Norwich PL, York Minster, Halle UL, Munich SB (2)*, Zurich ZB.

15. *Aetiologi/a. Roberti Watsoni/* Anglia, in qua explicatur, quare

APPENDIX FOUR 187

depre/hensus annum unum & menses pene/quatuor, propter
Evangeliu' incarce/ratus fuit: quena' interipsu' & eius An/
tagonistas in carcere habita fuit disce/ptatio, de Transubstan-
tione & reali/ Christi praesentia in Sacramentis: &/ quo pacto
corpore incolumi &/ illibata conscientia tandem/ expediuit eum/
Dominus.//
8o.   Col: A1–H8, I1–4. 68 ff. A variant edition.
Copies: Cambridge Trin.

16. Liturgy. *Ratio/ et forma/ publice orandi De/um, atque
administran/di sacramenta,/ et caet.// In Anglorum eccle/siam,
quæ Genevæ colligitur, recepta: cum iu/dicio & comprobatione
D. Iohannis Calvini.// Genevæ,/ apud Ioannem Crispinum,/
M.D.LVI.*
Crespin, Geneva, 1556. STC 16565. Translation by William
Whittingham.
8o.   Col: A1–E8.
Copies: London BL*, Oxford Bod, Bal, Ch Ch, Corpus, Jesus,
Cambridge UL, Trin, Edinburgh NL, Lincoln Cath, Leiden UB*,
Munich SB, Geneva NP; Boston PL, Harvard, New York Un-
ion.

17. John Foxe. *Christus Tri/umphans, comoe/dia apocaly/ptica;//
Autore Ioanne Foxo Anglo.// Accessit,/ in Christum trium/
phantem, Autoris eiusdem Pa/negyricon.// Basileae, per Ioan/
nem Oporinum.*
Oporinus, Basle, 1556 (March).
8o.   Col: A1–8, *1–4, B1–H8, J1–6.
Copies: London BL*, Oxford Bod (imp), BNC, Cambridge UL,
Trin, Edinburgh UL, Munich SB, Zurich ZB; Harvard, Illinois
UL, New York Union, Greenville Percy.

18. John a Lasco. *Epistolae/ tres lectu dignis/simæ,/ de recta et legi/
tima ecclesiarum Be/ne, instituendarum ratio/ne ac modo:// ad
potentiss. Regem/ Poloniæ, Senatum, reliquosque/ Ordines:// D.
Ioanne a Lasco Ba/rone Poloniæ, &c. autore.// Basileae, per
Ioan/nem Oporinum.//*
Oporinus, Basle, 1556 (March).
8o.   Col: A1–G8.
Copies: Oxford Bod* (2), Ch Ch, Manchester Ry, Leiden UB*,
Utrecht UB, Munich SB.

19. John a Lasco. *Purgatio mini/strorum/ in ecclesiis pe/regrin.
Francofurti,/ adversus eorum calumnias, qui ipso/rum doctri-
nam, de christi Do/mini in Coena sua præsentia, dis/sensionis*

accusant ab *au/gustana* Con/fessione.// Autore D. *Ioanne a La/ sco*, Barone Polono.// *Basileae, per Ioan/nem Oporinum.*//
Oporinus, Basle, 1556 (Dec).
8o.   Col: a1–c8, d1–10.
Copies: London Lam*, Oxford Bod*, Cambridge UL, Caius, Trin, The Hague KB, Amsterdam UB, Utrecht UB, Munich SB.

1557

20. *Defensio/ veræ et catholicæ do/ctrinae de Sacramento corporis & sanguinis/ Christi* Servatoris nostri, & quoru'dam/ in hac causa errorum co'futatio, verbo sanctissi/mo Domini nixa atq' fundata, & consensu anti/quissimorum Ecclesiæ scriptorum firmata, a Re/verendiss. in Christo Patre ac Domino *D./ Thoma Cranmero/* Martyre, Archiepiscopo Can/tuariensi, Primate totius/ Angliæ, & Me/tropolitano,/ scripta,/ ab autore in/ vinculis recognita/ & aucta.// *Iesus Chrittus.*// Embdæ, apud Gellium Ctematium./ M.D. LVII.//
Ctematius, Emden, 1557. STC 6005 (var.)
8o.   Col: A1–X8, Y1–4 (Y4 blank). 172 ff.
Copies: London BL, Lambeth*, Oxford Bod, Bal, Cambridge UL*, St J*, Edinburgh NL, Manchester Ry, St Andrews UL, Berlin SB, Göttingen UB, Munich SB*, Tübingen UB*, Stuttgart LB*, Amsterdam UL*, The Hague KB*, Copenhagen KB, Colmar ECA, Paris BN, St Gallen SB, Sibiu (Romania) BMB; Folger; Huntington; Chicago New; Minneapolis UL.

21. *Defensio/ veræ et catholicæ do/ctrinae de Sacramento corporis & sanguinis/ Christi* Servatoris nostri, & quoru'dam/ in hac causa errorum co'futatio, verbo sanctissi/mo Domini nixa atq' fundata, & consensu anti/quissimorum Ecclesiæ scriptoru' firmata, a Reve/rendiss. in Christo Patre & B. Martyre *D./ Thoma Cranmero/* Archiepiscopo Cantuariensi,/ Primate totius Angliæ,/ & Me/tropolitano,/ scripta, ab autore in vinculis recognita/ & aucta.// *Iesus Christus*// M.D.LVII.
Ctematius, Emden, 1557. STC 6005. A variant edition.
8o.   Col: A1–X8, Y1–3. 171 ff.
Copies: London BL, Oxford Bod, All Souls, Exeter, Cambridge Kings, Magd, St J (2)*, Edinburgh NL, UL, Eton, Shrewsbury S, York Min; Huntington, New York Union, Yale.

22. John Foxe. Ad inclytos ac/ præpotentes An/*gliae proceres,*/ Ordines, & Status, totamque e/ius gentis Nobilitatem, pro/

afflictis fratri/bus/ *supplicatio://* Autore *Ioanne Foxo/* Anglo.*//*
Basileae, per Io/annem Oporinum.
Oporinus, Basle, 1557 (March).
8o. Col: a1–d8, e1–4.
Copies: London BL* (2), Lam*, Oxford Bod, BNC, Corpus, Cambridge UL, Munich SB, Wolfenbüttel HAB; Folger, Chicago New, Harvard, Ohio UL.

23. John Foxe. Locorum Com/munium Tituli & Or/dines Centum quinquaginta, ad seriem Præ/dicamentoru' decem descripti: in quos, ceu/ certos nidos & capsulas, quæcunque sunt us/quam ex Autoribus colligenda, le/ctores congerant stu/diosi: Autore Ioanne Foxo Anglo.*//* ... *Basileae, apud Ioan/nem Oporinum.//*
Oporinus, Basle, 1557 (March).
8o. Col: α1–4, a1–b8, (c1–z8, A1–R8, S1–4), T1–8. (Headed pages, interleaved with blanks.)
Copies: London BL*, Oxford Bod, Cambridge UL, Munich SB, UB (imp), Zurich ZB.

24. John Foxe. De Predicamentis Tabulae.
8o. Listed as a separate work in *Librorum per Oporinum Excusorum*, 1567, but probably a confusion with no. 23, above. See Mozley, *Foxe*, p. 243.

25. John Foxe. Mira ac elegans cum primus Historia vel tragoedia potius, de tota ratione examinationis et condemnationis J. Philpotti Archidiaconi Wincestriae, nuper in Anglia exusti. Ab autore primum lingua sua congesta; nunc in Latinum versa. Interprete J.F.A. 1557? See John Strype, *Memorials of Archbishop Cranmer* (3 vols in 4, Oxford, 1848–54), vol. 3, p. 174. No copies found. Reprinted in *Rerum* (no. 39 below), pp. 543–631.

26. Martin Bucer. *De Regno Chri/sti Iesu servatoris nostri,/ Libri II. // Ad Eduardum VI. Angliae/ Regem, annis abhinc sex scripti:/ non solum Theologis atque Iurisperitis profutu/ri, verum etiam cunctis Rempub. bene & feliciter/ administraturis cognitu cumprimis/ necessarij.// D. Martino Bucero/ Autore.//* ... *Basileae, per Ioan/nem Oporinum.//*
Oporinus, Basle, 1557 (Sept).
fo. Col: a1–6, a1–z4, A1–G4, H1–6 (H6 blank).
Copies: Oxford Bod (2)*, Balliol, Magd, Queens, Cambridge UL (2), Cath, St J, Edinburgh UL, The Hague KB, Leiden UB*, Augsburg SB, Coburg LB, Wolfenbüttel HAB (2), Basle OB,

Bern StB, Zurich ZB, Strasburg BN, Copenhagen KB, UB, Debrecen Coll.

27. Peter Martyr Vermigli. *Disputatio/ de Euchari/stiae sacramento ha/bita in celeberrima uni/versitate Oxoniensi in Anglia, antea qui/dem illic excusa, iam vero denuo/ cum triplici Indice in lu/ cem edita.// Tiguri apud And. Gesne/rum, anno M.D.LVII.//*
Andreas Gesner, Zurich, 1557.
8o.   Col: + 1–8, A1–V8, Aa1–Cc8, Dd1–4.
Copies: Oxford Bod*, Cambridge Emma.

28. Peter Martyr Vermigli. *Petri Martyris/ Vermilii Florentini/ Viri doctissimi de sacra/mento eucharistiæ in celeberrima An/gliæ schola Oxoniensi ha/bita tractatio.// Tiguri apud And. Ges/ nerum, Anno M.D. LVII.*
Gesner, Zurich, 1557.
8o.   Col: a1–b8, A1–V8.
Copies: Oxford Bod*, Freiburg UL, Zurich ZB, Paris BN, Florence BNC.

29. John Ponet. *Dialla/cticon viri bo/ni et literati, de veri/tate, Natura atque Substantia Corpo/ris & Sanguinis Christi in/ Eucharistia.// ... Anno M.D.LVII.*
[Rihel, Strasburg], 1557.
8o.   Col:)(1–4, A1–O8, P1–4.
Copies: London BL*, Oxford Bod, Ch Ch (2), Cambridge UL, Edinburgh UL, Dublin Trin (2); Washington Con.

29a. John Ponet. Axiomata Eucharistiae.
A different book? See *DNB*, vol. 46, p.79.

30. Thomas Becon. *Gnomotheca/ Solomonis, ad vi/tam pie instituendam,/ dignosque Christiano homine mo/ses excole'dos longe utilissima: ex/ omnibus ipsius, qui quidem exta't,/ libris desumpta, atque in Locos dige/sta communes, per Thomam/ Beconum Anglum.// Basileae, per Ioan/nem Oporinum.*
Oporinus, Basle, [1557].
8o.   Col: a1–m8, n1–4.
Copies: Oxford Bod*, Munich SB, Vienna NB, Colmar AC; Folger.

30a. A number of other Latin works by Becon are listed by Bale, *Catalogus* (1557), p. 727: In Germania Latine congessit ... Introductionem ad pietatem; Miscellanea religionis; De authoritate verbi Dei, etc.
Whether these works were separately printed and published is not certain.

APPENDIX FOUR   191

31. John Bale. *Scriptorum il/*lustriu' maioris Britanniæ quam/ nunc Angliam & Scotiam vocant: mul/torumque aliorum, qui in eadem uixerunt & obierunt insula, Catalo/gus: a Iapheto per 3617 annos, usque ad annum hunc Domini 1556 ... in XII Centurias partitus.// Autore *Ioanne Baleo* Sudouolgio Anglo ... // *Basileae, apud Ioan/*nem Oporinum.//
    Oporinus, Basle, 1557 (September). A first printing of no. 32, below.
    fo.   Col: t/p, a1–z4, A1–Z4, aa1–zz4, Aa1–Zz4, Aaa1–4.
    Copies: London BL*.

32. John Bale. *Scriptorum Il/*lustriu' maioris Brytannie, quam/ nunc Angliam & Scotiam vocant: Ca/talogus: a Iapheto per 3618 annos, usque ad annu hunc Domini 1557./ ... ix Centurias continens://... Autore *Ioanne Baleo* Sudouolgia Anglo ... // *Basileae, apud Ioan/*nem Oporinum.//
    Oporinus, Basle, 1557 (September).
    fo.   Col: α1–6, β1–Γ4, a1–z4, A1–Z4, aa1–zz4, Aa1–Zz4, Aaa1–4.
    Copies: London BL (2), Oxford Bod (3), AS, Bal, Corp, Ch Ch, Eng, Hert, Magd, Mert, New, Queens, St J, Trin, Worc, Cambridge UL (2), Trin, Caius, Kings (2), Corp, Jesus, Magd, Queens, St J, Emma, Pet, Clare, Cath, Edinburgh NL, UL (2), New, Machester UL (2), St Andrews UL*, Aberdeen UL, Glasgow UL, Exeter Cath, The Hague KB, Leiden UB*, Utrecht UB, Berlin SB, Darmstadt LB, Erlangen UB, Frankfurt SUB, Göttingen UB, Hamburg SUB, Hannover KM, Karlsruhe LB, Lübeck SB, Munich SB, Mainz SB, Oldenburg LB, Stuttgart LB, Tübingen UB, Wolfenbüttel HAB, Weimar LB, Zurich ZB, Vienna NB, UB, Graz UB, St Gallen SB, Paris BN, Rome BA, Geneva UB, Wroclawin UB; Yale, Iowa UL, Baltimore PL, Princeton UL, New York PL, Penna BMC, Brown UL, Texas UL, Wisconsin UL. Many copies with no. 43, below. See also no. 42.

1558

33. John Bale. Acta Romano/*rum pontificum, a di/*spersione discipulorum Christi, usq'; ad/ tempora Pauli quarti, qui nunc in Eccle/sia tyrannizat: Ex Ioannis Balei Sudo/uolgii Angli maiore Catalogo Anglico/rum scriptorum desumpta, & in tres/ Classes, Libros vero se/ptem, divisa.// *Basileae.//*
    Oporinus, Basle, 1558 (July).
    8o.   Col: *1–***8, a1–z8, A1–V8.

Copies: London BL, Lam*, Oxford Bod, Exeter, Jes, Magd, Queens, Univ, Cambridge UL, Emma, Pem, St J, Magd (imp), Edinburgh UL, Aberdeen UL, Aberystwyth NL, The Hague KB, Berlin SB, Darmstadt LB, Detmold LB, Frankfurt SUB, Giessen UB, Göttingen UL, Halle UL, Munich SB, Nuremberg SB, Rostock UB, Weimar LB, Wolfenbüttel HAB, Zurich ZB, Paris BN, Sibiu (Romania) BMB, Vienna NB; Chicago UL.

34. Robert Barnes. *Senten/tiae ex doctori/bus collectae, per doctiss: virum R. Barni/ Anglum, sacrae theologiae/ doctorem*: Nunc longe quam antea emendatius edi/te ... // Authore Eberharto Haberkorn,/ Ursellanæ Ecclesiæ ministro./ Anno 1558.
Ursellis [i.e. Oberursel], excudebat Nicolaus Henricus, 1558.
8o.   Col: *,)(, **1–8, A1–4, B1–Q8, R1–4.
Copies: Cambridge Caius (imp), Emma, Berlin SB, Frankfurt SUB, Jena UB, Tübingen UB, Wiesbaden LB, Wolfenbüttel HAB, Woclawin BU, Vienna NB.

35. Simon Alexius [Pierre Alexandre]. *De/ origine/ novi Dei Missati/ ci, quondam in Anglia/ mortui, nunc denuo ab inferis excitati: Dialogi vii.// Simone Alexio Autore.//*
[Crespin, Geneva], 1558.
8o.   Col: A1–4, B1–I8, K1–4.
Copies: Oxford Bod*, Worc, Cambridge Caius, Aberdeen UL, Ghent UB, Paris BN.

36. Pierre Alexandre. *De/ origine/ novi dei missati/ci, quondam in anglia/ mortui, nunc denuo ab inferis excitati:/ dialogi vii.// ... Simone Alexio Authore.// Genevæ.*
[Crespin], Geneva, [1558]. Variant of above.
8o.   Col: A1–4, B1–I8, K1–4.
Copies: London BL, Lam (2)*, Cambridge UL, Dublin Trin, Amsterdam FU, Utrecht UB.

37. Peter Martyr Vermigli. *In epistolam S. Pau/li Apostoli ad Romanos, D. Petri/ Martyris Vermilii Florentini, Professoris/ divinarum literarum in schola Tigurina,/ commentarii doctissimi, cum tra/ctatione perutili rerum & lo/corum, qui ad eam episto/lam pertinent.// Basileæ/ apud Petrum Pernam./ M.D.LVIII.*
Pernam, Basle, 1558.
fo.   Col: α1–6, *1–4, a1–z6, A1–Z6, Aa1–Gg6, Hh1–4, α1–δ6 (δ6 blank).
Copies: Oxford Bod, Magd, New, Queens, Univ, Cambridge Corp (imp), Pem, Aberdeen UL, St Andrews UL(2)*, Tübingen UB, Arrau AKB, Basle UB, Neuchâtel BP, PasB, St Gallen SB,

Zurich ZB, Deventer AB, Utrecht UB, Paris BN, Florence BNC, Sarospatek RCL; Washington Con, St Louis Eden.

38. Thomas Becon. *Antholia/ Lactantii/ Firmiani, Ele/gantissimas sen/tentias, easque tam pietate, quam doctri/na illustres, complectens: recenter/ in locos digesta communes/ per Thomam Be/ conum.// Lugduni/ apud Clementem Baudinum/* 1558.
Clément Baudin, Lyon, 1558.
8o. Col: +1–8, *1–8, a1–q8.
Copies: Cambridge UL, St J, Durham UL, Paris BN, Maz, Avignon MuC.

1559

39. John Foxe. *Rerum/ in ecclesia ge/starum, quæ postremis & pericu/losis his temporibus evenerunt, maxi/marumq'; per Europam persecutionum, ac Sanctorum Dei/ Martyrum, cæterarumq'; rerum si quæ insignioris/ exempli sint, digesti per Regna & natio/nes Commentarij.// Pars Prima ... //* Autore *Ioanne Foxo* Anglo.// *Basileae, per Nicolaum/ Brylingerum, et Ioan/ nem Oporinum.//*
Brylinger and Oporinus, Basle, 1559 (Aug).
fo.   Col: A1–4, a1–z4, A1–Z8, aa1–qq4, rr1–8, ss1–zz4, Aa1– Ff4, Gg1–6, Hh1–Jj4, Kk1–6, Ll1– Yy4.
Copies: London BL, Lam*, Oxford Bod, AS, Bal, BNC, Ch Ch, Jes, Keble, Pem, Queens, Univ, Worc, Cambridge UL, Trin, Emma, Queens, Pet, Sid, Corp, Magd, Edinburgh NL, UL (2), Manchester Ry, Dublin Trin, Amsterdam UB, Deventer, Utrecht UB, Göttingen UB, Munich SB (2), St Gallen SB, Zurich ZB; Huntington, Harvard, Yale, Chicago New, Illinois UL, New York PL, Union, Pennsylvania UL, Princeton UL, Williamstown CL.

40. John Bale. Acta Romanorum pontificum, a dispersione discipulorum Christi.
Basle, 1559.
8o.
Copies: Cologne SUB, Dresden LB, Gotha LB, Jena UB, Stuttgart LB, Tübingen UB, Wolfenbüttel HAB, Rome BA, Vienna NB; Harvard, Yale.

41. John Bale. Scriptorum Brytannia catalogus.
Basileae apud Ioannem Oporinum [1559]
fo.

Copies: London BL, Kassel LB; Boston CL, New York PL.

42. John Bale. *Scriptorum Il/*lustriu' maioris Brytannie, quam/ nunc Angliam & Scotiam vocant: Ca/talogus: a Iapheto per 3618 annos, usque ad annu' hunc Domini 1557./ ... IX Centurias continens:// Autore *Ioanne Baleo* Sudouolgia Anglo ... // *Basileae, apud Ioan/nem Oporinum.//*
Oporinus, Basle, 1557 (September).
fo. Col: α1–5, [α2–6], β1–μ4, a1–z4, A1–Z4, aa1–zz4, Aa1–Zz4, Aaa1–4.
The edition of 1557 (no. 32) with a letter of dedication to Queen Elizabeth inserted.
Copies: London BL*.

43. John Bale. *Scriptorum il/*lustrium maioris Brytanniæ po/sterior pars, quinque continens Cen/*turias ultimas, quas author, Ioannes/* Baleus Sudouolgius, Anglus, ex Lelando Antiqua/rio, alijsque probis authoribus, non par/vo labore collegit.// ... *Basileae per Ioan/nem Oporinum.*
Oporinus, Basle, 1559 (February).
fo. Col: α1–6, β1–4, a1–z4, A1–T4.
Second part of no. 32.
Copies: London BL (2)*, Lam*, Oxford Bod (3), Cambridge UL (2), Trin, Caius, Kings, Corp, Jesus, Magd, Queens, St J, Emma, Pet, Clare, Cath, Edinburgh NL, UL (2), New, St Andrews UL*, Glasgow HM, Leiden UB*, Utrecht UB, Munich SB, Paris BN; Philadelphia LC.

44. John Bale. *Scriptorum il/*lustriu' maioris Brytannie, quam/ nunc Angliam & Scotiam vocant: Ca/talogus: a Iapheto per 3620 annos, usque ad annu' hunc Domini 1559,/ ex Beroso, Gennadio ... atque alijs authoribus collectus,/ & XIIII Centurias continens:// Autore *Ioanne Baleo* Sudouolgio Anglo ... *Basileae, apud Ioan/nem Oporinum.//*
Oporinus, Basle, 1559.
fo. Col: α1–6, β1–μ4, a1–z4, A1–Z4, aa1–zz4, Aa1–Zz4, Aaa1–4.
Copies: London Lam*, Canterbury CL.

45. Thomas Becon. *Coenae Sa/cro sanctae domini/ nostri Jesu Christi,* & Missæ Papisti/cæ, Comparatio ... // *Autore Thoma Beco/no Anglo.// Basileae, per Ioan/nem Oporinum.//*
Oporinus, Basle, 1559 (June).
8o. Col: α1–x8, A1–Q8 (Q8 blank).
Copies: London BL*, Lam*, Oxford Bod (2), Ch Ch, Linc,

Worc, Cambridge UL, Trin, Edinburgh UL, Dublin Trin, Exeter Cath, York Min, Ghent UB, Bonn UB, Berlin SB, Lübeck SB, Munich SB, Oldenburg LB, Tübingen UB, Wolfenbüttel HAB, Colmar CAC, Salzburg BSB, Vienna NB, Wroclaw UB.

46. Peter Martyr Vermigli. *Defensio/* Doctrinæ veteris & Apostolicæ/ de sacrosancto Eucharistiæ Sacramento, *D. Petri Martyris/* Vermilij, Florentini ... adversus Stephani Gardineri, quondam/ Vuintonien'. Episcopi, librum ... //
[Froschover, Zurich, 1559].
fo.   Col: *1–6, a1–z6, A1–Z6, Aa1–Xx6, Yy1–4, Zz1–6.
Copies: London BL, Lam*, Oxford Magd, Univ, Cambridge UL, Trin, Caius, St J, Pet, Corp, Edinburgh UL (3), Aberdeen UL, St Andrews UL, Groningen UB, Leiden UB*, Utrecht UB. Leiden UB copy col: *1–6, aa1–6, bb1–4 (index), a1– etc.

47. Peter Martyr Vermigli. *Defensio/ D. Petri Marty/ris Vermilii Florentini/ Divinarum literarum in Scho/*la Tigurina professoris, ad Riccardi Smythæi An/gli, olim Theologiæ professoris Oxoniensis/ duos libellos de Cælibatu sacerdo/tum, & Votis monasticis,/ Nunc primum in luce/ edita.// *Basileae apud Petrum Pernam.//* M.D.L.IX.
Pernam, Basle, 1559.
8o.   Col: *1–4, a1–z8, A1–L8, M1–4.
Copies: London Lam*, Oxford Bod, BNC, Ch Ch, Cambridge Trin, Sid, Corp, Dublin Trin, St Andrews UL, Utrecht UB, Ghent UB; Brown UL.

48. Peter Martyr Vermigli. *In Episto/lam S. Pauli A/postoli ad Romanos D./ Petri Martyris Vermilii Floren/*tini, Professoris divinarum literarum in schola Tigurina,/ commentarij doctissimi, ... // *Tiguri M.D.LIX.//*
[Gesner], Zurich, 1559.
8o.   Col: α1–8, β1–4, μ1–8, δ1–2, a1–z8, A1–Z8, Aa1–Yy8, a1–e8, f1–4.
Copies: Cambridge Caius, Emma, Edinburgh UL, St Andrews UL*, Dublin Trin, Munich SB, Neuchâtel BV, Budapest Academy.

49. Laurence Humphrey. De Religionis/ conservatione &/ reformatione/ vera:// Deque Primatu Regum &/ magistratuum, & obedientia/ illis ut summis in terra Chri/sti vicarijs præstanda,/ Liber:// Ad Nobilitatem, Clerum & po/pulum Anglicanum.// *Laurentio Hum/fredo autore.// Basileae, per Ioan/nem Oporinum.//*

Oporinus, Basle, 1559 (Sept).
8o.   Col: a1–g8.
Copies: London BL*, Cambridge UL (2), Caius, Emma, Munich SB; New York Union.

50. John Foxe. Germaniæ ad/ Angliam,/ *de Restituta* E/vangelij luce, Gra/tulatio.// *Basileae, per Io/annem Oporinum./* 1559.
Oporinus, Basle, 1559 (Jan).
8o.   Col: a1–d8 (d8 blank).
Copies: London Lam*, Munich SB, Basle UB.

APPENDIX FIVE

Two Letters of the Delegate of the Emden Reformed Church, from London, April/May 1559

Source: Emden, Archiv der Evangelische-Reformierte Kirche, Rep. 320 varia 14, 51. (Translation by Alastair Duke).

1. Anthony Ashe to the Consistory of the Reformed Church In Emden, 28 April 1559.

My beloved brethren. I wish you grace and peace of God our heavenly father with the inward power of the Holy Spirit by Jesus Christ our Lord and saviour.

You should know my dear and worthy brethren that I received your letter which master Wolter[1] wrote on 25 April and understand your intention concerning the request, which I shall perform, if I see some possibility of carrying out the same. But it is not yet time, as I wrote you in my last letter, for the religion here has made little progress, to the great sorrow of the pious and to the great insolence of the papists, who not only persist in their popery, but also begin to take some heart, boasting that change will not come, openly saying this in their churches. Such encouragement as they may have may well be exhausted. Master Scory[2] has been ordered in the Queen's name to draw up a list of all the scholars who have been or are still abroad and to present their names to the Council. For what purpose they know not, but they believe that it has been done on account of some who have written a book against the regiment of women and that women have no place in the office of the magistrate, on which account house-to-house searches have been made here and three have been imprisoned. The congregation which was here in the time of persecution

---

[1] Wouter Delenus, the recipient of letter two. Delenus was a former minister of the Dutch church at London (1550–1553) and now a leading member of the Emden Reformed community.

[2] John Scory (d. 1585), during the Marian exile superintendent of the English church in Emden. On his return to England he took part in the disputation with the Catholics on 31 Mar. He was appointed bishop of Hereford in July 1559.

continues to hold its general meeting where they used to, in private houses where they teach and administer the sacraments.[3] I am not able to write more to you, my beloved, since I replied at length in my last letter, and since that time not much has changed. If any change comes, I will inform you immediately. Parliament is still sitting and it is not known when it will break up. Pray yet that the Lord will overthrow and destroy the kingdom of Antichrist here in England so that his kingdom may be built up and all godly people may be comforted. Pray also for me that the Lord will grant me wisdom and good success in the matter of his congregation. Herewith I commend you to the Lord that you may be kept in complete health, harmony and unity of spirit, so that his Holy name may be magnified. Amen. London, 28 April 1559. From me, your brother and servant.

2. Anthony Ashe to Wouter Delenus, 2 May 1559.

I wish you grace and peace, my beloved brother and father ... Wouter, of God our heavenly father through Jesus Christ. Amen.

You should know, my beloved, that I received your letter and have returned an answer to the brethren, thanking you for visiting my wife in my absence. You will have learned that nothing has changed since I wrote to the brethren. People speak much about some reformation, but that is not certain since Parliament is still sitting. Further, I have today been to the Marshalsea to see some prisoners who were imprisoned for that same doctrine which you and certain brethren defended in the Gasthuis against master Schare and Watson,[4] and they complain that the extreme predestinarians have been the cause of their imprisonment. If this is so, God will forgive them, and they have kindly requested that I should write to you and those of Ophusen. Further they desire that Peter[5] were here, and many others with him too. I know of nothing else to write. Remain then commended to

---

[3] This presumably refers to a portion of the London stranger congregation who had remained in England during Mary's reign. Nothing further is known of these secret gatherings. See Chapter 2.

[4] This presumably refers to a disputation between Delenus and members of the Emden English congregation (John Scory and Robert Watson?) during the period of exile in Emden. Nothing further is known, either of the occasion of the dispute or the questions debated. The *Gasthuis* was the former home of the Emden Franciscan community, which in 1557 had been cleared and turned over to the use of the Reformed.

[5] Peter Delenus, son of Wouter, and currently a minister in East Friesland. Later in 1559 he would return to London to take on the ministry of the revived London Dutch church.

God. In great haste. Dated as above. Greet all those who love the truth from me, Antoenis Ashe.

Tell my wife that I have received encouragement with regard to Hubert's matter and that I shall hasten as soon as I can to give a fuller answer.

(On the reverse): To the honourable and learned Master Wouter Delenus, resident at Emden.

Bibliography

Anderson, Marvin, *Peter Martyr. A reformer in Exile* (Nieuwkoop, 1975).
——, 'Rhetoric and Reality: Peter Martyr and the English Reformation', *SCJ*, 19 (1988), pp. 451–69.
Bainton, Ronald H., 'The Heretic as Exile: Bernardino Ochino', in his *The Travails of Religious Liberty. Nine Biographical Studies* (Westminster Press, 1951), pp. 149–76.
Bartlett, Kenneth R., 'The English Exile Community in Italy and the Political Opposition to Queen Mary I', *Albion*, 13 (1981), pp. 223–41.
——, 'The Role of the Marian Exiles', in Hasler, P. W. (ed.), *The Commons, 1558–1603. Vol 1* (London, 1981), pp. 102–10.
Baskerville, E. J., *A Chronological Bibliography of Propaganda and Polemic published in English between 1553 and 1558* (Philadelphia, 1979).
——, 'Some lost works of propaganda and polemic from the Marian period', *The Library*, 6th ser., 8 (1986), pp. 47–52.
——, 'John Ponet in Exile; a Ponet letter to John Bale', *JEH*, 37 (1986), pp. 442–7.
Bauckham, Richard, *Tudor Apocalypse* (Abingdon, 1978).
Beer, Barrett L., 'John Stow and the English Reformation, 1547–1559', *SCJ*, 16 (1985), pp. 257–71.
——, 'London Parish Clergy and the Protestant Reformation', *Albion*, 18 (1986), pp. 375–91.
——, 'John Ponet's *Shorte Treatise of Politike Power* Reassessed', *SCJ*, 21 (1990), pp. 373–83.
Bindoff, S.T., *The House of Commons, 1509–1558* (3 vols, London, 1982).
Bowler, Gerry, 'Marian Protestants and the Idea of Violent Resistance to Tyranny', in Lake, Peter and Dowling, Maria, *Protestantism and the National Church* (Beckenham, 1987), pp. 124–43.
Brigden, Susan, *London and the Reformation* (Oxford, 1989).
Burns, J. H., 'Knox and Bullinger', *Scottish Historical Review*, 34 (1955), pp. 90–1.
Christianson, Paul, *Reformers and Babylon: English Apocalyptic Visions from the Reformation to the Eve of the Civil War* (Toronto, 1978).

Clark, Peter, *English Provincial Society from the Reformation to the Revolution: Religion, Politics and Society in Kent, 1500–1640* (Hassocks, 1977).

Colligan, J. H., *The Genevan Service Book of 1555* (Manchester, [1931]).

———, *The Honourable William Whittingham of Chester (?1524–1579)* (Chester, 1934).

Collinson, P., 'The authorship of A Brieff discours off the troubles begonne at Franckford', *JEH*, 9 (1958), pp. 188–208.

———, 'The role of Women in the English Reformation: illustrated by the life and friendships of Anne Locke', in Cuming, G. J. (ed.), *Studies in Church History*, 2 (1965), pp. 258–72.

———, *Archbishop Grindal, 1519–1583. The Struggle for a Reformed Church* (London, 1979).

———, 'Cranbrook and the Fletchers: Popular and Unpopular Religion in the Kentish Weald', in Brooks, Peter Newman (ed.), *Reformation Principle and Practice. Essays in honour of A. G. Dickens* (London, 1980), pp. 171–202.

———, 'Truth and Legend: the Veracity of John Foxe's Book of Martyrs', in Duke, A. C. and Tamse, C. A., *Clio's Mirror: historiography in Britain and the Netherlands* (Zutphen, 1985), pp. 31–54.

Cowell, Henry, 'English Protestant Refugees in Strasburg, 1553–1558', *Proceedings of the Huguenot Society*, 15 (1933–37), pp. 69–120.

———, 'The Sixteenth-Century English-Speaking Refugee Churches at Strasburg, Basle, Zurich, Arrau, Wesel and Emden', *Proceedings of the Huguenot Society*, 15 (1933–37), pp. 612–55.

Craig, John, and Litzenberger, Caroline, 'Wills as Religious Propaganda: The Testament of William Tracy', *JEH*, 44 (1993), pp. 415–31.

Danner, Dan, 'Christopher Goodman and the English Protestant Tradition of Civil Disobedience', *SCJ*, 8, no. 3 (1977), pp. 60–73.

———, 'The Marian Exiles and the English Protestant Tradition', in *Social Groups and Religious Ideas in the Sixteenth Century* (Kalamazoo, 1978), pp. 93–101.

Davies, W. T., 'A Bibliography of John Bale', *Oxford Bibliographical Society, Proceedings and Papers*, 5 (1936), pp. 201–81.

Davis, John F., *Heresy and Reformation in the South East of England, 1520–1559* (London, 1983).

Dawson, Jane E. A., 'Revolutionary Conclusions: The Case of the Marian Exiles', *History of Political Thought*, 11 (1990), pp. 257–72.

———, 'The Two John Knoxes: England, Scotland and the 1558 Tracts', *JEH*, 42 (1991), pp. 555–76.

———, 'Resistance and Revolution in Sixteenth-Century Thought: The Case of Christopher Goodman', in Van Den Berg, J. and Hoftijzer P. G. (eds), *Church, Change and Revolution* (Leiden, 1991), pp. 69–79.

———, 'The Apocalyptic thinking of the Marian exiles', in Wilks, M. (ed.), *Prophecy and Eschatology* (Studies in Church History, subsidia 10, 1994), pp. 75–91.

Dickens, A. G., 'Heresy and the Origins of English Protestantism', in Bromley, J. S. and Kossman, E. H., *Britain and the Netherlands*, vol. 2 (Groningen, 1964), pp. 47–66.

Fairfield, L. P., *John Bale: Mythmaker for the English Reformation* (West Lafayette, IN, 1976).

———, '*The vocacyon of Johan Bale* and Early English Autobiography', *Renaissance Quarterly*, 24 (1971), pp. 327–40.

———, 'The mysterious press of "Michael Wood" (1553–1554)', *The Library*, 5th ser., 27 (1972), pp. 220–32.

Firth, Katharine, *The Apocalyptic Tradition in Reformation Britain: 1530–1645* (Oxford, 1979).

Freeman, Thomas, 'Notes on a Source for John Foxe's Account of the Marian Persecution in Kent and Sussex', *Historical Research*, 67 (1994), pp. 203–11.

———, ' "A solemne contestation of divers popes": A work by John Foxe?', *English Language Notes*, 31 (1993–94), no. 3, pp. 35–42.

Garrett, Christina, *The Marian Exiles* (Cambridge, 1938).

———, 'John Ponet and the Confession of the Banished Ministers', *Church Quarterly Review*, 137 (1943–44), pp. 47–74, 181–204.

Haller, William, *Foxe's Book of Martyrs and the Elect Nation* (London, 1963).

Heinze, R. W., ' "I pray God to grant that I may endure to the end": a new look at the martyrdom of Thomas Cranmer', in Ayris, Paul, and Selwyn, David (eds), *Thomas Cranmer. Churchman and Scholar* (Woodbridge, 1993), pp. 261–80.

Houlbrooke, Ralph, *Church Courts and the People during the English Reformation, 1520–1570* (Oxford, 1979).

Hudson, Winthrop S., *John Ponet 1516–1556. Advocate of Limited Monarchy* (Chicago, 1942).

Isaacs, Frank, 'Egidius van der Erve and his English Printed Books', *The Library*, 4th series, 12 (1931–32), pp. 336–52.

Jagger, Meriel, 'Bonner's Episcopal Visitation of London, 1554', *BIHR*, 45 (1972), pp. 306–11.

Jones, Whitney R. D., *William Turner. Tudor Naturalist, Physician and Divine* (London, 1988).
King, John N., 'The Account Book of a Marian Bookseller, 1553–54', *British Library Journal*, 13 (1987), pp. 33–57.
Kingdon, Robert, 'Calvinism and Resistance Theory, 1550–1580', in Burns, J. H. (ed.), *The Cambridge History of Political Thought, 1450–1700* (Cambridge, 1991), pp. 193–218.
Leadam, I. S., 'A Narrative of the pursuit of English Refugees in Germany under Queen Mary', *TRHS*, n.s., 11 (1897), pp. 113–31.
Leaver, R. A., 'Coverdale and the Anglo-Genevan Liturgy of 1556', *Mededelingen van het Instituut voor Liturgiewetenschap van de Rijksuniversiteit te Groningen*, 18 (1984), pp. 30–4.
——, *The Liturgy of the Frankfurt Exiles, 1555* (Grove Liturgical Studies, 38; Bramcote, 1984).
——, 'A penitential hymn from the English Exile Congregation in Emden 1555', *The Hymn*, 41/1 (1990), pp. 15–18.
——, 'A unique broadsheet in the Scheide Library, Princeton', *Papers of the Bibliographical Society of America*, 83 (1989), pp. 337–52.
——, *'Goostly Psalmes and Spirituall Songes'. English and Dutch Metrical Psalms from Coverdale to Utenhove, 1535–1566* (Oxford, 1991).
Levin, Carole, 'Women in *The Book of Martyrs* as Models of Behaviour in Tudor England', *International Journal of Women's Studies*, (1981), pp. 196–207.
Loach, Jennifer, 'Pamphlets and polemics, 1553–1558', *BIHR*, 48 (1975), pp. 31–44.
——, 'The Marian Establishment and the Printing Press', *EHR*, 101 (1986), pp. 135–48.
——, *Parliament and the Crown in the Reign of Mary Tudor* (Oxford, 1986).
Loades, David, 'The Authorship and Publication of *The Copye*', *Transactions of the Cambridge Bibliographical Society*, 3 (1960), pp. 155–60.
——, 'The Essex Inquisitions of 1556', *BIHR*, 35 (1962), pp. 87–97.
——, *Two Tudor Conspiracies* (Cambridge, 1965).
——, *The Oxford Martyrs* (London, 1970).
——, 'The Sense of National Identity among the Marian Exiles', in his *Politics, Censorship and the English Reformation* (London, 1991), pp. 48–55.
——, 'John Foxe and the Traitors; the Politics of the Marian

Persecution', in Wood, Diana (ed.), *Martyrs and Martyrologies* (Studies in Church History, 30, 1993), pp. 231–44.

MacCulloch, Diarmaid, *Suffolk and the Tudors. Politics and Religion in an English County, 1500–1600* (Oxford, 1986).

———, *Archbishop Cranmer* (Oxford, 1996).

———, and Blatchly, John, 'Pastoral Provision in the Parishes of Tudor Ipswich', *SCJ*, 22 (1991), pp. 457–74.

McIntosh, M. K., 'Sir Anthony Cooke: Tudor Humanist, Educator and Religious Reformer', *Proceedings of the American Philosophical Society*, 199, 3 (1975), pp. 233–50.

Marcombe, David, 'Bernard Gilpin: anatomy of an Elizabethan Legend', *Northern History*, 16 (1980), pp. 20–39.

Martin, Charles, *Les protestants anglais réfugiés à Genève au temps de Calvin, 1555–1560* (Geneva, 1915).

Martin, J. W., *Religious Radicals in Tudor England* (London, 1989).

———, 'The Marian Regime's Failure to understand the importance of Printing', *Huntington Library Quarterly*, 44 (1981), pp. 231–47.

———, 'The Protestant Underground congregations of Mary's reign', *JEH*, 35 (1984), pp. 519–38.

———, 'Sidelights on Foxe's account of the Marian Martyrs', *BIHR*, 58 (1985), pp. 248–51.

———, 'Robert Crowley in Two Protestant Churches', in *Religious Radicals in Tudor England* (London, 1989), pp. 147–69.

Mason, Roger, 'Knox, Resistance and the Moral Imperative', *History of Political Thought*, 1 (1980), pp. 411–36.

———, *John Knox. On Rebellion* (Cambridge, 1994).

Mayhew, Graham, *Tudor Rye* (Falmer, 1987).

Neale, J. E., 'Sir Nicholas Throckmorton's Advice to Queen Elizabeth on her Accession to the Throne', *EHR*, 65 (1950), pp. 91–8.

Oxley, James E., *The Reformation in Essex to the Death of Mary* (Manchester, 1965).

Peardon, Barbara, 'The politics of polemic: John Ponet's *Short Treatise of Political Power* and contemporary circumstances, 1553–1556', *Journal of British Studies*, 22 (1982), pp. 35–49.

Penny, Andrew, *Freewill or Predestination? The Battle over Saving Grace in Mid-Tudor England* (Woodbridge, 1990).

Pettegree, Andrew, *Foreign Protestant Communities in Sixteenth-Century London* (Oxford, 1986).

Pijper, F., *Jan Utenhove, zijn leven en zijne werken* (Leiden, 1883).

Pineas, Rainer, 'William Turner and Reformation Politics', *BHR*, 37 (1975), pp. 193–200.

Ridley, Jasper, *Thomas Cranmer* (Oxford, 1962).
——, *John Knox* (Oxford, 1968).
Shakespeare, Joy, 'Plague and Punishment', in Lake, Peter and Dowling, Maria (eds), *Protestantism and the National Church* (Beckenham, 1987), pp. 103–23.
——, and Dowling, Maria, 'Religion and politics in mid-Tudor England through the eyes of an English Protestant woman: the recollections of Rose Hickman', *Bulletin of the Institute of Historical Research*, 55 (1982), pp. 94–102.
Shaw, Duncan, 'John Willock', in his *Reformation and Revolution. Essays presented to Hugh Watt* (Edinburgh, 1967), pp. 42–69.
Skinner, Quentin, *The Foundations of Modern Political Thought* (Cambridge, 1978).
Southgate, W. M., 'The Marian exiles and the influence of John Calvin', *History*, 27 (1942), pp. 148–52.
Sutherland, Nicola, 'The Marian Exiles and the Establishment of the Elizabethan Regime', *ARG*, 78 (1987), pp. 253–86.
Tudor, Philippa, 'Protestant Books in London in Mary Tudor's Reign', *London Journal*, 15 (1990), pp. 19–28.
Wabuda, Susan, 'Equivocation and Recantation during the English Reformation: the "Subtle Shadows" of Dr Edward Crome', *JEH*, 44 (1993), pp. 224–42.
——, 'Henry Bull, Miles Coverdale, and the Making of Foxe's *Book of Martyrs*', in Wood, Diana (ed.), *Martyrs and Martyrologies* (Studies in Church History, 30, 1993), pp. 244–58.
Williams, Neville, *John Foxe the Martyrologist. His Life and Times* (Friends of Dr Williams's Library, 29th lecture, 1975).
Wollman, David H., 'The Biblical Justification for resistance to authority in Ponet's and Goodman's polemics', *SCJ*, 13 (1982), pp. 29–41.

Index

Aachen 64
Abraham 26, 94
Acts of the Apostles 179
adiaphora 142
Adisham 161
Alexandre, Pierre 44, 192
Alley, William 112–13
Alread, Benedict 171
altars 142
anabaptists 156, 160
Anderson, Robert 170
Anna, Countess of East Friesland 59
Antichrist 23–4, 25, 26, 198
Antwerp 10, 11, 28, 30, 37, 64, 65, 68, 69, 89, 134, 155
   Calvinist churches in 74, 155
Apocalypse 128
Appleby, John 170
Ashe, Anthony 145, 148, 197–9
Augsburg Confession (1530) 67, 75, 76, 77, 82, 133–5
   Variata (1540) 81, 135
Augsburg, Peace of (1555) 72, 81, 152
Augustine 23, 24
Augustinians 89
Aylmer, John 138
   his writings 35

Baal 86, 166
Babylon 25
Bacon, Nicholas 103, 104, 107, 140
Bale, John
   his writings 31, 122–3, 126, 184, 191, 192, 193, 194
Baltic Sea 59
Banks, Robert 114
Barlow, William 16, 98
Barnes, Robert 123, 185, 192
Basle 80, 123, 128
   printing in 122, 124, 126, 128, 185, 187, 188–96
Bath and Wells 16
Baudin, Clément 193

Beale, Robert 35
Becon, Thomas 15, 98
   his writings 122, 183, 190, 193, 194–5
Bedford, Francis Russell, Earl of 107
Berne 76
Bernher, Augustine 33, 51
Bertie, Catherine, Duchess of Suffolk 148
Bertie, Francis 47
Beyer, Hartmann 70, 71, 78, 80
Beza, Theodore 10, 62, 135
   his writings 127, 148
Bill, William 113–14, 139
Bind, Thomas 171
Blake, Anthony 114
Bland, John 161–2
Bocher, Joan 5
Bocskai, Stefan 10
Bonner, Edmund 14, 43, 47, 108, 115
Book of Common Prayer 132
book trade
   in England 30–31, 163–5
Boughton, Thomas 97
Bourg, Anne de 157
Bradford, John 5
Braubach, Peter 71, 72, 78, 79, 184, 185
Bremen 59, 61, 71
Brylinger, Nicolaus 193
Brockelsby, Edward 171
Bruem, John 170
Bruges 64
Brussels 89
Bucer, Martin 39
   his writings 93, 96, 101, 121, 184, 189
Bugenhagen, Johannes 71
Bullinger, Heinrich 58, 61, 62, 63, 80, 83, 91, 96, 125, 136
   his writings 128
Bullingham, Nicholas 170
Buscoducensis 71

Calais 163
Calvin, John 8, 10, 19, 21, 33, 36,
    108, 136, 151, 156–7, 187
  his writings against Nicodemism 6,
    53, 90–92, 95–6, 154
  his *Institutes* 108
  other writings 63, 71, 72, 73, 79,
    148
  and sacramentarian controversy
    61–3, 78–84
  and foreign churches in Germany
    66–7, 73–8
  ecumenical initiatives 81
  and Elizabethan Settlement 137,
    143–6
  influence in England 148
Calvinism 152, 158, 159
Cambridge 17, 42, 107, 112, 113,
    115, 121
Cana 94
Canterbury 32
Cassander, George 68
catechisms 16, 23, 57
Cave, Ambrose 107
Cecil, William 6, 29, 109, 140, 145,
    146–7, 163
  and Elizabethan Settlement 35,
    106, 107, 113, 114, 115, 145
  religious attitudes 53, 109, 133,
    136, 140, 148
  conduct under Mary 103–5, 136–9
  and Calvin 144–8
Chaldee 94
Chambre Ardente 161
Charles V, Emperor 7, 104, 158
  attitude to heresy 89, 151, 157–8,
    164
Chateaubriand, Edict of (1551) 105,
    163
Cheke, Sir John 16, 126, 183
Chester 112
Cheyney, Richard 113
Christopherson, John 139
Church Fathers 31
clergy 1
Cleves 64
Clough, Richard 11
Chichester 14
Colchester 102
Coleman, Christopher 17, 170
Coligny, Gaspard, Admiral de 10

Cologne 69, 184
colporteurs 30
Commons, House of 104, 130, 131,
    140, 141
Consensus Tigurinus 61, 81–2, 136
Constantine, George 17, 98, 99, 170
Convocation 110, 113, 119, 124
Cooke, Sir Anthony 29, 63, 104,
    107, 121, 140
Cop, Nicolas 90
Copenhagen 16, 58, 59–60
Copley, Thomas 108
Corinthians, Epistle to 93
Cossye, John 110
Cottisford, Thomas, 16, 32
  his writings 16, 18, 19, 23, 25, 87,
    96, 98, 168
Council of Trent 151
Coverdale, Miles 147–8
Cox, Richard 137
Cranmer, Thomas 5, 16, 44, 120,
    136, 142–3
  his writings 15, 28, 31–2, 120–21,
    125, 126, 168, 169, 188
  his martyrdom 124, 157–8
Crépy, peace of (1544) 7
Crespin, Jean
  as martyrologist 28, 115
  as printer 147, 186, 187, 192
Crome, Edward 98
Cromwell, Thomas 86
Ctematius, *see* Erve, van der
Cyprian 23

Daniel, Book of 19, 26
Dathenus, Peter 71
Dauwe, Josias 62
Dawberry, Thomas 171
Daye, John 164
deacons
  in Emden 19, 62, 174, 175, 178
  in London 34, 57
Deborah 138
Delenus, Wouter (Gualter) 44, 57, 58,
    61, 85, 145, 197–9
Delenus, Peter 44, 71, 198
Delft 89
denizens, denization 44, 45, 48, 49
Denmark 13, 16, 56–9, 62, 72, 85
Dickinson, Christopher 171
discipline 18, 20, 27, 34

INDEX

Dover 43, 51
Dowley, John 20–22, 171, 172, 174
Downham, William 112
Dudley, Ambrose, Earl of Warwick 147
Dudley, Robert, Earl of Leicester 109, 147
Duisburg 64
Durham 147
Dutch Revolt 134, 160
Duval, Pierre 51

Early, Thomas 149
Early Church 24
East Anglia 102, 164
East Friesland 13, 15, 16, 17, 30, 37, 181
Edward VI, King of England 1–3, 5, 7, 8, 16, 17, 19, 23, 27, 39, 41, 46, 56, 57, 86–7, 96, 101, 103, 107, 108, 119, 127, 128, 138, 139, 153
  church under 24, 27, 56, 83, 88, 99, 126, 128, 142, 143, 167
Edmundes, William 110
Egenolff, Christian 72, 185
Egypt 94
elders 34
  in Emden 19, 22, 62, 173–82
  in London 57
Elijah 86, 93
Elisha 94, 97
Elizabeth, Queen of England 6, 8, 9, 11, 12, 15, 22, 36, 39, 46, 48, 55, 102, 106–7, 112, 113, 125, 129, 144, 146, 149, 162, 163, 166
  in Mary's reign 6, 53, 107, 109, 116, 137, 146
  attitude to religion 133–4, 136–8, 141, 143
Elizabethan Settlement 8, 34, 35, 106, 108, 130–50
Elsinore 58
Emden 40, 51, 59–64, 70, 74, 84, 144, 145
  English Church 4, 5, 10–38, 87, 172–82
  order of service 14, 18–19
  disputes in 20–22, 172–82

Dutch church 20–23, 30, 34, 74, 181, 197
French church 22, 64, 176, 181
printing 23–9, 31–2, 37, 88, 125–6, 185, 186, 188
Synod (1571) 37
Emmanuel College, Cambridge 107
Ephesians, Epistle to 181
Erasmus, Desiderius 89, 90
Erve, Gilles van der (Ctematius) 23, 28–9, 31, 32, 62, 164, 185, 186, 188
Esschen, Jan van der 89
Essex 102, 113
Estienne, Robert 184
Exeter 112
exiles, Marian 3, 4, 6–8, 12, 13, 18, 33, 52, 88, 94, 107, 131
  Latin writings 8, 31–2, 119–26, 183–96
Eye 162
Ezekiel, Book of 181

Farel, Guillaume 10, 71, 91
Feria, Count of 133, 138
First Book of Discipline 17, 36
Flanders 64, 100
Fleet prison 142
Foxe, John 126, 130, 138
  his *Book of Martyrs* 3, 4, 34, 51, 52, 113, 115–16, 122–5, 162, 184, 193
  distortions in 5, 159–60
  other writings 123, 125, 130, 184, 187, 188–9, 193, 196
France 7, 36, 42, 43, 53, 55, 56, 90, 91, 104, 106, 109, 151–5, 157, 159, 160, 163
Francis I, King of France 91, 151
Frankfurt 16, 32, 40, 64, 122
  English church in 12, 15, 16, 20, 33, 120
  Dutch church in 70
  French church in 65, 68–78, 81, 83, 120
  printing in 184, 185
Frankfurt Concord (1542) 73
Froschover, Christopher 125, 194
Fulnebery, Marmeduke 171
Fumée, Antoine 92

Gallars, Nicholas des 84, 145

INDEX

Galliart, Jan 120
Gardiner, Stephen 31, 43, 45, 52, 120, 125, 135, 136, 186
Garrett, Thomas 98
Gasthuis 198
Geneva 10, 12, 21, 42, 60–63, 73, 74, 82–4, 105, 136, 149, 157
  Academy 10
  English church in 10, 19, 33, 36, 147
  book trade 28, 30
  Company of Pastors 19
  printing in 144, 147, 184, 186, 187, 192
Germany 4, 7, 8, 13, 16, 56, 57, 73, 81, 85, 89, 125–6
  exile churches in 16, 27, 40
  see also Emden, Frankfurt, Wesel
  Lutheran churches in 81, 125, 134, 152
Gesner, Andreas 190, 195
Ghent 64
Glastonbury 68–70, 73, 120
Glauberg, John von 74
Gloucester 113, 142, 157
Goodman, Christopher
  his writings 26, 146–7
Grafton, Richard 164
Grand, Augustin le 66
Granvelle, Antoine Perrenot, Cardinal 137
Gravesend 42, 58
Green, Stephen 18, 170
Gresham, Sir Thomas 107
Grey, Lady Jane 1, 42, 107, 113, 119
Grindal, Edmund 13, 15, 106, 119, 125
  as bishop of London 33, 146, 147, 150
  literary activity 124–5, 127
Gualter, Rudolph 23, 137, 169
Guest, Edmund 112

Haddon, Sir Walter 108
Haemstede, Adriaan van 115
Hale, William 170
Hamburg 60–61, 71
Hanseatic towns 37
Hardenberg, Albert 61
Hedio, Caspar 89
Heenwich, Thomas 171

Henricus, Nicolaus 192
Henry II, King of France 151, 160–61
Henry VIII, King of England 1, 17, 23, 24, 39, 49, 86, 94, 98, 124, 153, 165, 166
Hereford 113
Heshusius, Tileman 81
Heydon 102, 115
Hickman, Rose 101
Hill, John 170
Hill, Nicholas (van den Berghe) 23, 28–9, 31, 164
Holstein 59
Hondebeke, Frederik 89
Hooper, John 5, 96, 99, 113, 142, 143, 156, 157
  his writings 97, 125, 127
Horne, Robert 75
  his writings 95, 96
Howe, William 171
humanism 154
Humphrey, Laurence 126, 195
Hungary 10

iconoclasm 139, 155, 165–6
Inns of Court 108
Ipswich 110, 114
Ireland 122
Isaiah 143, 144
Israel 24, 26
Italy 4, 154

Jacobson, Henry 170
Jerome, William 98
Jerusalem 83
Jewel, John 98, 137, 140, 147
Joseph of Arimathaea 90
Josiah 94
Josus, Balfredus 170
Judges, Book of 26, 121
Jülich 64

Katelyne, Joris van der 23
Keck, Thomas 170
Kent 6, 43
Knollys, Sir Francis 107
Knox, John 10, 17, 36, 106, 145, 146, 148–9
  his writings 26–7, 144–9, 168

Kolding 58-9

Lasco, John a 13, 14, 16, 18, 23, 32, 42-4, 51, 57-61, 81, 83
  his church order (*Forma ac Ratio*) 19-20, 27, 32-6, 38, 72, 78, 120, 168, 174, 185
  other writings 51, 60, 76, 136, 168, 169, 187
  and Sacramentarian dispute 62-3, 80
  and Wesel 66-7
  and Frankfurt 70-76
  relationship with Calvin 80
Latimer, Hugh 5, 51
  his writings 28
  his martyrdom 29, 124, 156
Latimer, William 114
Laud, William 54
Layfield 162
Lincolnshire 103
Locke, Thomas 101
Lollardy 97, 112, 124
London 11, 23, 28, 39, 51, 102, 161
  secret church in 5, 16, 30, 33, 34, 35, 87, 102, 112, 153
  stranger churches 5, 8, 14, 18, 19, 21, 32-4, 41-58, 66-8, 70, 83-4, 100-101, 145, 155
  book trade 30, 164
  Protestantism under Mary 100, 111-12
Lords, House of 131, 133
Lords of the Congregation 35, 146
Lorraine, Charles de Guise, Cardinal 134-5
Lübeck 60
Lucas, Thomas 108
Luther, Martin 2, 7, 60, 61, 81-2, 89
Lutheran churches 8, 56, 58-9
  in Germany 60-61, 64, 67-84, 134, 152
Lyon 151, 193

Magdalen College, Oxford 108
Maitland of Lethington 17, 146
Margaret of Parma 152
Marshalsea 145, 148, 198
Mary, Queen of England 1, 2, 3, 4, 6, 7, 11, 12, 15, 18, 24, 25, 28, 34, 36, 37, 39, 40-54, 56, 63, 86, 88, 94, 98, 103, 105, 106, 108, 109, 111, 118, 128, 137, 138, 151, 152, 155, 160, 167
marriage, clerical 1, 114
martyrs 3-7, 26, 28, 52, 156
Mass 1, 35, 44, 49, 51, 57, 87, 91, 95, 97, 102, 116, 119, 149, 156
  Protestant criticism of 91, 96, 99
Matthew, gospel of 21, 176
Maubert, Guillaume 51
May, William 113, 115
Melanchthon, Philip 77, 79, 80, 135, 142
Menno Simons 59-60, 183
Mennonites 59
Merchant Adventurers 11
Merrill, Michael 171
Micron, Marten 57, 71, 83, 183
  his writings 13, 18, 23, 168, 169
  disputes in Germany 58, 60, 61, 62
Mierdman, Steven 120, 164
Mildmay, Sir Walter 107
Miller, Robert 171
Morellus, Francis 65, 66
Morice, William 32
Mortaigne, Gerald 62
Mühlberg 7
Münster 160
Musculus, Wolfgang 76

Namaan 94, 97
Nantes, Edict of (1598) 152
  Revocation (1685) 55
Netherlands 7, 10, 30, 36, 42, 43, 47, 53, 55, 56, 61, 64, 81, 84, 92, 105, 106, 152, 155, 159, 160
  persecution in 89, 151, 157, 158, 163-4
Newhaven 147
Nicodemism, Nicodemites 6-7, 24-6, 53, 90, 92, 95, 97, 108, 146
  among London French congregation 49-53
  in England 88-9, 106, 154-5
Norden 71
Normandie, Laurent de 30
Northumberland, Edmund Dudley, Duke of 1, 103, 107, 109, 113, 119, 127, 138-9
Norton, Thomas 108-9
Norway 58

INDEX

Norwich 158
Noyes, John 162
Nuremberg 134

Oberursel 78, 192
Ochino, Bernardino 42
Old Testament 26, 93, 94, 99, 166
 see also Daniel, Judges, Psalms
Olde, John 15, 31-2, 170
 his writings 23-8, 88, 96, 168, 169, 185
Onsow, Richard 108
Oporinus, Johann 122, 123, 125, 185, 187, 188, 189, 190-92, 193, 194, 195-6
Orange, William of 10, 134
Ordinal 142
Ossory 122
Oxford 31, 42, 108, 115, 120, 121

Paget, William 139
Palatinate 82
Palmer, Humphrey 171
Paris 92, 154, 161
 Parlement of 155, 157, 161
Parker, Matthew 6, 53, 106, 113
Parliament 104-5, 129-31, 163, 198
Parr, Thomas 107
Parr, William, Marquis of Northampton 107
Parris, George van 5
Parry, Sir Thomas 107
Paul, Saint 93, 95, 99
Paul's Cross 114, 139
Payne, John 171
Percy, Simon 50
Pernam, Peter 192, 195
Perussel, François 57, 58, 65-8, 75-7
Peterborough 112, 114
Philip II, King of Spain 151, 153, 162
Philippians, Epistle to 99
Philpot, John 28, 169, 189
 his writings 95, 120, 124-5, 127, 183
Placards, Affair of (1534) 91
plague 20-22, 172-3
Plaice, Matthew 115
Poissy, Colloquy of (1561) 134
Poland 32, 72, 80
Pole, Cardinal 104, 127, 128, 160, 186
Ponet, John 14, 103
 his writings 26, 31, 122, 183, 190
Poullain, Valérand 69, 70, 73-8, 82, 92, 120
 his writings 120, 183-5
Prayer Book
 1549 1, 31, 130, 133, 135
 1552 1, 34, 44, 130, 135
 1559 136
presbyterianism 35
printing
 exile 12, 31-2
 in Emden 23-9, 31-2
Privy Council 41, 44, 48, 69, 103, 106-8, 138, 142, 197
puritan choir 130
puritanism 36

Queen's College 115

Ratheby, William 170
Reading 110
Renard, Simon 43, 45, 47
Rhineland 12, 36, 37, 64
Ridley, Nicholas 5, 13, 32, 98, 142, 143
 his writings 28, 29, 124, 168, 186
 his martyrdom 124-5, 156
Rihel, Wendelin 123, 184, 190
Ritter, Mattheus 70
Rochester 13, 32, 112
Roese, Joest 62
Rogers, Edward 109
Rogers, John 5, 156
Romans, Epistle to 121
Rome 24, 28, 87
Roningh, Robert 170
Rostock 59
Rotterdam 160
Rough, John 16, 30, 35, 52
Roussel, Gérard 91
Rowe, John 170
Rye 43, 110

Sackville, Thomas 107
St David's 18
Salisbury 97
Sandys, Edwin 52, 106
Savonarola, Girolamo 168
Saxony 134
Scambler, Edmund 112

schoolmasters 14
Scory, John 13–17, 19, 31, 32, 98, 145, 197, 198
  pastor in Emden 22, 170, 174
  writings 23–4, 26, 27, 168
Scotland 10, 17, 146, 147, 152
  English intervention in 35, 146
  Calvinist church in 36
Secelles, Jean de 76
Servetus, Michael 84, 156–7
Shepherd, William 102, 115
Simpson, David 16, 170
Singleton, Hugh 164
Six Articles, Act of (1539) 86
Smith, Richard 31, 121
Smith, Sir Thomas 108
Somerset, Edward Seymour, Duke of 16, 68, 108, 138
Southwark 50, 51
Spain 55
Stationers' Company 30
Stephanus, Robert see Estienne, Robert
Strasbourg 12, 42, 121, 123–4
  exile church in 36, 69
  printing in 126, 184, 190
Stratford-le-Bowe 52
Suffolk 110, 148, 162
Sussex 110
sustainers 29
superintendent
  in Emden 14
  in England 33–6, 42, 69
Switzerland 4, 7, 12, 81, 125
Symson, Cuthbert 34
Syria 94

Taylor, Rowland 5, 156
Thirlby, Thomas 137
Thomason, Thomas 171
Throckmorton, Michael 168
Throckmorton, Sir Nicholas 103, 109, 111
Timann, Johann 71, 73
Timothy, Book of 179–80
Tournai 92
Tracy, Henry 110
Tracy, William 110
Tremellius, Emmanuel 121
Turner, William 16
  his writings 23, 25, 168

Tyndale, William 97

universities 4, 39, 115
  see also Cambridge, Oxford
Utenhove, Jan 13, 58, 59, 80, 83, 85

Valenciennes 92
Vauville, Richard 57, 70, 73, 74
Vergerio, Pier Paulo 128
Vermigli, Peter Martyr 39, 42, 91, 120–21, 125, 137, 140, 147
  his writings 120–21, 190, 192, 195
vestments 142, 143, 148, 149
Viret, Pierre 92
Visscher, Wilhelm de 62
Voes, Heinrich 89

Waad, Armigail 35
Warnemünde 59
Watson, Robert 16, 32, 98, 198
  his writings 26, 168, 186
Wesel 40, 69
  English church in 12, 16, 19, 20, 33, 68, 75
  printing in 28, 126
  French church 64–8, 74, 76–8, 81, 83
Westphal, Joachim 60–63, 71, 73, 78–82, 84
Whitchurch, Edward 164
Whitehead, David 16
White Horse Tavern 17
Whittingham, William 36, 125, 147, 186, 187
William, Edmund 170
Willock, John 16–17, 98, 170
Wilslow, Henry 115
Winchester 122
Wismar 59–60
witches 157
Wittenberg 60, 71, 79, 123
Woodman, Richard 115
Worms 80
Worms, Edict of 89
Württemberg, Duke of 133
Wyatt, Sir Thomas
  his rebellion 17, 44, 87, 103, 109, 116, 138, 163
Wycliffe, John 123

York 15

Young, Elizabeth 30
Young, Thomas 15, 19, 170
　minister in Emden 22, 174, 176, 177, 179, 181

Zurich 60–63, 80–83, 121, 125, 136, 137
　printing in 125, 190, 195
Zwingli, Ulrich 19, 23, 80, 136, 168